&

MODI

REFORMER'S IDEAS
PERFORMER'S IMPLEMENTATION

AMBEDKAR
&
MODI

REFORMER'S IDEAS
PERFORMER'S IMPLEMENTATION

Compiled by

BlueKraft Digital Foundation

Foreword : **Ilaiyaraaja**

PRABHAT
PRAKASHAN

Published by
PRABHAT PRAKASHAN PVT. LTD.
4/19 Asaf Ali Road,
New Delhi-110 002 (INDIA)
e-mail: prabhatbooks@gmail.com

ISBN 978-93-5521-372-3
AMBEDKAR & MODI
Compiled by BlueKraft Digital Foundation

Edition
First, 2022

Price
₹ 295.00 (Rupees Two Hundred Ninety Five only)

Printed at
R-Tech Offset Printers, Delhi

Dedicated to
Aspirational New India

Foreword

Bharat Ratna Dr. Babasaheb Ambedkar is a giant who is remembered by society for his intellect and battle against discrimination. We have all learnt about the greatness of his work, the rights he has ensured to all of us through our Constitution. He has been an inspiration to many people who want to overcome all odds and succeed. Many historical personalities are seen as great people during their own lifetime, but are forgotten soon after. Some other people had very little impact during their own times, but acquired relevance much later. But Dr. Babasaheb Ambedkar is a rare leader who made history during his own times and is still being read and followed widely, decades after his time.

A few years ago, I read in the news that Prime Minister Narendra Modi called Dr. B.R. Ambedkar the architect of India's water and river navigation policy. It was surprising to me to learn that Dr. Babasaheb Ambedkar had played a role in creating some important institutions related to water and irrigation. It is best to know about this in Prime Minister Modi's own words from the speech he gave in 2016 at an investment summit.

"Many of us may not know that Dr. Babasaheb Ambedkar created two powerful institutions related to water, navigation and power. They were: The Central Waterways, Irrigation and Navigation Commission and The Central Technical Power Board. His observations while setting up these two organisations is a testimony to his great foresight. I quote from his address on 3rd January, 1945: "Objects which have led to the setting up of two

organisations are to advise on how the water resources can be best utilised and how a project can be made to serve purposes other than irrigation."

"Dr. B.R. Ambedkar had emphasised the importance of the new waterways policy in order to lay the foundation for a regime of prosperity for the millions of poor of our country. I am happy to state that we have embarked on the development of National Waterways in keeping with Dr. Babasaheb Ambedkar's vision and foresight. With a GDP growth rate of more than 7%, India is the fastest growing major economy today. The IMF and the World Bank have indicated even better prospects in the days to come. We are taking aggressive steps to ensure that our process of growth is both fast as well as inclusive. This summit is another step to realise Dr. Babasaheb Ambedkar's dream of an economically strong, socially empowered and technologically equipped India."

However, it is not enough that one merely knows more about Dr. Babasaheb Ambedkar. It is equally, or perhaps more important, to imbibe his values and also encourage those who are implementing his ideas. While there are no limits to one's imagination, there are several hurdles one faces in implementation and only a true leader with commitment and passion to serve the people, can ensure logical and meticulous execution there by leaving the stamp of his legacy behind.

In this vein, this book also attempts to study the intersection of India's development journey under Prime Minister Narendra Modi with the ideals and vision of Dr. B.R. Ambedkar. This is done across various domains ranging from industrialisation to social justice to women empowerment.

As far as industrialisation is concerned, the Prime Minister's 'Make in India' policy has resulted in many achievements, especially in mobile manufacturing. India is also becoming well known for its effort to build world-class infrastructure, from roads and railways, to metros and expressways.

When it comes to social justice, Prime Minister Narendra Modi has strengthened the legal safeguards for socially marginalised communities through a number of laws and constitutional protections and setting up of the long-pending OBC Commission. He has also spearheaded a large scale effort to change the lives of the poor by building toilets, constructing homes and opening bank accounts–these are steps that help the poorest of the poor, many of whom are from socially disadvantaged communities. Right from ensuring better living conditions through housing, sanitation and electricity access to financial inclusion, a number of flagship policy successes are directly empowering crores of poor and marginalised people.

Recently, I read in news reports that the Prime Minister Modi government took a decision to raise the marriageable age of women, a step that would give more freedom for women to pursue further studies, especially in rural areas. This apart, the scheme that provides free LPG connections and the Prime Minister's message to society on saving the girl child come to mind when one thinks of his work for the progress of women. Pro-women legislations such as the banning of Triple Talaq and the rise in sex ratio due to the historic 'Beti Bachao Beti Padhao' movement, which has brought in social transformation is something that Dr. B.R. Ambedkar would have been proud of.

BlueKraft Digital Foundation's work on this book is an acknowledgement of the continuing importance of Dr. Babasaheb Ambedkar's ideals.

The book also brings out some striking parallels between the personalities of Dr. B.R. Ambedkar and Prime Minister Narendra Modi. Both these striking personalities succeeded against odds that people from socially disempowered sections of society face. Both saw poverty and stifling social structures from close quarters and worked to dismantle them. Both dreamt big for India, but both are also practical men who believe in action rather than mere thought exercises.

I also hope that it informs people on how India is moving in the direction of fulfilling his dreams. It is notable that this book is coming out in the 75th year of India's independence. The Atmanirbhar Bharat that Prime Minister Modi is building is a fitting tribute to the dreams of our freedom fighters.

I especially recommend this book to the youth of our country for it will inform them of the legacy of a great son of our soil and also how a New India is being built which seamlessly fuses the vision of our freedom fighters with the aspirations of our future generation.

I wish the book all the success.

9th April, 2022

—Ilaiyaraaja

Contents

	Foreword	7
1.	Dr. B.R. Ambedkar's Legacy and Modi's Mission	13
2.	Industrial Growth: A Social Liberator	30
3.	Labour Rights in Dr. B.R. Ambedkar and Modi Era	58
4.	Development through Self-reliance	80
5.	New Infrastructure for New India	91
6.	Urbanisation: Powering Social and Economic Mobility	114
7.	Jal Se Hi Jeevan: How Drinking Water is Transforming Lives	129
8.	Waterways as Pathways of Development	147
9.	Education: The Great Social Leveller	159
10.	Social Empowerment through Development for All	183
11.	Gender Equality: Empowering Women	197
12.	Team India: Building a Nation	217
	Reference	234

1

Dr. B.R. Ambedkar's Legacy and Modi's Mission

The greatest tragedy of Indian history is that it was written to please the powers that be at the Centre, instead of presenting a more factual account of events that transpired. It came at the cost of losing our historical icons in the pages of history while one family's name continued to fill the textbooks. Year after year, book after book, speech after speech, we were told about the indispensability of the Nehru-Gandhi family in the making of Independent India. The same was consumed on a mass scale and reproduced across generations. The exercise was repeated till the slate was left bereft of any outsider, no matter how big the contribution was.

One such legacy was that of the architect of the Constitution of India, Dr. B.R. Ambedkar, who not only faced injustice while he was alive, but even after his death. It was not an aberration, a mistake, or a misnomer, but a systematic attempt to obliterate the legacy of a man who stood tall despite many attempts to silence him.

Dr. Babasaheb Ambedkar: The Crusader for the 'Man at the Last Mile'

Dr. Babasaheb Ambedkar was the fourteenth child of Subedar Ramji Sakpal serving in the British Indian Army. Considered to be from the 'untouchable' Mahar caste, he faced discrimination in every sphere of life, starting from childhood. His later writings would reflect this discrimination and exclusion based on caste interactions that he experienced at a personal level. One of the instances that Dr. Babasaheb Ambedkar narrates is of the time when he was a school student. As a person of 'lower' caste, he was not allowed to directly take water from the school tap for the fear of 'polluting' it. Every time he would want a drink, he had to wait for the school peon to give him water.

Despite all the hurdles, Dr. Babasaheb Ambedkar displayed sheer determination and went on to complete his education from the world's top universities. He obtained degrees from universities in Mumbai, New York and London, dwelling deep into law, economics and political science. On his return to India, he used the knowledge to work for the repressed classes and liberate society from the taint of casteism. His unflinching resolve made Dr. Babasaheb Ambedkar a voice of the marginalised, the downtrodden and the exploited.

A Voice of Reason

From the beginning, Dr. Babasaheb Ambedkar believed in the power of electoral politics as a tool to achieve social and political reform. In 1936, he formed the Independent Labour Party and won 15 seats in the 1937 elections to the Provincial Legislative Assembly of the then Bombay Province. He continued as a vociferous opponent of caste prejudices and socio-economic inequalities.

Between 1942 and 1946, Dr. Babasaheb Ambedkar was part of the Viceroy's Executive Council as Labour Member. During these years, he made good use of the office to introduce a series of labour reforms, laying down his vision in actionable format. He was given responsibilities that covered the domains of labour, irrigation, water resources, public works, minerals and power, and was directly involved in framing the objectives and strategy of economic planning, water and electricity policy. Here is an account from the second edition of the study[2] by the Central Water Commission on Dr. Babasaheb Ambedkar:

"Being a member of the Central Cabinet, he (Dr. Babasaheb Ambedkar) was also a member of the Reconstruction Committee of the Council (RCC), President of the Policy Committee for Irrigation and Power and was also associated with its Official Committee. The task of the Policy Committee and its Official Committee was to study the problems affecting the development of irrigation and hydroelectric power and suggest practical ways of solving them. By virtue of his position in all the three bodies, Dr. Babasaheb Ambedkar significantly helped in formulating the policy and action plan for the optimal development of water and power resources in India...

"Though the RCC was the ultimate approving authority for the plan, the ministries concerned were to do the ground work. At the department level, the Policy Committee and Official Committee, of which Dr. Babasaheb Ambedkar was President, were required to prepare four statements, namely: (a) a statement regarding the broad policy of post-war reconstruction and economic development; (b) a detailed statement of policy on subjects within the department's jurisdiction, namely irrigation and power; (c) an action plan; and (d) policy stand on certain basic questions, such as (i) the question of State versus private ownership of irrigation and hydroelectric projects and others; (ii) role of the State and the Centre in the development of irrigation and power; and (iii) areas for Central Government intervention or participation in these two subjects, which were under the jurisdiction of the states."

The above excerpt points to the central role Dr. Babasaheb Ambedkar played in defining and shaping India's post-Independence policy framework. These policy interventions are discussed in greater detail in the subsequent chapters of the book.

Dr. Babasaheb Ambedkar's Discomfort with Nehru's Congress

Dr. Babasaheb Ambedkar's appointment in the Viceroy's

Council was not welcomed by the Congress, which continued with its efforts to isolate him. However, that did not deter him from his path, as he made a significant impact on the framing of a pan-Indian policy for development, industrialisation, uplift of the depressed classes and urbanisation.

Such was his impact that despite being at variance with the Congress, Dr. Babasaheb Ambedkar was made the Chairman of the Drafting Committee of the Constitution in 1947. This too did not come without difficulty. The Congress Party did not allow Dr. Babasaheb Ambedkar to be elected to the Constituent Assembly when it was first formed. However, he got himself elected from the Bengal Province, allegedly with the help of the Muslim League.

French author Christophe Jaffrelot writes in his book, Dr. Babasaheb Ambedkar and Untouchability:[3] *"In 1946, Dr. Babasaheb Ambedkar had contested elections to join this body [Constituent Assembly] not in Bombay, where Congress was the ruling party; but in Bengal, where he was elected after winning the support of the Muslim League."* His disappointment with the Congress was palpable after his party's poor performance in the polls, which he expressed as:

> *"Having led the untouchables against the Congress for full five years in the Round Table Conference and in the joint Parliamentary Committee, I could not pretend to be unaffected by the results of the elections. To me the question was – Had the untouchables gone over to the Congress? Such a thing was to me unimaginable. For, I could not believe that the untouchables – apart from a few agents of the Congress who are always tempted by the Congress fold to play the part of the traitor – could think of going over to the Congress enmasse, forgetting how Mr. Gandhi and the Congress opposed, inch by inch up to the very last moment, every one of their demands for political safeguards."*[4]

After the Partition of India, Dr. Babasaheb Ambedkar lost his seat. However, possibly under the instructions of Mahatma

Gandhi, he was re-elected from Bombay Province and given the Law Ministry. His education and experience on matters of legal, political and economic importance, coupled with heightened social consciousness, made him a perfect fit to be the Chairman of the Drafting Committee of the Constitution, and had Mahatma Gandhi's backing. Surpassing expectations of a nation that had fought years of colonialism that had impoverished and divided the country, Dr. Babasaheb Ambedkar gave India a Constitution that became instrumental in its reconstruction. The world that saw Indian democracy with scepticism, foreseeing a fate leading to its Balkanisation, was proven wrong because India's Constitution encapsulated the highest ideals of humanity.

Yet, the principal architect of the Indian Constitution, Dr. Babasaheb Ambedkar resigned from the Law Ministry, disenchanted with the Nehru government. Here is an excerpt from Dr. Babasaheb Ambedkar's resignation speech from the Union Cabinet on October 10, 1951. In his speech, he states:[5]

"As a result of my being amember of the Viceroy's Executive Council, I knew the Law Ministry to be administratively of no importance. It gave no opportunity for shaping the policy of the Government of India. We used to call it an empty soap box only good for old lawyers to play with. When the Prime Minister made me the offer, I told him that besides being a lawyer by my education and experience, I was competent to run any administrative department and that in the old Viceroy's Executive Council, I held two administrative portfolios, that of Labour and C.P.W.D., where a great deal of planning projects were dealt by me, and would like to have some administrative portfolio. The Prime Minister agreed and said he would give me, in addition to Law the Planning Department which, he said, he was intending to create. Unfortunately, the Planning Department came very late in the day and when it did come, I was left out.

"During my time, there have been many transfers of portfolios from one minister to another. I thought I might be

considered for any one of them. But I have always been left out of consideration. Many ministers have been given two or three portfolios so that they have been overburdened. Others,like me, have been wanting more work. I have not even been considered for holding a portfolio temporarily when a minister in charge has gone abroad for a few days.

It is difficult to understand what is the principle underlying the distribution of government work among ministers which the Prime Minister follows? Is it capacity? Is it trust? Is it friendship? Is it pliability? I was not even appointed to be a member of main committees of the Cabinet, such as Foreign Affairs Committee, or the Defence Committee.

"When the Economic Affairs Committee was formed, I expected, in view of the fact that I was primarily a student of Economics and Finance, to be appointed to this committee. But I was left out. I was appointed to it by the Cabinet, when the Prime Minister had gone to England. But when he returned, in one of his many essays in the reconstruction of the cabinet, he left me out. In a subsequent reconstruction, my name was added to the committee, but that was as a result of my protest."

In his speech, Dr. Babasaheb Ambedkar accused Jawaharlal Nehru of favouritism, a charge that has now become synonymous with the Congress party. Despite his qualifications, he was kept out of important committees that were dedicated to shape the institutions of modern India.

Another reason given for his resignation was the way the Nehru government had treated backward classes and their rights. Dr. Babasaheb Ambedkar said:

"The Prime Minister's whole time and attention is devoted for the protection of the Muslims. I yield to none, not even to the Prime Minister, in my desire to give the Muslims of India the utmost protection wherever and whenever they stand in need of it. But what I want to know is, are the Muslims the only people who need protection? Are the Scheduled Castes, Scheduled

Tribes and the Indian Christians not in need of protection? What concern has he shown for these communities? So far as I know, none and yet these are the communities which need far more care and attention than the Muslims."[6]

Later, in his resignation speech, he severely criticised Nehru for his foreign policy, saying:

"On the 15th of August, 1947, when we began our life as an independent country, there was no country which wished us ill. Every country in the world was our friend. Today, after four years, all our friends have deserted us. We have no friends left. We have alienated ourselves. We are pursuing a lonely furrow with no one even to second our resolutions in the United Nations. When I think of our foreign policy, I am reminded of what Bismarck and Bernard Shaw have said. Bismarck has said that 'politics is not a game of realising the ideal. Politics is the game of the possible.' Bernard Shaw, not very long ago, said that good ideals are good; but one must not forget that it is often dangerous to be too good. Our foreign policy is in complete opposition to these words of wisdom uttered by two of the world's greatest men."

The final straw that broke the camel's back was the non-passage of the Hindu Code Bill, which led to the resignation of Dr. Babasaheb Ambedkar from Nehru's Cabinet.

Dr. Babasaheb Ambedkar tendered his resignation to Prime Minister Jawaharlal Nehru in 1951, just months before India's first General Elections in 1952. He participated in the election process as a candidate of the Scheduled Caste Federation Party (this later became the Republican Party of India) from the North Bombay constituency, but was defeated by a Congress candidate. Nehru aggressively campaigned against Dr. Babasaheb Ambedkar in these elections.

Ramachandra Guha writes in his book,India after Gandhi: *"The prestige and hold of the Congress, and the fact that Nehru made several speeches in Bombay, carried Kajrolkar to victory."*

In the Bhandara (Maharashtra) by-election, Dr. Babasaheb

Ambedkar re-contested, only to be defeated once again by a Congress candidate.

When he was alive, Dr. Babasaheb Ambedkar differed with the Congress' point of view on many occasions, including the way the Partition of India was conducted, or the way the Kashmir issue was handled. On Partition, he wrote:

"The question that concerns the Hindus is how far does the creation of Pakistan remove the communal question from Hindustan? That is a very legitimate question and must be considered. It must be admitted that by the creation of Pakistan, Hindustan is not freed of the communal question. While Pakistan can be made a homogeneous State by redrawing its boundaries, Hindustan must remain a composite State. The Musalmans are scattered all over Hindustan–though they are mostly congregated in towns– and no ingenuity in the matter of redrawing of boundaries can make it homogeneous. The only way to make Hindustan homogeneous is to arrange for exchange of population. Until that is done, it must be admitted that even with the creation of Pakistan, the problem of majority vs. minority will remain in Hindustan as before, and will continue to produce disharmony in the body politic of Hindustan."[7]

Dr. S.N. Busi, in his work on Dr. Babasaheb Ambedkar's role in the framing of the Indian Constitution, highlighted a certain reported view of his on Article 370. As per Busi, Dr. B.R. Ambedkar was categorical on the subject:

"You wish India should protect your borders, she should build roads in your area, she should supply you food-grains, and Kashmir should get equal status as India. But, the Government of India should have only limited powers and Indian people should have no rights in Kashmir. To give consent to this proposal, would be a treacherous thing against the interests of India and I, as the Law Minister of India, will never do it."[8]

On many matters of national importance, Dr. Babasaheb Ambedkar differed with Nehru and anybody who disagreed had to face a similar fate of being treated as a pariah by the ecosystem built around the man. In his resignation speech, he said, *"We have our newspapers. They have their age-old bias in favour of some and against others. Their judgements are seldom based on merits. Whenever they find an empty space, they are prone to fill the vacuum by supplying grounds for resignation, which are not the real grounds; but which put those whom they favour in a better light and those not in their favour in a bad light. Some such thing I see has happened even in my case."*

Dr. Babasaheb Ambedkar's revelation reflects the status quo of those times. Patronising the media and using it against the opponents was not a practice that began recently. In fact, it was a model practised by the colonisers and co-opted by the Congress party to suppress voices of dissent.

Forgetting Dr. Babasaheb Ambedkar in Life and Death: A Congress Vice

If one thought that Dr. Babasaheb Ambedkar's ill-treatment at the hands of the Congress ended upon his death, they would be in for a surprise. The manner in which Nehru-led Congress maintained a distance from the great icon when he was alive, later became a norm in the party as it continued to distort his legacy.

Dr. Babasaheb Ambedkar's memory was sidelined during decades of Congress rule. Even his portrait in the Central Hall of Parliament was unveiled when a non-Congress politician, V.P. Singh, became the Prime Minister of India. He was awarded the country's highest civilian honour, the Bharat Ratna, 34 years after his death by the National Front government. It was similar to the fate of other national icons who were awarded Bharat Ratna posthumously, including Sardar Patel who was awarded the honour 41 years after his death, and Maulana Abul Kalam Azad, 33 years after his death. Contrasting the delay in recognising the builders of modern India, Jawaharlal Nehru was conferred Bharat Ratna in 1955 and Indira Gandhi in 1971 during their own tenures as Prime Ministers.

In an interview to a newspaper,[9] the grandson of Dr. Babasaheb Ambedkar, Prakash Ambedkar made sharp criticism of the way the Congress Party treated his grandfather. During the interview, he asked the Congress as to why they forgot to celebrate Dr. Babasaheb Ambedkar's 100th birth anniversary. He further said:

> *"Today, the Congress is battling for survival. Their affection for Dr. Babasaheb Ambedkar is to regain the support of Dalits and consolidate their vote-bank, but people are no longer going to be fooled by such gimmicks. Let them explain what they have done to keep the legacy of Dr. Babasaheb Ambedkar alive when in power at the Centre and in Maharashtra. Not a single book was republished. None of his writings that were kept under wraps has been made public. The greatest injustice ever done to Dr. Babasaheb Ambedkar when he was alive was by the Congress."*

The questions raised by Prakash Ambedkar were not his alone–it was a sentiment running across the socially-deprived sections of the country as well as those aware of Dr. Babasaheb Ambedkar's role in India's making.

Celebrating Dr. Babasaheb Ambedkar's Legacy: Modi Era

Narendra Modi was born in a humble family belonging to a community that is classified as OBC (Other Backward Class). He had first-hand experience of the double blow that poverty and social discrimination can inflict on the people from disadvantaged sections of society. The growth of Modi in public life and the important roles he has been given by the people are an example of the social mobility that Dr. Babasaheb Ambedkar envisioned. Even he has made the point many times that it was the impact of Dr. Babasaheb Ambedkar's work that made it possible for people like him to rise in social life.

One of the striking patterns that can be observed by any serious analyst who studies the trajectory of Modi's life is his unwavering values and lifelong commitment to certain principles.

This shows in his commitment to the values of Dr. Babasaheb Ambedkar as well as the cause of social equality. The typical politician is said to change his likes and dislikes according to the direction of the political winds, but Modi is starkly different.

Modi's passion for social equality showed even at a very young age. As a young boy, he wrote a play called Peelu Phool (Yellow Flower) in Gujarati, which raised awareness against the practice of untouchability. When he was in his thirties and working with the Rashtriya Swayamsevak Sangh, he was a vital cog in the Sangh's response to the Meenakshipuram incident of 1981, due to his work on Dalit issues.

As Bharatiya Janata Party's (BJP) General Secretary in Gujarat, in 1987, one of the first initiatives of Modi was to mobilise the party organisation to install statues of Dr. Babasaheb Ambedkar at various places and honour him by garlanding them. He made this a part of regular political consciousness of the BJP workers at a time when Dr. Babasaheb Ambedkar's legacy had been almost erased at the national level by the Congress-dominated political ecosystem. Strikingly, this was at a time when political parties, claiming to be votaries of Dr. Babasaheb Ambedkar's ideals, had not gathered any electoral heft.

The same year, Modi was the architect of the Nyay Yatra that galvanised the people of Gujarat against injustice. There were many issues that were at the centre of this movement, including farmers' issues, drought relief and a demand to end atrocities on Dalits, among others.

Modi built his political party into a winning unit in Gujarat and eventually went on to become the Chief Minister of the state. As Chief Minister, in 2007, he constructed Ambedkar Bhavans in various places across Gujarat. His speeches at this series of inauguration events offer a deep insight into the way he perceives Dr. Babasaheb Ambedkar–as one of the most important makers of modern India. CM Modi had observed that because Dr. Babasaheb Ambedkar's goal was social revolution, he was not just an individual, but synonymous with the entire struggle against inequality, He also compared Dr. Babasaheb Ambedkar to Martin Luther King and lamented the fact that while Dr. King was celebrated worldwide, a lot of injustice had been done to the memory of Dr. Babasaheb Ambedkar by the entrenched established elite of India taking decades to even honour him with a Bharat Ratna.

CM Modi also organised a Samvidhan Yatra in 2010, celebrating the sixtieth anniversary of the adoption of the Constitution. As part of this yatra, he flagged off a procession of a giant replica of the Constitution, beginning from a statue of Dr. Babasaheb Ambedkar. The replica was placed on a decorated elephant, which carried it across the city, even as the Chief Minister himself walked alongside the elephant, with his ministers and thousands of other people who had joined.

As Chief Minister of Gujarat, a number of his governance schemes had Dr. Babasaheb Ambedkar as their inspiration. For example, the Babasaheb Ambedkar Awas Navinkaran Yojana provided financial assistance to disadvantaged sections to become house owners.

CM Modi also holds in high regard the ideal of samajik samrasta or social harmony, something that Dr. Babasaheb Ambedkar had always propounded and practiced. As CM Modi observed in one of his speeches, Dr. Babasaheb Ambedkar was a leader who fought for social equality, but his movement was never characterised by negativity; instead, he was always for the reform of society where even the most marginalised sections couldlead a life of dignity. CM Modi has ingrained this ideal in both himself and his party– building a society where everyone is cared for, no one is discriminated against, and the disadvantaged sections get a helping hand. Therefore, ensuring social empowerment and social harmony have been the top priority for CM Modi's party and his government.

It is no wonder then, that as he rose to the national level, the representation of the disadvantaged sections of society within his party also began to rise. In the 2014 Lok Sabha elections, out of the 131 Member of Parliament (MP) seats reserved for Scheduled Castes and Scheduled Tribes, the BJP contributed 67. In 2019, this number increased sharply– the BJP has 97 Lok Sabha MPs belonging to the SC and ST communities who won from the reserved seats. The BJP also sent 81 OBC MPs in 2014 and 113 OBC MPs in 2019. This is a clear sign of the radical expansion of the BJP's social base in PM Modi's era as well as the popularity of PM Modi Modi among these communities.

Ever since the National Democratic Alliance (NDA) government led by PM Modi was elected in 2014, there has been a revival of the legacy of marginalised heroes in the public consciousness. Necessary institutional support to this cause has made the initiative long-lasting and not something that would be overturned with a change in government.

The NDA government under the leadership of PM Modi took the important decision of developing places of historical importance that were closely related to Dr. Babasaheb Ambedkar's life as Pancha Tirthas:

- His birthplace in Mhow, Madhya Pradesh.
- The place in London where he stayed while studying in the UK.
- Deeksha Bhoomi in Nagpur, Maharashtra.
- Mahaparinirvan Sthal in Delhi.
- Chaitya Bhoomi in Mumbai, Maharashtra.

This was the first of the many steps taken by the dispensation to create a substantive stock of institutions fully dedicated to keep the legacy of Dr. Babasaheb Ambedkar alive for generations to come. On 19th November, 2015, the government declared 26th November as 'Constitution Day' in honour of Dr. Babasaheb Ambedkar. Next, in April 2018, PM Modi inaugurated the Dr. Babasaheb Ambedkar National Memorial at Delhi's Mahaparinirvan Sthal which is spread over nearly two acres. The memorial was first proposed by the previous NDA government led by the late Atal Bihari Vajpayee. However, the project was stalled when UPA came to power, only to be revived by another NDA government.

Even in the governance-related vision of the government, in PM Modi's own words, Dr. Babasaheb Ambedkar is one of the foundational thinkers. As discussed above, the Congress-led government failed to imbibe the vision laid down by Dr. Babasaheb Ambedkar. In fact, he faced neglect and exclusion under the Nehru regime, while his legacy was abandoned after his death by successive Congress governments. Correcting the historical wrongs, Dr. Babasaheb Ambedkar's work has been brought to the forefront by the BJP-led government. His thoughts could be observed in the priorities laid down by PM Modi who, during his 'Mann Ki Baat' radio address, drew people's attention to the areas in which his government has drawn inspiration from Dr. Babasaheb Ambedkar's vision and acted to honour his legacy:

"My dear countrymen, 14th April is the birth anniversary of Dr. Babasaheb Ambedkar. Years ago, Dr. Babasaheb Ambedkar spoke of India's industrialisation. According to him, the industry was an effective medium by which jobs could be made available to the poorest of the poor and the poorer. Today, the campaign of 'Make in India' is progressing successfully in consonance with Dr. Babasaheb Ambedkar's dream of India as an industrial super-power – that vision of his has become our inspiration today.

"Today, India has emerged as a bright spot in the global economy and today the highest Foreign Direct Investment or FDI in the world is flowing into India. The whole world is looking at India as a hub for investment, innovation and development. That the development of industries could only be possible in the cities was the kernel of the idea of Dr. Babasaheb Ambedkar and that was the reason he banked upon urbanisation of India. In continuance with his vision, Smart City Mission and Urban Mission were kick-started in the country so that all kinds of amenities, be it good roads, water supply, health facilities, education or digital connectivity are available in the big cities and small towns of the country.

"Dr. Babasaheb Ambedkar had a strong faith in self-reliance. He did not want anybody to languish in poverty forever. He also believed that poverty cannot be ameliorated by mere distribution of capital among the impoverished. Today, our monetary policy, Start Up India, Stand Up India initiatives have become the seedbed for our young innovators and young entrepreneurs. In the 30s and 40s, when only roads and railways were being talked about in India, Dr. Babasaheb Ambedkar mentioned about ports and waterways. It was Dr. Babasaheb Ambedkar who envisaged water power as 'nation power'. He stressed the utilisation of water for the development of the nation. The genesis of different river valley authorities, different water related commissions– all these were possible due to the vision of Dr. Babasaheb Ambedkar. Today, there are landmark efforts being embarked upon for waterways and ports in our country. New seaports are being constructed on a number of seaways of India and infrastructure is being strengthened at old ports.

"In the era of 40s, while most of the discussions were centred around the Second World War, the looming Cold War and the Partition– it was during those times that Dr. Babasaheb Ambedkar had laid the foundation of Team India's spirit in a way. He had talked about the importance of federalism, federal system and stressed on Centre and states working together for the uplift of the country. Today, we have adopted in all aspects of governance, the mantra of co-operative federalism and going a step further, we have adopted competitive co-operative federalism; but, most importantly, Dr. Babasaheb Ambedkar is an inspiration for millions of people like me, who belong to backward classes.

"He showed us that to succeed it is not necessary for the person to be born in an illustrious or rich family, but even those who are born to poor families in India can also dare to dream their dreams and realise those dreams by achieving success. And, of course, this is exactly what happened as many people mocked

Dr. Babasaheb Ambedkar, tried to pull him back and made every possible effort to ensure that the son of an impoverished and backward family would not progress in life, be something and succeed in life.

"But, the picture of New India is altogether different. It is an India, which is Dr. Babasaheb Ambedkar's India, of the poor and the backward."[10]

Why is This Book Needed?

Dr. Babasaheb Ambedkar's contribution to the making of India as we know today is immense. However, by design during the decades of Congress rule in early years of our republic, and by writing and historical research later, full justice was not done to Dr. Babasaheb Ambedkar's contribution and legacy.His degrees on diverse subjects, each in itself worthy of a speciality, has also been under-appreciated. This has been in part by design due to the ecosystem of the Congress, which has always placed one family over every other national icon, and in part due to accumulated neglect that builds in academic circles from lack of institutional opportunity.

It is vital that continuous research and publications are produced on Dr. Babasaheb Ambedkar's thoughts and works so that our history and amalgamation of ideas truly represent our legacy and diversity and do not become appendage to just one family.

In modern times, PM Modi has had to face similar opprobrium from the Congress-nurtured ecosystem, as Dr. Babasaheb Ambedkar faced during his lifetime and later. It is not a coincidence that both came from humble backgrounds and yet both scaled the peak of their chosen vocations while still displaying immense fair play and justice in the public roles they were called on to discharge. From a policy standpoint as well, Dr. Babasaheb Ambedkar and PM Modi's thoughts and ideas on economics, social justice, empowerment of the weak and the poor, and social and financial empowerment of women are broadly in alignment and have resonance.

This book, which delves into these subjects, from scholarly perspective, would be an important contribution in the policy landscape of the country as also in balancing the scales when it comes to recognising the contribution of our icons.

□

2

Industrial Growth: A Social Liberator

"Industrialisation of India is the soundest remedy for the agricultural problems of India. The cumulative effects of industrialisation, namely, a lessening pressure and an increasing amount of capital and capital goods will forcibly create the economic necessity of enlarging the holding. Not only this, but industrialisation by destroying the premium on land will give rise to few occasions for its sub-division and fragmentation. Industrialisation is a natural and powerful remedy."

—*Dr. B.R. Ambedkar*[11]

The towering intellect of Dr. B.R. Ambedkar is conspicuous in his writings, in Constituent Assembly debates and speeches. Like most of the erudite thinkers of the past, his views were very clear across spectrums, be it economy, religion, policy, law or constitutional jurisprudence. This chapter explores his vision of an 'industrialised India' and its relevance in present times.

Dr. Babasaheb Ambedkar had a firm belief that industrialisation of the Indian economy would be a solution to most of its problems, particularly poverty and fragmentation of agriculture. He maintained that as long as people depended on land for their livelihoods, thinking about formation of any kind of industry was unfathomable. He observed:

"Why is industrialisation necessary? And you will have the full significance made clear to you at once; for the answer to

the question is– we want industrialisation in India as the surest means to rescue the people from the eternal cycle of poverty in which they are caught. Industrialisation of India must, therefore, be grappled with immediately."[12]

As we know, post-colonial India had been a predominantly agrarian economy. The diversification of economy– from agrarian into multiple forces of production– did not happen as it should have.

Though Dr. Babasaheb Ambedkar considered agriculture as one of the primary industries, his emphasis was more on the production of capital goods. Explaining the facets of industrialisation, he said that the production of capital goods (the base of any manufacturing industry), involving multiple factors of production, has high division of labour and certainly more per capita productivity than agriculture. The industries are, therefore, capable of producing enormous capital. India, according to him, with a growing population, needed commodities and capital with a simultaneous increase in the purchasing power. Dr. Babasaheb Ambedkar, therefore, advocated extensive use of machinery, which would result in the production of commodities on a mass scale.

Make in India

"'Make in India': This is the step of a lion."[13]

—Prime Minister Narendra Modi

Dr. Babasaheb Ambedkar's unflagging and unapologetic support to industrialisation is quite visible in his writings. His unwavering belief that agriculture alone cannot empower the poor gave teeth to his suggested reforms for the Indian economy. As he gained education in the West and was gradually informed of their work culture and economy, Dr. Babasaheb Ambedkar realised the potential of industrialisation in India's overall prosperity. That is why, undoubtedly, one of the biggest and pre-eminent policy launches of the Prime Minister Narendra Modi led government was 'Make in India'– a grand initiative to unleash massive industrialisation in the country and to reform the industrial process for a prosperous India.

To fulfil Dr. Babasaheb Ambedkar's vision of an industrialised India, the Modi government has enacted several important reforms to further boost 'Make in India'. A massive cut in corporate taxes, which fixes the rate at just 15% for new manufacturing units, makes India one of the most competitive economies in the world. Labour code reforms that streamline and consolidate more than 44 laws into four codes and the continued success of the Insolvency and Bankruptcy Code are just some of the path-breaking reforms undertaken by the government since it assumed office in 2014. The very unpopular Angel Tax, introduced by the UPA regime, was removed in 2019 as part of an effort to help start-ups raise additional money to put into their businesses. Indian companies are now allowed to directly list themselves overseas as part of an effort to give them a chance to access funds from abroad and, at the same time, compete with and forge business relationships with global players.

Unlike the previous industrial reforms, 'Make in India' embodies a paradigm shift, since it invites the world to invest and manufacture in India. It opens India to the world, so that it can become an inextricable part of a global supply chain. Dr. Babasaheb Ambedkar once talked about the prospering West while comparing it with India. Today, not only the West, but the whole world is looking to invest in India. His concerns about shrinking industrialisation in India have also been addressed with an initiative such as 'Make in India', with its emphasis on indigenous manufacturing. The scheme is bound to bridge the gap between the service sector and agriculture sector.

With the 'Make in India' programme, there is sustained focus on making India a hub of manufacturing and innovation in order to attract more foreign investment as well as transfer of technology. Since its launch, the programme has made significant achievements and is now focusing on 27 sectors under 'Make in

India' 2.0. As we go further, we will look into individual sectors that have registered impressive growth due to the government's push to promote manufacturing.

Atmanirbhar Bharat

> *"When India speaks of becoming self-reliant, it doesn't advocate a self-centred system. In India's self-reliance, there is concern for the whole world's happiness, co-operation and peace."*[14]
>
> **—Prime Minister Narendra Modi**

India has been one of the top global economies with the fastest rate of economic growth among major nations in the last few years. However, with the onset of the Covid pandemic, there was a disruption. To handle this disruption as well as strengthen the economy, the Modi government announced the landmark 'Atmanirbhar Bharat' package in May 2020 as part of the Prime Minister's larger vision to create a self-reliant India.

The five pillars of a self-reliant India, as described by the Prime Minister, are:

(i) Economy, which brings in quantum jump and not incremental change.

(ii) Infrastructure that becomes the identity of India.

(iii) Systems based on 21st century technology-driven arrangements.

(iv) Vibrant demography being the source of energy for a self-reliant India.

(v) Demand, to achieve full utilisation of the power of 'demand and supply'.

As part of the Atmanirbhar Bharat Abhiyaan, an economic package worth Rs. 20 lakh crore was announced (equivalent to 10% of India's GDP) to inject the economy with the much-needed funds, a new direction for development and provide relief to struggling businesses. The package focuses on land, labour, liquidity and laws and caters to various sections, including cottage industry, MSMEs, labourers, middle class, industries, among others. These reforms promote business, attract investment and further strengthen the 'Make in India' initiative.

From the beginning, PM Modi has stressed that self-reliance does not mean cutting India off from the world; instead, it is about creating a unique opportunity to tap into the potential of what the youth of the country have to offer to the rest of the world. Part of the 'Atmanirbhar Bharat' vision is to be 'vocal for local' and create an environment that promotes local products among the common man.

During the Covid pandemic when the global supply chain was disrupted, the importance of the local industry in fulfilling the needs of the common man, and also towards the industrial ecosystem became evident. It is, therefore, not surprising that PM Modi pushed for local industries to expand production. At the same time, he emphasised on the importance of making India a huge local market and spoke about the country's potential to take its local products global.

The call was reiterated when he flagged-off the Azadi Ka Amrit Mahotsav to mark 75 years of Independence. PM Modi tweeted:

> *"Today's #AmritMahotsav programme begins from Sabarmati Ashram, from where the Dandi March began. The march had a key role in furthering a spirit of pride and atmanirbharta among India's people. Going #VocalForLocal is a wonderful tribute to Bapu and our great freedom fighters.*[15]
>
> *"Buy any local product and post a picture on social media using #VocalForLocal. A charkha will be installed near Magan Niwas at Sabarmati Ashram. It will rotate full circle with each Tweet related to atmanirbharta. This shall also become a catalyst for a people's movement."*[16]

PM Modi believes that, in times of crisis, the importance of local manufacturing, local market and local supply chain is key to fulfilling the country's demands. He is of the view that all global brands were once local; however, when people started using and promoting them, did they become global. The government has amended existing rules to encourage local manufacturing of goods and services and enhance income and employment opportunities. Procurement has also been used to promote indigenous manufacturing of the MSME sector, which forms the backbone of the economy. As part of the Atmanirbhar Bharat package, the decision was taken to prioritise procurement from domestic MSME players for tenders of value up to Rs. 200 crore.[17]This serves as an assured base of MSME players, who can then obtain capital to fulfil such orders or for expanding their goods and service ambit.

In order to give a fillip to the telecom sector, a number of decisions were taken to transform the domestic manufacturing industry.[1] The move has re-energised a sector that was heavily dependent on imported equipment at costly rates.

A milestone in implementing the 'vocal for local' vision was the Production Linked Incentive (PLI) scheme of 2020 that focused on giving substantial boost to India's manufacturing capabilities and exports. The scheme is primarily aimed at making India a manufacturing hub by providing incentives to various companies for a specific time period. The PLI scheme was originally formulated to lower India's dependence on imports of electronic equipment. However, it has now been expanded to include 14 high-value sectors, including automobiles and auto components, pharmaceuticals, food products, high-efficiency solar PV modules, drones, etc. Also, a PLI scheme is being considered for new sectors like 5G technologies, as was revealed in Parliament during the presentation of Budget 2022-23.

PM Modi's vision for achieving atmanirbharta has also extended to building up our defence manufacturing capabilities to be self-reliant when defending the borders of our country. The government came out with Positive Indigenisation List for the Indian Armed Forces[19] in December 2021 to help identify the areas of focus for domestic manufacturers. This list helps create an assured market for those eager and willing to undertake such specialised manufacturing in India.

In his 87th edition of 'Mann Ki Baat' in March 2022, PM Modi gave the call of 'local for global' to celebrate the quantum jump in Indian exports. Praising the country for achieving a record export target of $400 billion, PM Modi said:[20]

> *"Today, India has reached $400 billion. In a way, this means that the demand for items made in India is increasing all over the world...New products from all corners of the country are reaching foreign shores. Leather products from Hailakandi in Assam or handloom products from Osmanabad, fruits and vegetables from Bijapur or black rice from Chandauli– the exports of all of these are increasing. Now, you will also find the world-famous apricot of Ladakh in Dubai too and in Saudi Arabia; you will find bananas shipped from Tamil Nadu. Most importantly, an array of new products are being sent to ever newer countries."*

These measures alongside other provisions have contributed significantly in not just reviving the economy, but also propelling it much higher than even pre-Covid levels in terms of growth and expansion.

Production-linked Incentive Schemes

Government of India notified the National Policy on Electronics (NPE) 2019 on February 2019 with the objective to promote domestic manufacturing in the entire electronics manufacturing value chain to achieve a turnover of over Rs. 30 lakh crore by 2025, including a targeted production of 100 crore mobile phones.[2] A Production Linked Incentive (PLI) scheme was rolled out in April 2020 to integrate manufacturing capabilities so that the sector could meet the demands of the global supply chain and exports. The scheme aims to position India as a global manufacturer by encouraging and driving capabilities in the country for developing core components, including chipsets, and creating an enabling environment for the industry to compete globally.

After the resounding success of a Production Linked Incentive scheme for the mobile and electronics sector introduced in 2020, which saw investment worth Rs. 35,541 crore by April 2021, the Modi government decided to introduce similar incentive schemes for 14 other key sectors.[22]PLI schemes give the much-needed push to domestic manufacturing with an initial outlay of Rs. 1.97 lakh crore across different sectors of core competency over five years. The government is looking to create a positive environment in the manufacturing sector that will lead to overall growth in the economy and create huge employment opportunities. Indian manufacturers will emerge as globally competitive, capable of attracting large investments and cutting-edge technology, which will, in turn, reduce the country's import dependency.

The sectors covered include: (i) advance chemistry cell battery; (ii) electronic/ technology products; (iii) automobiles, auto components &drones; (iv) pharmaceuticals drugs; (v) telecom &networking products; (vi) textile products; (vii) food products; (viii) high-efficiency solar PV modules; (ix) white goods (ACs & LED); (x) speciality steel; (xi) medical devices; (xii) large-scale electronics manufacturing; (xiii) key starting materials/ drug intermediates/active pharmaceutical ingredients; and (xiv) semiconductors.

Disinvestment and Increased Private Sector Participation

For much of its history since Independence, India remained a mixed economy based on a combination of capitalism and socialism, with an overbearing presence of the State in economic activity. The strategy employed by the Congress governments was to take charge of major sectors, such as banking, coal, oil and gas, steel, telecom, transport, defence, education, manufacturing and healthcare, and create public sector organisations to run them. The dominance of the public sector was so large that the typical Indian seemed to be either a farmer or was employed by the government in one form or another. In contrast, the size of the private sector was small and insignificant, besides being heavily regulated. An initial privatisation process that began in the early 1990s saw some economic activity open for private players, but it needed more reforms for it to be able to show its full impact.

One of the key focus areas for PM Modi has been to push the privatisation of key public sector companies that have been undergoing losses for decades to ensure increased private sector participation in major economic spheres. Privatisation, which till now had been attempted only on an ad-hoc basis, has finally been put into a well-defined structural framework that seeks to capitalise on the expertise and mobilisation abilities of the private sector to generate greater economic growth. From mining to money management, the government has prepared a list of areas where private sector will be allowed to invest more, even translating it on the ground in the form of auctions and disinvestment deals. Already, disinvestment of Air India, long considered the touchstone of reforms, has been completed. With this, India's aviation sector is completely privatised and now the government has started formalising the details for the disinvestment of LIC as the next step.

The privatisation process is expected to speed up India's economic growth by attracting big private players to invest in these loss-making PSEs, giving a chance to upgrade their ailing infrastructure, making them market-competitive and bring their workforce at par with the rest of the country.

Defence Manufacturing

The growth of domestic manufacturing is an imperative for the Indian economy to grow with 'Make in India' and 'Atmanirbhar

Bharat' giving major impetus during planning and procurement of equipment for the Indian Armed Forces. One of the many objectives is to achieve atmanirbharta in defence by creating a state-of-the-art manufacturing infrastructure in the country so that there is a reduced dependence on imports. India, having the third-largest military in the world,is the sixth-biggest spender on defence with nearly 60% of the country's defence requirements being met through imports.

India's defence manufacturing sector is covering new ground with greater impetus on 'Make in India'. In addition to procuring defence equipment, such as radar, ballistic helmets, artillery guns, bulletproof jackets and ammunition from local vendors, India is capably manufacturing air-to-air and surface-to-air missile systems, advance light helicopters and light combat helicopters, etc. The country has also ventured into manufacture of Main Battle Tanks (MBT).

India is not only producing bullet-proof jackets that provide 360-degree protection, but is also exporting them to more than 100 other countries. With this, it has become the fourth country after the US, UK and Germany to have its own national standard on bulletproof jacket.[23]

To provide autonomy and enhance efficiency, the Ordnance Factory Board has been converted into seven defence public sector undertakings.

However, appointment of the Chief of Defence Staff (CDS) and creation of the Department of Military Affairs (DMA) remain the most significant and transformative reforms undertaken by any government since India's Independence. The DMA will spearhead future reforms towards ensuring optimum utilisation of scarce national resources, enhancing synergy between the three Services and steering the modernisation of the Indian military force.

Modernisation of the Indian Army in the face of emerging

threats is a must. From the economic as well as security point of view, indigenous manufacturing of defence equipment puts India at an advantage. Therefore, considering a big component of the 'Make in India' policy is the technology transfer, the focus is on building capacity among the Indian players, especially among the MSME sector. In view of acquiring the best technology, the government had allowed 100% FDI in defence sector, out of which up to 74% is under automatic route. FDI above 74% is permitted through the government route on case-to-case basis where it is likely to result in access to modern technology. The government came out with Positive Indigenisation List for the Indian Armed Forces[24] in December 2021 to help identify the areas of focus for domestic manufacturers. This list helps create an assured market for those eager and willing to undertake such specialised manufacturing in India. This effort gets complemented by the push for defence industrial corridors in Uttar Pradesh and Tamil Nadu that aim to create an end-to-end ecosystem for aerospace and defence sector development covering design, engineering and manufacturing.[25]

In order to create a level-playing field for the private sector to thrive in a capital-intensive defence sector, preferential treatment in excise duty or customs duty, given to Public Sector Undertakings (PSUs), has been discontinued. Further, the customs duty exemption on import of defence equipment has been removed to encourage imports and incentivise domestic manufacturing.

On the one hand, import of defence equipment has been arrested and on the other, removal of customs duty exemption is incentivising domestic manufacturing.

There is also great emphasis on developing the defence sector manufacturing to make India a major exporter of defence equipment in the world. About 50 Indian companies in the private sector have contributed to defence exports. Some of the major export destinations for defence products include Italy, Maldives, Sri Lanka, Russia, France, Nepal, Mauritius, Sri Lanka, Israel, Egypt, etc. The major defence items being exported are personal protective items, offshore patrol vessels, ALH helicopter, SU avionics, Bharati Radio, coastal surveillance systems, Kavach MoD II Launcher and FCS, spares for radar, electronic system andlight engineering mechanical parts,etc.The efforts to making India a major exporter received a shot in the arm with the Philippines placing a major order for India-made BrahMos supersonic cruise missiles, on January 28, 2022.[26]

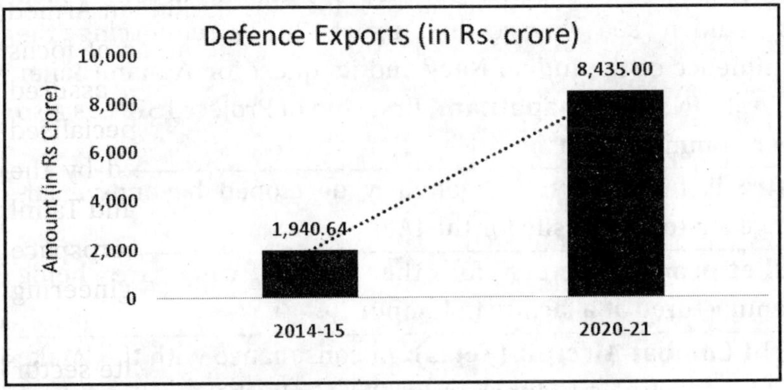

(Source: Ministry of Defence/news reports)[27]

Several initiatives have also been undertaken by PM Modi towards empowering women in the Services and permanent commission of women officers has finally been implemented in the Armed Forces with a particular focus on their management of technology. The first batch of women naval operations officers were inducted into the rotary wing and joined the helicopter squadron INAS 336 at 'INS Garuda', Kochi in 2021.

'Make in India' Wonders
'INS Kalvari' became India's first 'Make in India' Scorpene-class submarine to be commissioned into the Indian Navy. A joint venture between private entity Mazgaon Docks Ltd. and a French company is constructing six submarines, of which four have now been inducted, one is undergoing sea-trial and the sixth is still under construction.
BrahMos is a JV between DRDO and Russia's NPOM for the development, production and marketing of the supersonic cruise missile.
Indigenous aircraft carrier **'Vikrant'** successfully accomplished its maiden sea voyage in August 2021, reinforcing the confidence of the Indian Navy and its quest for 'Atmanirbahar Bharat'. **'INS Visakhapatnam',** first ship of Project 15B, has also been commissioned.
Astra is India's first indigenously developed beyond-visual-range air-to-air missile for the IAF.
Bullet-proof helmets for the Indian Army are being manufactured at a facility in Kanpur.
Light Combat Aircraft (Tejas): In consonance with the 'Make in India' campaign launched by PM Modi, the first Squadron of Tejas, an advanced multirole aircraft with state-of-the-art avionics, was formed.
16 **Apache** advanced choppers for Indian Army, by Boeing, are said to be the world's most advanced attack helicopter. Under 'Make in India', AH-64 Apache fuselages and other aero-structures are being manufactured at the Tata Boeing Aerospace joint venture facility in Hyderabad.
Hercules C-130J-30: IAF has inducted additional six C-130J all-weather transport aircraft which are designed for Special Operations.

The **Defence Production and Export Promotion Policy 2020** aims to make India amongst the leading countries of the world in the defence sector, including aerospace and naval shipbuilding sectorsand expects defencegoods and services to accountfor a turnover of Rs. 1.75 lakh crores by 2025.

In the Midst of a Mobile Revolution

Not only defence, indigenous electronics manufacturing has made huge strides under 'Make in India'. There has been a positive outlook towards Indian manufacturing.

Till 2014, India had only two mobile manufacturing units; by 2019, the number stood at 268 with one of the biggest mobile manufacturing units openedat Noidain Uttar Pradesh. It has been estimated that almost 90% of the hand phones being sold in India were domestically manufactured by 2020. The export of mobile phones has increased from Rs. 1,440 crore in 2017-18 to Rs. 12,240 crore in 2021 (April 21-September 21), while imports decreased from Rs. 25,200 crore in 2017-18 to Rs. 3,600 crore in 2021 (April 21-September 21). As a result of mobile and mobile components being manufactured in India, Rs. 3 lakh croreare being saved in imports as per a study done by the India Cellular and Electronics Association (ICEA). It is estimated that about 7.5 lakh persons have been employed (directly and indirectly) by the units manufacturing mobile phones and its components.

The Production Linked Incentive scheme has given an additional thrust to India's mobile manufacturing industry. According to India Cellular and Electronics Association (ICEA), the industry had projected to hire about 50,000-60,000 people in 2021. This could turn into a

Rs. 13,680 crores opportunity by 2025 with the country looking to export 600 million mobile phones worth Rs. 8 lakh crore, both in the entry level as well as high-priced segments, to markets like Europe, North America and Africa.

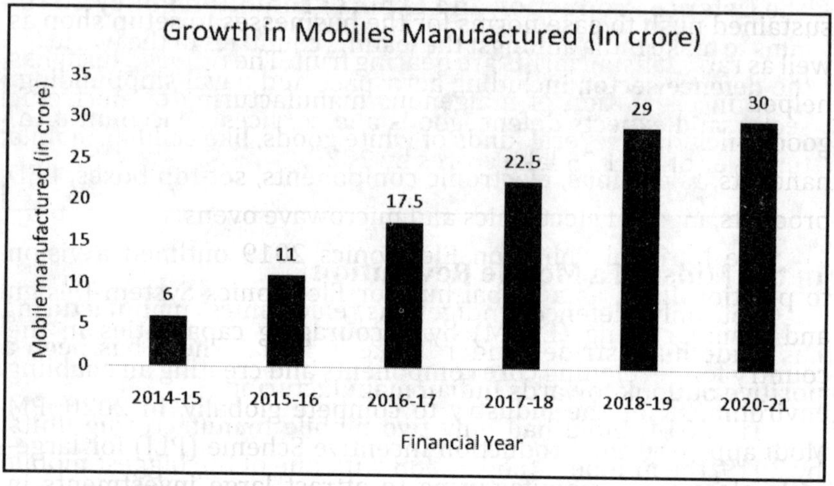

(Source: News reports/Websites)[28]

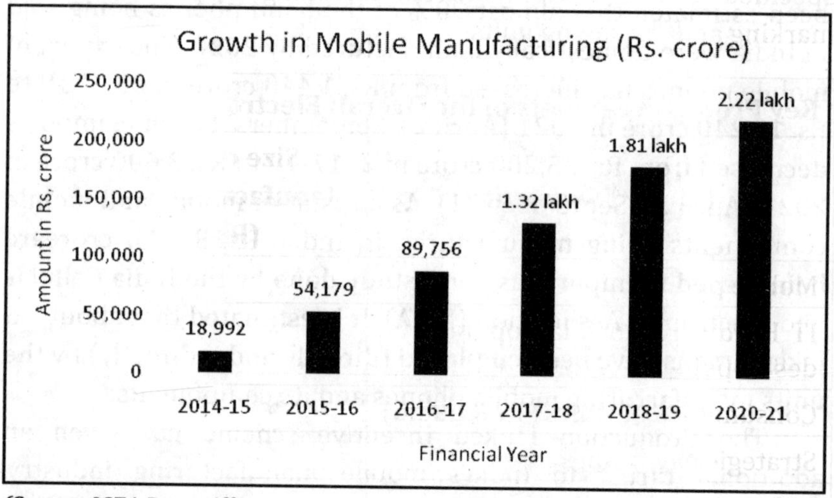

(Source: ICEA Report)[29]

Rise in Electronics Manufacturing

The appetite for electronics has been growing in the country with an increase in incomes. Majority of this demand used to be fulfilled by importing the components and assembling them in the country, since India's consumer electronics manufacturewas at its nascent stage before 'Make in India' came into the forefront. The sustained push to ease norms for the businesses to setup shop as well as rationalising tariffs are bearing fruit. The reduced tariff has helped in promotion of indigenous manufacturing of electronic goods, including several kinds of white goods, like cellular mobile handsets, televisions, electronic components, set-top boxes, LED products, medical electronics and microwave ovens.

The National Policy on Electronics 2019 outlined a vision to position India as a global hub for Electronics System Design and Manufacturing (ESDM) by encouraging capabilities in the country for developing core components and creating an enabling environment for the industry to compete globally. In 2020, PM Modi approved the Production Incentive Scheme (PLI) for large-scale electronics manufacturing to attract large investments in specified electronic components, including assembly, testing, marking and packaging units.

Key Product Segments of the Overall Electronics Industry[30]

Product Segment	Size of Domestic Manufacturing 2020-21 (Rs. crore)
Mobile phones	2,160
IT Hardware (incl. laptop, tablets, desktops)	216
Consumer electronics (TV & audio)	684
Strategic electronics	288
Industrial electronics	756
PCBA	36
Auto electronics	432
LED lighting	158.4
Electronic components	648
Total	Rs. 5,378.4 crore

(Source: Indian Cellular & Electronics Association)

Industrial Corridors

The 'Make in India' initiative aims at promoting India as an investment destination and establishing the country as a global hub for manufacturing, design and innovation. In order to further strengthen thecountry's position as a favoured investment destination, the government has developed or is in the process of developing the following 11 industrial corridors (as of December, 2021)[31] with 32 projects to be developed in four phases, forming part of the National Infrastructure Pipeline (NIP):

1. Delhi Mumbai Industrial Corridor (DMIC).
2. Chennai Bengaluru Industrial Corridor (CBIC).
3. Bengaluru Mumbai Industrial Corridor (BMIC).
4. Amritsar Kolkata Industrial Corridor (AKIC).
5. East Coast Industrial Corridor (ECIC) with Vizag Chennai Industrial Corridor (VCIC) as Phase 1.
6. Extension of CBIC to Kochi via Coimbatore.
7. Hyderabad Nagpur Industrial Corridor (HNIC).
8. Hyderabad Warangal Industrial Corridor (HWIC).
9. Hyderabad Bengaluru Industrial Corridor (HBIC).
10. Odisha Economic Corridor (OEC).
11. Delhi Nagpur Industrial Corridor (DNIC).

These industrial cities would distinguish themselves with world-class modern infrastructure, such as high-speed transportation (rail, road) network, ports with state-of-the-art cargo-handling equipment, modern airports, special economic regions or industrial areas, logistic parks or trans-shipment hubs, knowledge parks focussed on feeding industrial needs, complementary infrastructure such as townships or real estate, and other urban infrastructure along with enabling policy framework.

These clusters of manufacturing or export-oriented business units boost economic activity with the creation of state-of-the-art infrastructure, connectivity and new green-field smart cities as global manufacturing hubs, thus leading to large-scale employment opportunities.

Strengthening the Mining Sector

Mining is one of the major economic activities that contributes to the GDP and generates significant number of employment opportunities. As the Labour Member in the Viceroy's Executive Council, Dr. Babasaheb Ambedkar had pushed for a mineral policy that could drive the industrialisation of the country. He proposed a legislation, on behalf of the Government of India, to establish control of the country's mineral resources. He stated:

"In defining the limits of legislative control over the minerals, we propose to take into consideration the following circumstances: One, the importance of the mineral from the defence point of view on all India mineral development; Two, the technical nature of the mineral; Three, the purposes for which the mineral is used; Four, the value of the mineral or of the products into the making of which the mineral enters. Our legislative provisions will fall into two classes, or rather divide the minerals into two classes: Those which will be subjected to general control; and under general control we propose to confine ourselves to the granting of prospecting and mining leases, the terms and conditions of such licenses and termination thereof.

"The detailed control will include, besides the power to grant licenses, the power to control the method of mining, of processing, of grading, of standardising, to direct improvement of mining and procuring methods, and also the power to initiate research for increased utilisation and for other necessary purposes."[32]

To fulfil India's industrial aspirations, the Modi government has freed the mining sector from corruption and administrative lethargy. It has duly recognised that as a source of raw material, the mining sector is not only an engine of core industries– a necessary prerequisite for infrastructure building, but is also instrumental in generation of growth and employment.

The red tape and bureaucratic inertia that mired the sector has been done away with and a single window clearance portal launched for the coal sector. The government has expedited environment and forest clearances through due process making,land identification, leasing and acquisition easier and faster. In 2019, the government introduced commercial coal mining. The move energised the coal mining sector, delinked it from captive usage and put traders and users at par when it came to allocation of coal mines. The first-ever successful auction of commercial mining was held in 2020 with the allocation of 19 coal mines. So far, 28 coal blocks have been auctioned in the States of Chhattisgarh, Jharkhand, Madhya Pradesh, Maharashtra and Odisha.[33]

The Modi government also approved the National Mineral Policy, 2019 to ensure more effective regulation. Auction of concessions for major minerals (other than coal, petroleum and natural gas) was done for the first time in the history of mineral administration in the country and 53 blocks were successfully allocated.[34] As of February 2022, the Ministry of Mines has auctioned a total of 145 blocks across 11 states.[35]

Power for All as an Opportuntiy

Dr. Babasaheb Ambedkar, while highlighting the importance of electricity in the progress of industrialisation, had emphasised: *"Without cheap and abundant electricity, India's efforts at industrialisation can't succeed."*[36]

More than 60% of India's electricity generation,through thermal power plants, is produced by burning of coal. In a historic move, the Modi government in February 2018, opened up the coal-mining sector to private firms for commercial useas till now it was a monopolised activity of the government.

This move, which is surely an embodiment of a shift from monopolisation towards competition in the coal sector,is unprecedented. Apart from greater energy security, it will ensure assured coal supply, increased domestic production, reduced dependence on imports and lowering of power tariffs. The foreign exchange saved by the increased production of coal could be invested in the social infrastructure elsewhere in the country.

Meantime, PM Modi's commitment towards fighting the threat of climate change is being fuelled by renewable energy. India has set a target to meet 50% (500 GW) of its energy requirements from renewable energy by 2030. This will help it to reduce the total projected carbon emissions by 1 billion tonnes, starting 2021 and till 2030. Already, more than 155 GW of clean power capacity is online with substantial capacity under development.

The government's commitment to green technologies has resulted in a number of regulatory reforms including 100% FDI under automatic route, creation of green energy corridors, introduction of competitive bidding, etc. India has maintained its 10th rank for the second year running in the Climate Change Performance Index 2022 (CCPI) Report, and is already on track to meet the 2030 emissions target. The report states that the country will achieve its NDC target of 40% non-fossil fuel-based installed power capacity by 2030; and is on course to 33-35% reduction in energy intensity.[37] The country achieved the 40% target in November 2021 itself. India was in fact the only G20 nation on track to meet 2°C global warming targets as agreed to under the Paris Accord.[38]

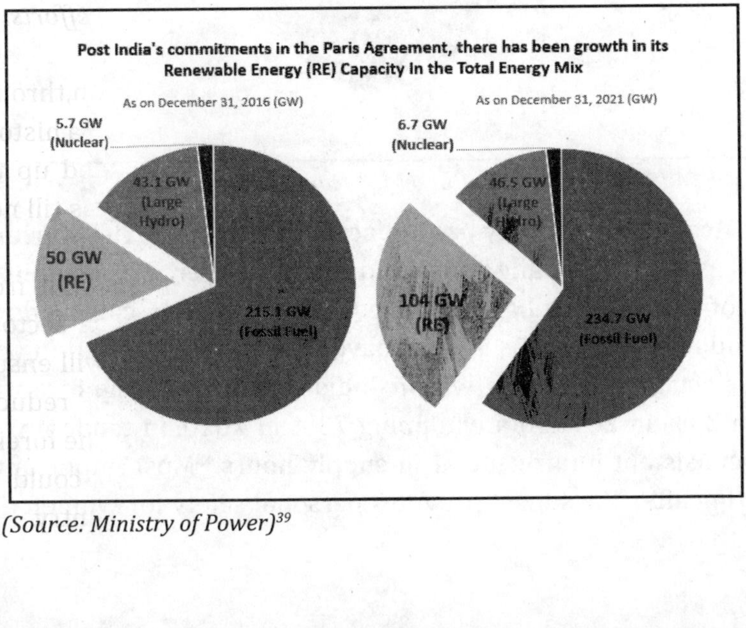

(Source: Ministry of Power)[39]

PM Modi's commitment towards uplifting the poor by providing them with the basic amenities is as strong as his vision of energy-independent India. Since becoming the Prime Minister of the country, he has focused on a number of schemes which ensure that the poorest in the remotest part of the country has access to power. The 'Sahaj Bijli Har Ghar Yojana' (SAUBHAGYA) is one of the world's biggest universal electrification initiatives launched in 2017. The aim of the SAUBHAGYA scheme is to provide power to all by ensuring last mile connectivity and electricity connections to all un-electrified households in the country. Since the launch of the scheme, 99.1% households have access to electricity,[40] including 90% off-grid houses. This in fact also generated positive spinoffs, as evidenced by the strong growth in the transmission wires and cables business in India over the years.[41]

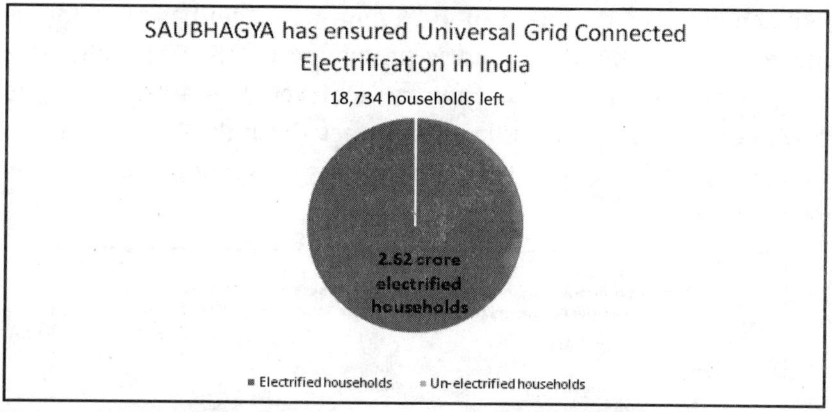

(Source: SAUBHAGYA Dashboard, as on 15th March, 2022)

Access to electricity has impacted the quality of life of people in all aspects, be it daily household chores or overall development. Use of kerosene for lighting purposes has reduced, cutting down on indoor pollution. As studies have shown, the satisfaction with the electricity situation within India has jumped significantly– from 23% in 2015 to a whopping 73% in 2020, in tandem with the consistent improvement in supply hours.[42]Most importantly, lighting after the sunset provides personal safety for women and helps children to spend more time on studies.

Another scheme–Unnat Jyoti by Affordable LED for All (UJALA), promotes the efficient usage of energy at the grassroot level. It addresses concerns, such as high electrification cost and inefficient lighting. In a short span, the scheme has become one of the world's largest zero subsidy domestic lighting programmes. LED bulbs are being distributed at subsidised rates to every grid-connected customer with a metered connection. Till date, over 36 crore LED bulbs, 72 lakh LED tubelights and 23 lakh energy-efficient fans have been distributed by EESL across India. The scheme has transformed the lives of tens of thousands of people. It has not only made affordable energy accessible to all, but also led to massive energy savings for the middle and lower middle-class households. Thanks to this effort, India has also become a major hub for LED bulb manufacturing, achieving the scale and cost that few countries can match and touching 4 crore LED bulbs a month.[43]

Focus on Micro-Small & Medium Enterprises (MSMEs)

Dr. Babasaheb Ambedkar was of the view that for an industrialised economy, the diversion of labour from agriculture to non-agricultural avenues was indispensable. While talking about the productivity of labour, he mentions the diversion of labour to non-agricultural channels of production. He said:

> *"If we succeed in sponging off the labour in non-agricultural channels of production, we will at one stroke lessen the pressure and destroy the premium that at present weighs heavily on land in India. Besides, this labour when productively employed will cease to live by predation as it does today, and will not only earn its keep, but will give us surplus; and more surplus is more capital."*[44]

The MSME sector has the potential to absorb non-agricultural labour on a massive scale in the country. The sector is the backbone of the Indian manufacturing industry, providing employment to millions in India. India has approximately 6.3 crore MSMEs that contribute about 29% towards the GDP through its national and international trade.[45] With over 11 crore people employed in the sector,[46] these small and medium businesses are growth engines that fuel the economy. They are the seeds through which innovation and employment take birth on the ground.

In 2018, the government came out with an incentive plan to help MSMEs overcome cash crunch, gave technological push to the sector, ensured ease of doing business and was a step forward in ending inspector raj, allowing our MSMEs to perform and thrive. From faster loans through 59-minute online portal to lowering of interest rates by 2% than the market rates for every GST-registered unit, the government came out with 12 different reforms were meant to strengthen the sector further.

An MSME-Champions scheme has been formulated by merging all six components of erstwhile Technology Upgradation Scheme (TUS) in an effort to unify various schemes with a single purpose. The idea is to pick up clusters and enterprises and modernise their processes, reduce wastages, sharpen business competitiveness and facilitate their national and global reach and excellence.

Today, the primary obstacle for a small unit or a micro enterprise, in a village or town, to thrive and grow, is the lack of credit. 'Pradhan Mantri MUDRA Yojana' through collateral free loans is helping create capital in the MSME sector by taking care of the credit crunch. With nearly 33 crore loans valued at more than Rs. 16 lakh crore sanctioned to entrepreneurs so far, MUDRA is helping achieve Dr. Babasaheb Ambedkar's vision of diversified forces of production. The scheme specially addresses the needs of the marginalised sections, such as SCs/STs and gives them an opportunity to bring to life their enterprising ideas and set up a business capable of not only providing them a decent earning and a life of dignity; it also creates further jobs.

Also, to help alleviate the credit crisis arising from the Covid pandemic, the Emergency Credit Line Guarantee Scheme (ECLGS) of the Modi government came to the rescue of the sector, saving livelihoods and lives. As on March 11, 2022, a total of 117.87 lakh businesses have been supported with 100% guaranteed collateral free loans under ECLGS of which about 95.21% were MSMEs.[47] The impact had been significant. A study done by the State Bank of India had shown that MSME loan accounts worth Rs 1.8 lakh crore were saved from slipping into NPA, an equivalent of 14% of the outstanding MSME credit as of December 2021. If these units had turned non-performing, then 1.5 crore workers would have become unemployed. Therefore, the ECLGS ended up saving the lives and livelihood for 6 crore people (assuming each job saved impacted a family of four), highlighting the prescience of the scheme.[48]

Accompanying MUDRA, 'Prime Minister's Employment Generation Programme' (PMEGP) has helped create multifarious self-employment opportunities in rural and urban areas to the artisans, unemployed youth and dispersed labour, over the years, by sharing the cost of setting up a non-farm enterprise. Between the period 2014 to 2022, micro-enterprises have been given a subsidy of Rs. 9,098 crore and the programme has created jobs for nearly 16 crore people.[49]About 80% of the units assisted are in rural areas and about 50% units are owned by SC/ST and women.[50]

The Government e Marketplace (GeM) portal was launched in the year 2016 by the Modi government. The primary goal of the portal was to enhance transparency, efficiency and speed in public procurement. The portal serves as a facilitator for online procurement of common use goods and services across various arms of the government and its subsidiary bodies while ensuring best value for the expenditure they incur.

Since 2016, 40.25 lakh sellers and service providers have registered themselves on the GeM portal.[51] Together, they cater to 59,365 buyer organisations. To date, Rs. 2.2 lakh crore of business has been conducted through this portal and more than 56% of all order by value have been delivered by the MSE sector, which has been listed as a priority with respect to purchases on this portal. The momentum it has particularly generated in the post-Covid economic growth is witnessed by the fact that during 2021-22, more than Rs. 1 lakh crore of procurements happened through the portal.

Attributing the success of 'Make in India' drive to farmers, artisans, weavers, engineers, small entrepreneurs and MSME sector, among others, PM Modi said:[52]

> *"It is only due to their hard work that the goal of exporting to the tune of $400 billion has been achieved and I am happy that this power of the people of India is now reaching new markets in every nook and corner of the world. When each and every Indian is vocal for local, it does not take long for the local to become global. Let's make the local 'global' and augment the prestige of our products further."*

Ease of Doing Business

Dr. Babasaheb Ambedkar was keen on reforming and easing processes that could facilitate industrial progress in the country. He went to the extent of suggesting a reduction in corporate tax to enable the growth of an industrial enterprise. He observed:

> *"It seems to me that if we agree that industrialisation is a very important thing for the prosperity of India, and if we further agree that, for industrialisation, the incorporation of capital is also necessary, then I am afraid that we cannot increase this tax to a very large extent, for fear of penalising incorporation."*[53]

For any industrial activity to grow and prosper, it needs an enabling environment that is being taken care of by the Modi government. In fact, the 'Make in India' initiative not only calls enterprises to industrialise; it also gives them apposite environment to do business. Providing ease of doing business is the sine qua non for a healthy industrialisation process. From invoking minimum import price (MIP) in the steel sector to boost export and protect domestic manufacturers, to introducing a system of fixed-term employment across all sectors, the government's vision of reforming the industrial process is aligned with Dr. Babasaheb Ambedkar's vision of giving freedom to businesses without penalising them through unreasonable laws.

While FDI norms have been relaxed in various sectors, a National Single Window System (NSWS) has been introduced as a one-stop-shop to help investors and businesses secure fast approvals and clearances. A number of tax reforms have also been initiated to bridge the trust deficit between the government and wealth creators. Also, efforts have been made to reduce litigations in the direct tax payments through the 'Vivad Se Vishwas' scheme, even as the transformational faceless assessment and appeals mechanism coupled with the tax charter seek to secure the rights of taxpayers and prevent their harassment. Perhaps the biggest tax reform so far undertaken by the Modi government for easing the process of doing business in the country, is the landmark Goods and Services Tax (GST) that replaced a complicated multiple tax regime.

Enabling maximum ease of doing business and better compliance, 1,500 old and obsolete laws have been repealed since 2014, and a number of offences under the Companies Act have been decriminalised. The removal of the retrospective tax will create a positive environment for foreign investors to do business in India.

With the reforms unleashed, India jumped to 63rd rank in 2019 from 142nd rank in 2014 in the World Bank's Ease of Doing Business Report 2020, a meteoric rise of 79 ranks. The country has emerged as the clear leader after securing the first position among the South Asian countries. The change did not happen overnight. The rapid stride in global rankings under the Modi government displays the serious work done to make India conducive for enterprise. With the launch of Ease of Doing Business 2.0 through the 2022-23 Budget, the Modi government has signalled its intent to not drop the ball on this critical issue.

Job Creation

The heightened manufacturing activity in India has resulted in creation of lakhs of direct and indirect jobs. EPFO subscription in eight months of 2021-22 at 82.4 lakh saw more addition than in the three years preceding it. Between 2018-19 and 2020-21, there were 3.1 crore net additions, of which 1.5 crore were noticed in the pandemic period starting 2020. Of these, 1 crore were first-time job seekers, a clear sign of the rapid pace with which jobs have been created in the Indian economy.

Similarly, we have seen how startups, as per NASSCOM data, created 23 lakh direct and indirect jobs between 2017 and 2021. Of these, more than 9 lakh have been created since 2019 – a clear sign of the tailwinds of the Indian economy.[54]For the first time, India's exports crossed the $400 billion mark in FY2021-22due to a healthy performance across industries, including petroleum products, engineering goods, apparel, etc.[55]This is another indication that new jobs are being created in high volume sectors, like engineering goods and apparel, which are job intensive and directly impact MSMEs associated with them.

From Fragile Five to Fastest Growing Economy

It is not only the 'Ease of Doing Business' rankings, but in other global parameters as well that India has been shining bright. In the period from 2014-20 and later post-pandemic in 2021, India emerged as one of the fastest growing economies.

In World Economic Forum's (WEF) Global Competitiveness Index, India was at 71st rank in 2014. Since then, the country has been steadily moving up to be on the 43rd rank in 2021. India has jumped 35 places from 2015 on the Global Innovation Index to 46th rank in 2021. The country has been ranked 49th in the Chandler Good Government Index 2021 among 104 countries in terms of government capabilities and outcomes.

The best of the best in the world want to engage with India. Despite the ongoing global pandemic, India received Foreign

Direct Investment (FDI) worth $60.3 billion in FY2021-22 (till December 2021).[56]

Dr. Babasaheb Ambedkar's wisdom and vision are seen in the colossal collection of his speeches and written work. His views on industrialisation of the Indian economy are pertinent and find meaning in the structural reforms initiated by this government. Industries, as Dr. Babasaheb Ambedkar believed, would end the cycle of poverty and push the nation towards greater social mobility. It is heartening to see that the Modi government shares the same vision as was seen by the father of our Constitution and has been able to unleash policy initiatives like 'Make in India' and 'Atmanirbhar Bharat', with an unwavering conviction in the process of industrialisation.

> *"Nothing can open possibilities of making agriculture in India profitable except a serious drive in favour of industrialisation. For it is industrialisation alone which can drain away the excess of population, which is exerting such an enormous pressure on land into gainful occupation other than agriculture."*[57]

—Dr. B.R. Ambedkar

□

3

Labour Rights in Dr. B.R. Ambedkar and Modi Era

The idea that industrial growth and labour rights are always at variance with each other is a problematic proposition. In fact, both the entities are highly co-dependent on one another. Industry needs labour to grow and expand, while labour needs industry to generate income and assure prosperity.

Prime Minister Narendra Modi's government, in its first and second terms, has not shied away from overhauling the cumbersome codes and processes hindering growth, while ensuring that labour rights are strengthened. When presenting the Budget on the floor of the Parliament in 2019, the Finance Minister announced the government's intent to merge 44 labour laws into four labour codes. These codes relate to wages, safety, health, working conditions and industrial relations. This step was a culmination of a series of labour reforms already initiated in the first term of the Modi government and reflects the vision of Dr. B.R. Ambedkar.

Dr. Babasaheb Ambedkar had a long and deep-running involvement with the labour cause, first as a labour leader and then as a policymaker. Therefore, his vision for empowering the labour force of India can be seen in his action and advocacy as a labour leader and also as an administrator.

Dr. B.R. Ambedkar and Labour Welfare

In 1934, Dr. Babasaheb Ambedkar became the President of the Bombay Municipal Karmachari Sangh and, later in 1936, he founded a new political party named Independent Labour Party (ILP). In 1942, he was appointed as the Labour Member (minister) in the Viceroy's Executive Council, a post that he held for four years and during which he enacted a wide range of pro-labour reforms. These years were remarkable for labour legislation and rights in the country.

In 1943, he introduced the Indian Trade Union (Amendment) Bill in the then Legislative Assembly. The bill ensured recognition of the trade union by the employer and also imposed certain conditions on the trade unions to make them worthy of recognition.

As the Labour Member, Dr. Babasaheb Ambedkar successfully lobbied for an increase in the Labour Welfare Fund allotted under the Mines Act of 1944 for coal-mine workers by doubling the tax on the extraction of coal. The fund was aimed at safety and health of the workers as well as other welfare activities, like education. Other labour welfare funds for coal mines and one each for iron and manganese were also established.

The same year, while amending the Factories Act of 1934, he tried to include the recommendations of the International Labour Conference of 1936 to ensure better working conditions for labour, like right to holiday, earned leave facility, washing facilities and appropriate working hours. He also ensured that problems, such as lockouts, sickness, accident, legal strike, etc., which were beyond the control of the labour, would be counted while calculating the continuous length of service. He opposed the proposal of 12 working hours and followed the then British pattern of 48 work hours in a week as the optimum work. The Workmen Compensation Act, 1923, was also amended to increase the compensation paid in case of death or disability.

Dr. Babasaheb Ambedkar also moved the Payment of Wages (Amendment) Bill in 1944 that defined wages, authorised and unauthorised deductions, increments, etc., and fixed a specific day (7th day) of the month on which wages must be paid.

In 1946, he moved a bill for the protection of minimum wages. This provided for the constitution of an advisory committee and advisory board with equal representation of labour and employers to advise the government on the matter. The bill became a law in 1948. He also introduced a social insurance scheme comprising workmen's compensation, sickness insurance, etc.

Dr. Babasaheb Ambedkar championed the cause of equal rights for women. He successfully advocated the lifting of ban against their employment in coal mines. He also ensured that the principle of 'equal pay for equal work' was enacted in the mines. He also moved the Mines Benefit (Amendment) Bill for providing maternity benefits to women working in the mines. In 1946, he successfully pushed through an Act focused on labour welfare in the mica mines. This Act also provided amenities to female labour, like better working hours and work conditions. Later, he got the Mica Mines Act amended twice to ensure favourable conditions, such as cradle facility and maids for day care were available for women labour. Dr. Babasaheb Ambedkar also got the Maternity Benefit Act passed.

Labour Welfare in the Modi Era

For decades, those wanting economic reform have also called for changes in India's multiple, archaic, rigid, and procedure-bound labour laws. Under the leadership of PM Modi, within months of taking charge of the affairs of the country, the government came out with major labour reforms with the objective to ensure 'Ease of Doing Business', helping industrial growth by easing compliance, ending 'Inspector Raj', and most importantly, empowering the workers of India.

"Long due and much awaited labour reforms have been passed by Parliament. The reforms will ensure the well-being of our industrious workers and give a boost to economic growth. They are also shining examples of 'Minimum Government, Maximum Governance'."[58]

—Prime Minister Narendra Modi

Particularly during the period of the Covid pandemic, multiple initiatives outlined in this chapter have helped to preserve the rights of the poor workers and give them a chance to secure an income to continue maintaining a life of dignity. The changes brought about pertain to the area have been further detailed below.

Simplifying Labour Laws

PM Modi believes that empowering workers is key to an 'Atmanirbhar Bharat'. For a long time, it was well known that majority of workers are employed in the unorganised sector and do not have access to social security, and any substantial action to protect them was negligible. It is for the first time that any government has cared for not only the big companies and factory owners, but also the workers and their families.

The four labour codes: (i) Code on Wages; (ii) Industrial Relations; (iii) Social Security; and (iv) Occupational Safety, Health and Working Conditions, are aimed at simplifying, amalgamating and rationalising the existing Central Labour Laws.

The Code on Wages[59] paved the way for statutory protection for minimum wages and timely payment of wages to approximately 50 crore workers of organised and unorganised sectors. It also ensures equal wages for both male and female workers.

The Social Security Code[60]secures the legal framework that ensures the right of workers for insurance, pension, gratuity, maternity benefit, etc. The Labour Code on Occupational Safety, Health and Working Conditions[61] focuses on the security of workers engaged in factories, mines, plantations, motor transport sector, bidi and cigarette workers, contract and migrant workers, etc. The Industrial Relations Code[62] is key to safeguarding the interests of trade unions as well as the workers. All possible steps have been taken to ensure that disputes do not arisein future.

The importance of the creation of labour codes cannot be emphasised enough. Many think that labour codes are only about the employees, but that is telling merely half the story. Often, an employer feels hassled in terms of compliance with a maze of laws that are difficult to track and keep pace with. In such a scenario, a consolidation helps to not only reduce the number of necessary approvals that have to be sought; it also makes the compliance process significantly easier. This works in favour of the employees, who are more assured about the protection of their rights.

Equal Rights for Women

Just like Dr. Babasaheb Ambedkar, PM Modi has laid a lot of stress on empowering women in work environment and giving them equal opportunities to prove their capabilities. The Prime Minister firmly believes that women play an important role in the growth of a nation.

The Code on Wages ensures that there is no discrimination on the grounds of gender in matters relating to wages by an employer, in respect of the same work done by both men and women. Under the Social Security Code, maternity benefit is now available to women employed in factories, mines, plantations and in other establishments. A woman cannot be dismissed from work or be given a notice for dismissal during the time when she is on maternity leave. Even if she is dismissed, she will still be entitled to maternity benefit.

As per the Working Conditions code, women are now entitled to be employed in all types of work. They have been given the right to work at night with their consent, and it has also been ensured that the employer would make adequate arrangements to provide safety and facilities to women workers at night.

The Maternity Benefit (Amendment) Act of 2017 has increased the duration of paid maternity leave from 12 weeks to 26 weeks. Its benefits now also extend to mothers who adopt and who are entitled to 12 weeks of maternity leave from the date of adoption. It also makes mandatory the provision for crèche facility for every establishment employing 50 or more employees and women employees would be permitted to visit the crèche four times during a day.

Increased Minimum Wage and Formalisation

Walking on the road shown by Dr. Babasaheb Ambedkar, the Modi government accepted the recommendations of the Minimum Wages Advisory Board and increased the day wages for the unskilled non-agriculture workers to Rs. 350 in non-urban areas. This 42% increase in the wages, in one stroke, brought significant improvement in the standard of living for 55 lakh workers and their families.

Similarly, the wage threshold for determining eligibility of employees for bonus has been revised from Rs. 10,000 to Rs. 21,000 per month, covering a larger pool of employees. The Bonus Act applies to every factory and establishment that employs 20 or more persons, and unlike other performance-linked incentives offered by companies, the bonus payable under this law is not linked to the performance of the employee. All employees earning up to the wage threshold (increased to Rs. 21,000 by an amendment) and who have worked in the establishment for not less than 30 working days in the year, are eligible to receive this statutory bonus.[63]

Not only this, but the cover of the Employees' State Insurance (ESI) Scheme has also been extended to bring in additional 50 lakh members by increasing the wage limit to Rs. 21,000 from Rs. 15,000. The existing insured personscan continue their membership even if their salary crosses the limit of Rs. 21,000 per month. The ESI Scheme is financed by contributions from employers and employees. The rate of contribution by employer is set at 4.75% of the wages payable to employees. The employees' contribution is set at the rate of 1.75% of the wages payable to an employee. ESI Corporation has also extended the benefits of the ESI Scheme to the workers deployed on construction sites located in the implemented areas under ESI Scheme w.e.f. 1st August, 2015.[64] Furthermore, new ESIC hospitals directly run by the Centre are now coming up to expand the scope of the service[65] in view of demand from both workers and employees and with the objective to provide better medical services to beneficiaries.

Sometimes, ESI beneficiaries would face hardships in availing medical services because there was no availability of ESIC's health care infrastructure in the form of a hospital or dispensary or insured medical practitioner within a radius of 10 km of their residences. To ameliorate this challenge, the government amended the ESI provisions, such that ESI beneficiaries can now avail medical care services from nearby ESIC empanelled hospitals (pan-India) without the need for any referral from an ESI dispensary or hospital.[66]

A Universal Account Number has also been provided for workers to ensure portability across accounts so that employees do not lose their hard-earned security benefits due to change of job. It has been designed to be an umbrella number of a member during his employment with different establishments in the organised sector.

Till March 2021, around 3.3 crore people had registered under ESI to avail the benefits.[67]

Better Working Conditions for Labour Force

The Modi government has been silently but steadily not only building upon the foundations laid by Dr. Babasaheb Ambedkar, it is also taking path-breaking steps to spur skill development, enabling affordable education by expanding scholarships for the disadvantaged sections of the society and integrating education and industry for better employability.

On October, 16, 2014, the government launched the 'Shram Suvidha' portal to consolidate information of labour inspection and its enforcement. It is aimed at transparency and accountability in inspections. This is to ensure that labour laws are easily complied with, in the absence of which, employees do not always receive what they are entitled to under these laws. Similarly, the National Career Service was launched on July, 20, 2015, as part of government's focus on providing right skills and generating employment. It is the converging point for Government of India's three major initiatives– Skill India, Digital India and Make in India that aim to provide skilled manpower, improve digital infrastructure and generate employment opportunities for all. The service will also provide information, counselling and job assistance services to the youth.

The 'Pradhan Mantri Rozgar Protsahan Yojana' was launched in August 2016 and aims to incentivise employers for employment generation with the government paying the employers' EPS contribution of 8.33% for the new employees for the first thre eyears of their employment, and is proposed to be made applicable for the unemployed semi-skilled and unskilled persons. Going a step further, the Government of India decided to make full employer's contribution (EPF and EPS both), i.e. 12% with effect from April, 1, 2018, for a period of three years to the new employees as well as to the existing beneficiaries for their remaining period of thre eyears. Again, the move pushed the unorganised sector towards greater formalisation and encourages employers to hire new talent, without bearing the extra cost associated with it.

The scheme was estimated to benefit 20 lakh beneficiaries. However, as on 27th November, 2021, benefit has been provided to 1.21 crore persons through 1.53 lakh establishments.[68]

Further, the government set up the eSHRAM portal for creating a National Database of Unorganised Workers (NDUW), with special provision for seeding accounts with Aadhaar. This is the first-ever national database of unorganised workers, including migrant workers, construction workers, gig and platform workers, etc. With the eSHRAM portal, each subscriber account contains details about the specified unorganised worker that will help them understand their employability and also help avail the benefits of the social security schemes to them.[69] Any unorganised worker, aged between 16-59 years, can register in the portalso long as the worker is not a member of EPFO/ESIC or NPS. The portal has already received traction, with 33.17 lakh registrations being completed by 21st March, 2022.[70] The utility of the portal can also be gauged by the following indicators:

- 54.18% of all registered personnel are women. Given the fact that women dominate the unorganized workforce,[71] this initiative gains even more importance.
- OBC, SC and ST form nearly three-fourths of the total registrants on the portal at a little over 72%. This matches the broader pattern.

Transparent System Aiding Rural Employment

The 'Mahatma Gandhi National Rural Employment Guarantee Act' (MGNREGA) that was meant to promise rural employment, became a source of moneymaking for middlemen. Delayed payments became a regular feature, so much so that the number of SC/ST beneficiaries began falling across the country, in a reversal of the rising trend seen in the earlier phase of MGNREGA. The slide between 2009 and 2012 was 46.5% among SCs and 39.6% in STs.[72] In 2014-15, the percentage of wage payment within a period of 15 days stood at a mere 26.85%. However, post-2015, the situation improved significantly, with the number crossing 96.24% in 2020-21.[73] Through the e-payment mode, 99.7% payment of MNREGA wages are now being paid.[74] This success has been enabled by the successful rollout of the JAM Trinity, in turn eliminating middlemen and minimizing avenues of corruption.

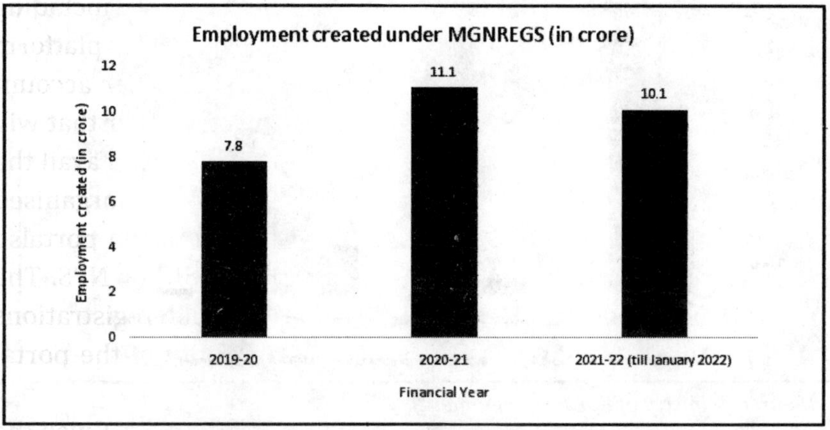

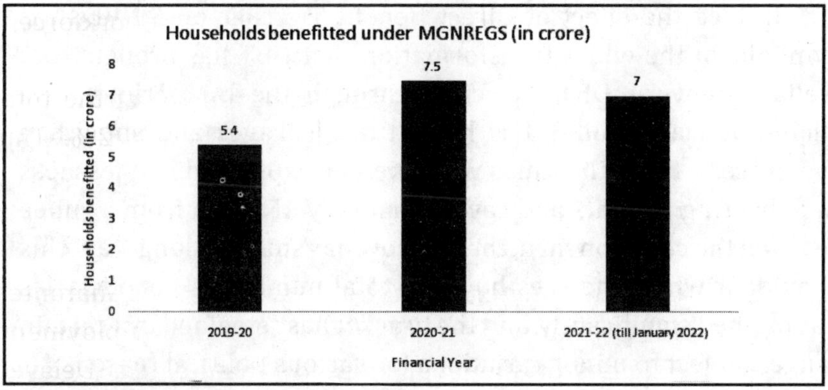

(Source: NREGA)

Through the 'Pradhan Mantri Garib Kalyan Rojgar Abhiyan' (PMGKRA),[75] a conscious effort is made to provide meaningful employment while achieving saturation of government initiatives, creating a win-win situation. Its effectiveness can be gauged from the fact that more assets were created across several categories in this 120-day campaign than in all of 2013-14.

Major Agricultural and Allied Works under MGNREGA

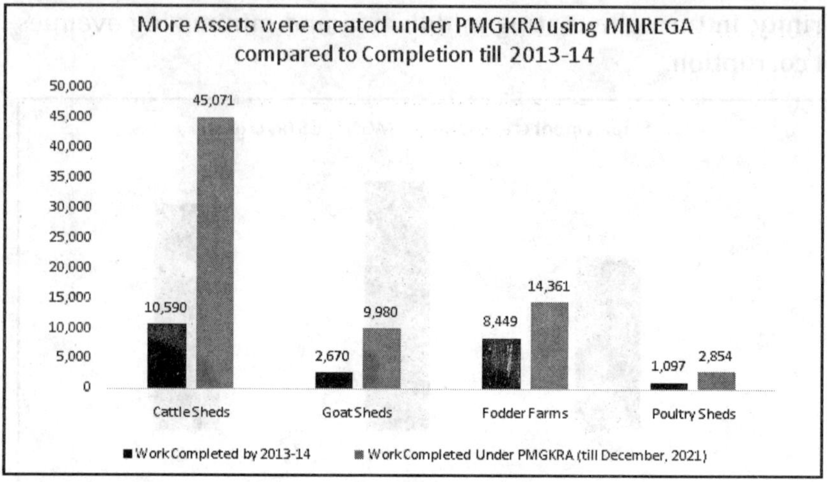

(Source: Ministry of Rural Development)

In fact, the effect of Direct Benefit Transfer on MNREGA is symbolic of the wider transformation that DBT has brought into welfare delivery. DBT, exercised through the JAM Trinity (Jan Dhan-Aadhaar-Mobile), has helped tap leakages and smoothen the process. From the times when people expressed helplessness in delivering benefits and saying that only 15 paisa from a rupee reached the common man, the window has shifted a long way. This is evident when one sees how the total number of beneficiaries has jumped significantly, and the bracket has remained in a certain range, subject to minor variations for various political reasons.

Empowering Labour during Covid Pandemic

The onset of Covid pandemic drastically impacted the economy and disrupted many sectors, but corrective measures introduced by the Modi government have resulted in creation of new jobs. Even during the Covid period, MGNREGS kept the rural economy moving with more than Rs. 2 lakh crore being allocated for the years 2020-21 and 2021-22.[76] Aided by DBT-based payments, this became a means of keeping the rural economy going. During the financial year 2021-22, multiple opportunities were provided for the rural poor to earn a respectable living and overcome the hardships brought forward by the ongoing pandemic. Subsequently, employment under MGNREGS had been provided to more than 10 crore people, benefitting around 7 crore households till January 2022.[77]

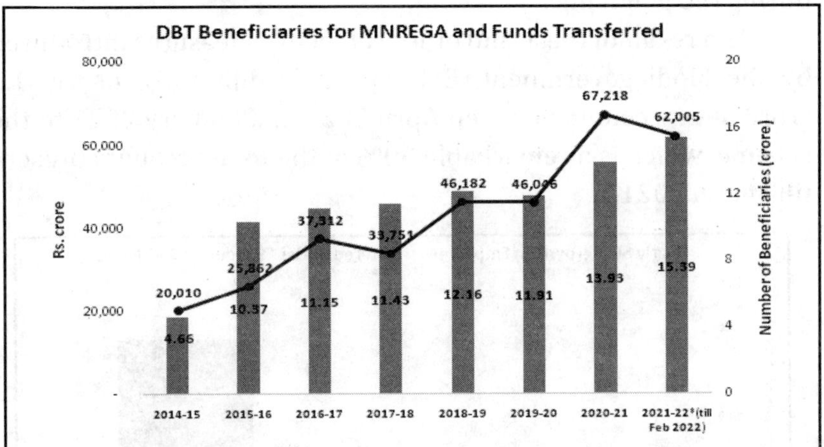

(Source: DBT Bharat)

MGNREGS was also deployed as part of the 'Pradhan Mantri Garib Kalyan Rojgar Abhiyan (PMGKRA).[78] It focused on 116 districts across six states. These districts were marked by the fact that they had a concentration of 25,000 and more returnee migrant workers on an average.

PRADHAN MANTRI GARIB KALYAN PACKAGE

More than 42 crore poor people received financial assistance of Rs. 68,820 crore

(As on 7th September 2020)

Rs. 30,952 cr	Rs. 2,814.5 cr	Rs. 17,891 cr	Rs. 4,987 cr	Rs. 2,476 cr	Rs. 9,700 cr
Given to 20 crore Jan Dhan women account holders	Given to 2.81 crore elderly, widows and Divyang	Instalment of PM-KISAN to 8.94 crore farmers	Support given to 1.82 crore to construction workers	24%EPF contribution transferred to 43 lakh employees	Given under Ujjwala Yojana for free LPG refills

(Source: Finance Ministry)

The Direct Benefit Transfer (DBT) emerged as the primary source of transfer of funds that helped the people during the pandemic, with more money transferred in the year 2020-21,[79] thanks to the Pradhan Mantri Garib Kalyan Package (PMGKP). This, alongside free ration, ensured money in the hands of the people, thus enabling a significant number of families to survive during the pandemic.[80]

As a result of these and other corrective measures introduced by the Modi government, ESI reported addition of nearly 1.6 crore new accounts between April 2021 and January 2022 to the scheme, which is a remarkable 50% of the total accounts present till March 2021.[81]

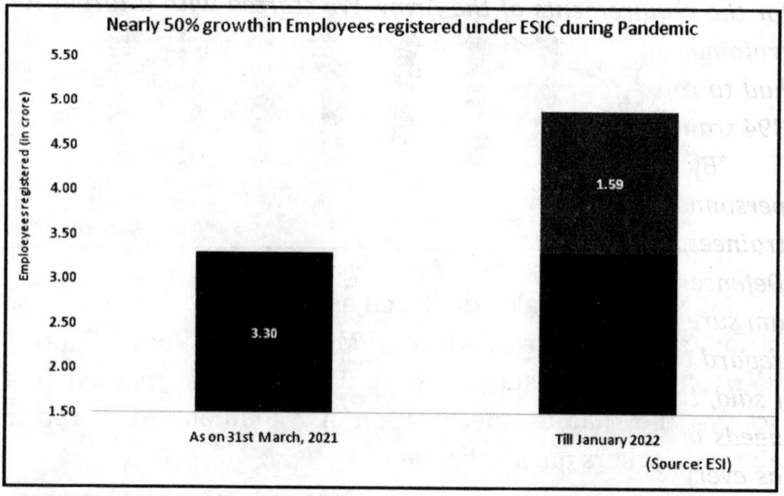

Need for Skill-based Training

Dr. Babasaheb Ambedkar, while addressing the Technical Training Scheme Advisory Committee in Calcutta on August 24, 1944, in his capacity as the Labour Member, Government of India, underlined the need to provide scientific and technical training as a nation planning its future development in the 'age of machine'. In a post-war scenario, the committee was deliberating on the future of skilled labour that was inducted in the Army.

In his speech, Dr. Babasaheb Ambedkar expounded on the unique opportunity India had in strengthening her human resource to fuel the nation's growth:

"You have assembled here today to consider the future of our Technical Training Scheme, which was introduced as an emergency measure to cater to the technical needs of the Army and has resulted in providing India with semi-skilled manpower to an extent unheard of before. Just to give you an idea of the magnitude of the work done in the field of technical training, I might refer briefly to the history of the Technical Training Scheme from its early stages. It was started three-and-a-half years ago to overcome one serious obstacle– the lack of technical personnel for the requirements of the Army. We started with a target for training about 3,000 men at a time; but, within two years we had to raise this figure to 48,000, which required setting up of 394 training centres.

"By the end of 1942, we had already supplied 54,000 trained personnel to the Army. By June, 1944, we had turned out 75,000 trainees, of whom 63,000 joined the technical branches of the Defence Services and 3,000 went to the ordnance factories. I am sure you will agree that this is no mean achievement having regard to the period within which it has been accomplished. As I said, this Technical Training Scheme was started to meet the needs of the Army, which had arisen out of the war. The war, as everybody can see, is coming to a close and the demand for technical training which came for the Army will abate."[82]

Dr. Babasaheb Ambedkar envisioned skill development and technical training to become a permanent fixture of India's educational system. However, he emphasised that in order to ensure success of the scheme, one had to understand that there was a mismatch between the skills imparted and the requirements of the industry. He implored the civil industry to hire untrained workmen in large numbers and train them in job-specific skills over time. He said: *"What changes can be made in our Technical*

Training Scheme to make it serve fully and completely the present-day needs of civil industry? It involves the consideration of the long-term policy of providing trained technical personnel for the post-war industrial development of the country."[83]

There was a need for the educational institutes, government training centres and the industry to come together and ensure compatibility between the needs of the industry and the skills being imparted. He proposed that training courses be tailored accordingly to ensure greater employability.

As one of the strongest proponents of ending caste hierarchies, Dr. Babasaheb Ambedkar saw access to education and skill development as a must to ensure social, economic and professional mobility. He envisioned the oppressed castes to enter into modern professions of the emerging economy.

On 29th October, 1942, Dr. Babasaheb Ambedkar submitted a 'Memorandum on the Grievances of the Scheduled Castes' to the Governor-General of India. The memorandum presented the political, educational and other grievances of the Scheduled Castes. It highlighted extremely low representation of Scheduled Caste youth in education of science and technology. He was of the view that education in arts and law were not of much help to the Scheduled Castes. They would benefit more from advanced education in science and technology. As course correction, he proposed creating the following scholarships:

- An annual grant of Rs. 2 lakh for Scheduled Caste students taking science and technology courses at universities or other scientific and technical training institutions in India.
- An annual grant of Rs. 1 lakh for scholarships in foreign universities in England, the Dominions, in Europe and America.

Dr. Babasaheb Ambedkar believed that the government hadan important role to play in raising the level of technical education among the masses and that government support and policy could play a central role in skill development in the country. He proposed: *"The Government of India can do a lot for improving the future of the Dalits. The SC boys can be kept as apprentices in such industrial units [such as the government printing press or railway workshops], which are under the control of the Government of India or are run by it, where there is a possibility of giving technical education."*[84]

To that extent, a series of efforts in the direction of skill development have been pursued by the government. While the ITI network was expanded to ensure that there is an ITI in every block of the nation,[85]the Pradhan Mantri Kaushal Vikas Yojana (PMKVY) in its third iteration is pushing for skill development throughout the country to address the industry needs, meet the market demands, impart skills in services and in new-age job roles that have become crucial in the post- pandemic era.[86] That the programme is adapting to requirements can be seen in the primary objectives of PMKVY 3.0, which include the following:

- Create an ecosystem for the youth to make informed choices on the available skilling avenues.
- Provide support to youth for skill training and certification.
- Promote sustainable skill centres for greater participation of private sector.

Pradhan Mantri Kaushal Vikas Yojana (PMKVY) has been able to provide the necessary skill training to 1.34 crore candidates since its inception in 2016 on pan-India basis.[87] The third phase of PMKVY was launched in January 2021, with a target of training 8 lakh youth across the country, including the North Eastern Region (NER), with an outlay of Rs. 948.9 crore. Despite the Covid pandemic's disruption, 4.45 lakh candidates have already been trained/oriented till December 31, 2021 under the scheme.[88]

Similarly, the ITI network's expansion has resulted in 14,736 ITIs being operational in the country by 2019, with 35.05 lakh seats being available all over India.[89]

A Common Platform for Employment Opportunities

Dr. Babasaheb Ambedkar was insistent on quality education and imparting of skills to the vast masses, but his vision was much larger than that. He envisaged that a common platform should exist where the employment seekers and employers can find a common place to interact. Moreover, there was a need to resettle the discharged war workers and demobilised security personnel after the Second World War got over.

As the Labour Member in the Viceroy's Executive Council, he strove to set up Employment Exchanges as a place where potential employers have an accessible organisation to search for labour. Dr. Babasaheb Ambedkar, Labour Member, Government of India, in his address to the Chairmen of National Service Labour Tribunals laid out his vision:

> *"I should like to emphasise that in addition to a very necessary service for ex-service demobilised personnel, the main purpose of the organisation that we propose to set up is to lay the foundation of an efficient employment service in this country. The important feature of such a service is a coordinated system of Employment Exchanges."*[90]

The efforts yielded results. While answering a question in the Legislative Assembly, Dr. Babasaheb Ambedkar informed about the progress of Employment Exchanges:[91]

> *"Employment Exchanges have been established at 10 centres in India, viz. Bombay, Ahmedabad, Nagpur, Madras, Calcutta, Dhanbad, Cawnpore, Delhi, Lahore and Karachi.*
>
> *"Up to 31st December, 1944, the Exchanges had found employment for 5,909 workmen."*

Taking the vision ahead, the PM Modi-led government established the National Career Service portal, an online platform to provide a variety of employment related services, like job matching, career counseling, vocational guidance, information on skill development courses, etc., which are offered through the Employment Exchanges.[92]

Firming up the Social Security Net

While addressing the Andhra Chamber of Commerce, Dr. Babasaheb Ambedkar, as the Labour Member in the Viceroy's Executive Council,referred to the social security programme pointing out that unless they organised the resources of the country in such a manner as it produces more wealth, it would be hardly possible to give effect to all measures of social security which the Government of India has in contemplation. He added: *"Government must undertake a definite policy of raising those who were socially, economically downtrodden so that welfare would not become the privilege and monopoly of any particular class."*[93]

In order to create the much-needed social security net for the poor and working class in the lower income bracket, the Modi government has launched ambitious schemes to provide health and insurance to the masses. For a poor household with a single wage earner, these schemes provide necessary protection from any untoward event. In case of a sudden death or accident of a wage-earning member, the entire process of social mobility for the family takes a jolt. The need for a safety net cannot be emphasised upon more, especially in order to minimise uncertainty from the lives of the poorest of the poor.

Pradhan Mantri Jeevan Jyoti Bima Yojana (PMJJBY) was launched in 2015 wherein the insured receives Rs. 2 lakh cover against an annual premium of Rs. 330 each year. Up till January 2022, the scheme saw an enrolment of 12.1 crore and over 5.4 lakh claims had been disbursed.[94] The scheme has particularly seen significant growth in women beneficiaries – 3.4 crore till December 2021.[95]

The accidental risk coverage scheme, Pradhan Mantri Suraksha Bima Yojana was launched in 2015 under which in case of accidental death or full disability, the payment to the nominee will be Rs. 2 lakh and in case of partial permanent disability, Rs. 1 lakh. As of January 2022, more than 27 crore people had been enrolled into the scheme and over 93,000 claims had been disbursed.

To provide pension benefits to the workers in the unorganised sector, the government launched the Atal Pension Yojana in 2015. The minimum age of joining APY is 18 years and maximum age is 40 years. The age of exit and start of pension would be 60 years. The scheme is specifically critical for the section of the labour population that is not part of the organised sector, sometimes living off a day's pay without any security provision or any future savings. As of January, 2022, 3.76 crore people from the informal sector have subscribed to the scheme. Earlier, the scheme was formalised for four years only. However, on the mass response it received, the government decided to extend the scheme indefinitely.

One of the most important provisions for building a safety net that remains underappreciated is the pension coverage on offer for the unorganised sector. The Pradhan Mantri Shram Yogi Maandhan Yojana is a voluntary and contributory pension scheme. Under this, the beneficiary would receive a minimum assured pension of Rs. 3,000 per month after attaining the age of 60 years.[96] If the beneficiary dies, the spouse of the beneficiary is entitled to receive 50% of the pension as family pension. Applicants between the age group of 18 to 40 years will have to make affordable monthly contributions ranging between Rs. 55 to Rs. 200 per month till they attain the age of 60. Already, 4.25 lakh unorganised workers, who essentially earn less than Rs. 1,500 a month, thus working with the hope that their old age is certainly going to be one of dignity.

A security cover for the working class, poor and downtrodden is a tool for empowerment that has finally been extended to the people at the bottom of the pyramid. Adding another dimension to the safety net, the government launched the world's largest health insurance, Pradhan Mantri Jan Arogya Yojana-Ayushman Bharat in the mix. The scheme offers a benefit cover of Rs. 5 lakh per family per year and more than 10 crore families belonging to the poor and vulnerable population are benefitting from the scheme. As of February 2022, 2.89 crore hospital admissions have taken place under the scheme and approximately 17.6 crore were PMJAY cards issued.[97]

Also, the need for ensuring affordable, quality rental housing for labour force and their family members, especially given their migrant status, has been felt in recent times. This has prompted the government to announce the Affordable Rental Housing Complexes (ARHC) Scheme. ARHCs will provide them dignified living with necessary civic amenities near their place of work, thus preventing from exploitation by unscrupulous landlords without pinching their pockets and hurting their disposable incomes.[98] The scheme has managed to provide cover to 46.52 lakh people so far, who earn less than Rs. 1,500 a month.[99]

Most of the categories covered under the scheme pertain to occupations involving the most vulnerable sections of the society. In the rural areas, SC/ST households are covered automatically. For a productive labour force, it is of utmost importance that affordable as well as quality healthcare is made accessible. Considering the escalating cost of quality healthcare in the country, it was mostly out of reach for the poor. In case a member of the family does get ill, it would push the family into a cycle of poverty and debt. With the healthcare intervention, the government has ensured that the poor are not left at the mercy of exploitative informal debt structures, but are ensured proper treatment and a promise of health.

An important but underappreciated measure undertaken by the Modi government has been the efforts taken up for the gig and platform workers. Most workers qualifying as per this definition would not, in any other country, have any rights or protections granted to them. However, through his government's budget, for the first time globally, social security benefits were made available to them.[100] This step would go a long way in preventing exploitation while bringing dignity to the lives of these people.

Ending Exploitation

In 1946, Dr. Babasaheb Ambedkar was able to get the Industrial Employment (Standing Orders) Bill passed. The bill aimed to have the terms and conditions of the employment certified by a competent officer as it would serve as documentary evidence in case of any dispute. He also wanted to form a commission on the forced labour in agriculture under the chairmanship of V.V. Giri, but the commission could not be established due to the protests by the Princely States.

In pursuance of his dream to see all the bonded labourers liberated, the Modi government has revamped the Centrally-sponsored Plan Scheme for Rehabilitation of Bonded Labourers with effect from 1st May, 2016. The revamped scheme is known as the Central Sector Scheme for Rehabilitation of Bonded Labourers, 2016. Under this scheme, financial assistance has been increased from Rs. 20,000 to 1 lakh per adult male beneficiary; Rs. 2 lakh for special category beneficiaries such as children, including orphans or those rescued from organised and forced begging rings, or other forms of forced child labour and women; and Rs. 3 lakh in cases of bonded or forced labour involving extreme cases of deprivation or marginalisation, such as transgenders, or women and children rescued from ostensible sexual exploitation, such as brothels, massage parlours, placement agencies, etc.; or in cases of differently abled persons, or in situations where the District Magistrate deems fit.

It also provides for the creation of a Bonded Labour Rehabilitation Fun dat the district level by each state with a permanent corpus of at least Rs. 10 lakh at the disposal of the District Magistrate for extending immediate help to the released bonded labourers.

The government also piloted the Child Labour (Prohibition and Regulation) Amendment Act, 2016. The Act prohibits the engagement of children in all occupations and to prohibit the engagement of adolescents in hazardous occupations and processes as well as the matters connected therewith or incidental thereto.

The norm, when it comes to highlighting labour rights, has been to keep labour rights and private sector interests at variance with each other. Usually, government initiatives towards labour reforms are always met with scepticism. However, it is for the first time that both labour welfare and ensuring ease of doing business are going hand in hand. While the government has time and again shown its deep commitment to the interests of the working class, it has also made sure that the businesses thrive by simplifying compliance, removing 'inspector raj' through randomised computer sampling and offloading the security benefits to encourage new hiring. Ultimately, reforms that ensure ease of doing business are going to further benefit the working class with increased employment opportunities as well as lead to greater formalisation.

□

4

Development through Self-reliance

"If you believe in living a respectable life, you believe in self-help which is the best help."

—Dr. B.R. Ambedkar[101]

One of the tools of India's fight for freedom against centuries of colonialism was self-reliance. It was to be the ideal on which a national consciousness was awakened. The strength to hold a sustained struggle against a powerful enemy, in fact, emanated from the self-confidence that India could rise on its own. There was popular upsurge in favour of swadeshi. As India moved towards realising political freedom, the concern for millions languishing in poverty, too, was writ large.

Dr. B.R. Ambedkar understood the realities facing the nation. As a thinker and a maker of modern India, he inspired people to become self-reliant. He had said: *"We will attain self-elevation only if we learn self-help, regain self-respect and gain self-knowledge."*[102] It became a basis of his philosophy to lift millions out of social and economic deprivation. He perhaps understood that for India to fly, its people need to gain the confidence to come out on their own and become an engine of growth.

Prime Minister Narendra Modi, drawing inspiration from the national icon, said: *"Dr. Babasaheb Ambedkar has shown us that it is not necessary for a person to be born in a rich family, but those who are born in poor families in India can also dream and strive to fulfil those dreams."*[103]

There is an understanding within the Modi government that India's window of opportunity to be part of the big league of the nations has finally arrived. At this point it is important that the development process, which had earlier focused on a top-down approach, has to be reformed to make it inclusive and broad-based. Each and every one needs to be empowered to become part of the growth momentum, especially those who, till now, had remained at the margins.

Giving a glimpse of his vision to utilise this opportunity, PM Modi rememberes Dr. Babasaheb Ambedkar: *"He had strong faith in self-reliance. He did not want anybody to languish in poverty forever. Dr. Babasaheb Ambedkar also believed that poverty cannot be ameliorated by mere distribution of capital...Today our monetary policy, Start Up India, Stand Up India initiative have become seedbed for our young innovators and young entrepreneurs."*[104]

India's Window of Opportunity

India's advantage lies in its demographic dividend. We are the youngest nation in the world. By 2020, the average age of an Indian was 28.1, which was quite low when compared to global economies, such as 37 in China and the US, 45 in Western Europe, and 49 in Japan.[105] It surely is both an opportunity and a challenge.

An economy fuelled by the concerted efforts of its youth is a force to reckon with. India, standing at such a juncture, is looking ahead to reap the benefits of its demographic dividend for the next 25 years.

Skilling the Unskilled

The expansion of the manufacturing sector is hinged on a million skilled young hands propelling the economy on the growth trajectory. Not only nationally, but also globally, the demand for skilled labour is on the rise, opening up new frontiers for the youth to cross, if equipped with right skills and expertise. In such a scenario, a programme like 'Skill India' becomes pertinent to prepare a highly skilled workforce, which is in tune with industry needs.

The objective of the government is to narrow down the gap between knowledge and employability and encourage differentiation through skill specialisation. It would not only lead to expansion of opportunities, but also accelerate innovation in respective fields. High competence in specialised vocations cultivates dignity of labour, ensuring better standards of living for the gainfully employed. Those who were earlier left out of the limited opportunity spectrum due to lack of aptitude or demand constraints, are now being comfortably accommodated in jobs or enterprises necessitating technical know-how.

In order to fine tune the process of skill development, that too, on an unprecedented scale, the chaos in the skilling ecosystem was corrected by bringing over 50 skill development schemes and programmes from 20 different ministries or departments under one ministry. Secondly, the National Policy for Skill Development and Entrepreneurship, 2015, the first-ever comprehensive policy framework, was put in place to standardise skilling processes all across the country and achieve skilling at scale with speed and efficiency. 'Kaushal Bharat, Kushal Bharat' has been adopted as the governance mantra, thus reiterating the importance of skilling the youth in the grand strategy towards a resurgent India.

The government's flagship scheme, Pradhan Mantri Kaushal Vikas Yojana (PMKVY) seeks to incentivise industry-driven skill training by providing financial rewards to 1 crore candidates who successfully complete approved skill-training programmes. More than half the number of beneficiaries of the scheme belong to SC/ST/OBC categories, showing the extensive reach of the scheme within socially disadvantaged groups. Women, too, availed the scheme in large numbers, making up 50% of the target beneficiaries. The skill development scheme greatly enhances women's employability and provides competencies that would enable them to become self-employed. Since the starting of the scheme in 2016, around 1.34 crore candidates have been trained across the country.[106]

Recognition of Prior Learning (RPL) programme focuses on re-skilling and up-skilling in prominent trades. The programme works on the skillsets required by the unorganised workforce of the country to be upgraded as per the standardised National Skill Qualification Framework (NSQF). Already, 65 lakh candidates have been trained under the programme. According to the study conducted by the National Skill Development Corporation, about 47% people admitted to an increase in income levels after undertaking RPL training. Till mid-2021, more than 9 lakh women had been certified in multiple sectors, ranging from garment manufacturing to aerospace.[107]

Jan Shikshan Sansthan (JSS) scheme is being implemented through NGOs with 100% grants from the Government of India. The scheme provides vocational skills in non-formal mode to non-literate, neo-literates and school drop-outs in the age group of 15-45 years. However, the priority groups are women, SC, ST, minorities and other backward sections of the society. JSSs are reaching to the unreached areas to cater to the needs of the poorest of the poor. They work at the doorstep of the beneficiaries with a minimum infrastructure and resources. More than 3.5 lakh beneficiaries have been trained so far.[108]

Startup India– Funding the Unfunded

The vision to educate and skill youngsters gains strength if adequate job opportunities or conducive entrepreneurial eco-system are provided along with it. Continuous engagement with the industry is being undertaken to ensure job opportunities for skilled workforce. However, more than the job seekers, the government is looking towards job creators to come forward and accelerate the growth process. The government has taken various policy initiatives, such as Startup India and Stand Up India to invigorate the startup culture and channelise the talent of India's youth for the betterment of the nation. For the first time, a policy framework for startups has been instituted and the concept has expanded to provide maximum benefit to the new wave of start-up ventures.

India's startup culture is on a rise with the number of DPIIT-recognised startups crossing 65,000 by February 2022,[109] as compared to 2,200 in 2013.[110] To encourage growth in the startup culture, the government offers over 400 tax exemptions, along with a fund-of-funds and special arrangements for female applicants. The Startup India portal launched by the government is a one-stop platform for startups to interact with each other, exchange ideas and form successful partnerships.

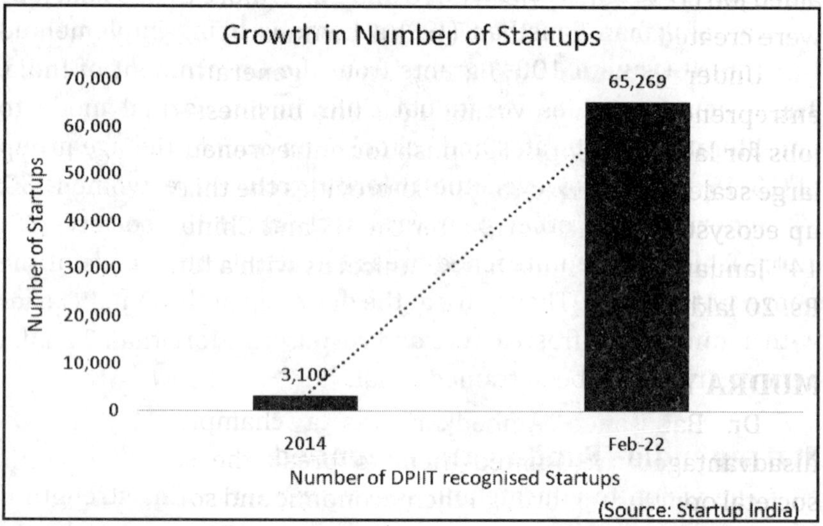

(Source: Startup India)

The Indian startup ecosystem is a signifier of a rising neo-middle class. The aspirational class is aiming to become the driver of India's growth. There has been continuous support from the government, which has made necessary policy interventions to make it convenient to not only start a business, but also exit in case it fails. An improved Intellectual Property Rights regime has encouraged registration of 11.6 lakh trademarks in the last four years, as compared to 11 lakh registrations in the last 75 years.

India's startups are the key reason behind the country's rise in the Global Innovation Index from 76 in 2014 to 46 in 2021. Today, startups are present in 55 industries, spread across 633 districts with at least one startup from every state/UT of the country, and 45% of the startups from Tier-2 and Tier-3 cities. Up to 46% startups are founded by women entrepreneurs; notably, almost four startups are recognised in India every hour. In 2021 itself, 44 unicorns came up in the country. This is more than the number of unicorns India saw in all the years before 2021! The momentum in the first two months of 2022 has also been scorching– one unicorn in every five days! Such growth has also aided job creation. Between 2018 and 2021, more than 6 lakh jobs were created with 2 lakh jobs in 2021 alone.

Under Startup India, a new generation of Indian entrepreneurs are converting ideas into businesses and creating jobs for lakhs of people.The push for entrepreneurship at such a large scale has ensured that India provides the third largest start-up ecosystem in the world after the US and China. Further, as of 14th January, 2022, India has 83 unicorns with a total valuation of Rs. 20 lakh crore.[111]

MUDRA Yojana

Dr. Babasaheb Ambedkar was a champion of socially disadvantaged. He wanted them to break the shackles of the societal oppression through their economic and social rise. Taking a cue from Dr. Babasaheb Ambedkar's vision, PM Modi launched a large-scale programme of financial inclusion. Equipped with a bank account of his/her own, Aadhaar card and a mobile phone in hand, the door of the economic mainstream is now made open to the person at the last mile.

Knowing that opening the bank accounts is not enough to sustain financial empowerment, the government concurrently came out with the Micro Units Development and Refinance

Agency (MUDRA) bank scheme. According to the NSSO survey of 2013, there were 5.77 crore small business units, mostly owned by people belonging to Scheduled Caste, Scheduled Tribe or Other Backward Classes. In light of the fact that only 4% of such units receive institutional finance, providing 'micro-finance' access to such micro/small business units owned by the socially disadvantaged communities has been the biggest achievement of MUDRA scheme.

Under Pradhan Mantri MUDRA Yojana (PMMY), the government had given out nearly 33 crore loans till January 2022. Of the total loans disbursed, 22.3 crore beneficiaries were women, 16.9 crore beneficiaries belong to SC, ST and OBC communities, and 7.2 crore beneficiaries were new entrepreneurs.[112]

An important feature of the scheme is that there are no agents or middlemen engaged for availing of MUDRA loans, thus making the loans easily accessible to those in need. There has been a slew of success stories of MUDRA beneficiaries standing up on their own feet, not only supporting their families, but also employing others and helping them earn a livelihood. Three of such stories are shared at the end of the chapter to provide a sense of the scale of transformation the MUDRA scheme has unleashed.

Stand Up India and Other Initiatives

Over the years, PM Modi has taken a number of initiatives to promote a spirit of entrepreneurship in the socially backward communities. While Startup India was an umbrella scheme to promote entrepreneurship amongst the youth in India, Stand Up India went a step ahead in specifically focussing on the women and SC & ST members of the community. The benefits to the disadvantaged communities include collateral free loans through credit guarantee scheme; simplified online application (through the www.standupmitra.in portal); handholding support and designated nodal officer for SUPI, etc.

The scheme offers bank loans of Rs. 10 lakh to Rs. 1 crore for

Scheduled Castes and Scheduled Tribes as well as women setting up new enterprises. After the initial resounding of the scheme, in 2019, the government extended the scheme till 2025. Now loans for businesses dealing in agriculture and related services are also eligible. Over 17,000 help centres and 24,750 hand-holding agencies have been set up across India to facilitate guidance for loans under the scheme.[113]

Since its inception, up to 1.3 lakh loans had been sanctioned till January 2022 by banks under the Stand Up India scheme[114] Notably, more than 80% (1 lakh) of these loans were given to women, while just over 24,800 were released to SC/STs.

Modi government introduced the Venture Capital Fund for SCs (VCF-SC) in 2014-15 with the aim to develop entrepreneurship amongst the SC youth to enable them to become 'job-givers'. Building upon Dr. Babasaheb Ambedkar's vision to uplift SC youth to become self-reliant and a part of mainstream economy, the government launched the 'Ambedkar Social Innovation and Incubation Mission' (ASIIM) in 2020 under VCF-SC. Up to 1,000 youth with start-up ideas will be identified in the next four years through the Technology Business Incubators (TBIs) in various higher educational institutions and provided funds of up to Rs. 30 lakh to help translate their start-up ideas into businesses.

A National SC/ST Hub was also established in October 2016 to promote entrepreneurship among SC/ST communities by strengthening market access/linkage, monitoring, capacity-building, leveraging financial support schemes and sharing industry-best practices, and so on. Till December 2021, around 55,800 SC/ST candidates were given assistance and an additional 26,800 candidates were trained under the programme.[115]

The aspirational 'new India' is a nation that believes in making things happen, rather than waiting for things to happen. It is the India of opportunities and possibilities. At the heart of 'new India' lies PM Modi's vision of skill and innovation-driven growth with the youth playing a pivotal role.

PM Modi has ensured that even those who have remained on the margins of development till now, are provided with opportunities that will merge them with mainstream India.

Success Stories of MUDRA[116]

Name of the Beneficiary: Shri Jayprakash Narayan S.S.
Location: Manipur
Bank: Vijaya Bank, Chikkabanavara, Bengaluru (Rural Karnataka)
Activity: Tea Shop
Loan Category: Shishu
Amount Disbursed: Rs. 30,000
His Story:

Jayprakash, a physically challenged person, never allowed his weakness to come in the way of his zeal for life. He worked hard, everyday, to earn a living for himself. Jayprakash owned a small tea shop in Chikkabanavara, near Vijaya Bank and supplied tea to the branch. One day he discussed his plans with one of the bank employees at his tea stall and, to his surprise, realised that the government had recently launched a MUDRA scheme to support people like him. He went to the bank and in a few days, applied for the loan. After fulfilling the formalities, he got a loan of Rs. 30,000. With the loan amount, he purchased a gas stove, some utensils, coffee powder, small chocolates, etc. With that, the business started growing and income increased. His sale proceeds are credited to the MUDRA card account daily and his loan account is regular.

Name of the Beneficiary: Smt. Pushpa Babaji Bansode
Location: Kharghar, Navi Mumbai
Bank: Bank of India, Kharghar, Navi Mumbai
Business Activity: Manufacturing silver-coated paper bowls and plates used for distribution of prasad in temples

Loan Category: Kishor
Amount Disbursed: Rs. 3 lakhs
Her Story:

Smt. Pushpa Babaji Bansode, aged 40 years, hailed from a lower middle-class SC family. With a dream to establish herself as a first-generation entrepreneur, she sought to venture into the manufacturing sector. She realised that the demand for manufactured products was immense and with the support of a bank loan, she would be able to cater to this demand. Seeking funding, she visited the Bank of India branch near her home where the staff briefed her about the PMMY scheme.

Today, she has a flourishing business of manufacturing silver-coated paper plates and bowls, which are used in temples for distributing prasad. She has received a five-year contract from Om Sai Enterprises and Gruha Udyog, New Panvel for supplying her products to them. Smt. Pushpa is now a confident entrepreneur and manages her business efficiently with the help of two people she has employed. With the revenue she generates from her business, she supplements her family income. This contributes to a better standard of living.

Name of the Beneficiary: Shri Dhaneswar Patangia
Location: Ghatuwa village, P.O. Tezpur, Dist. Sonitpur, Assam
Bank: State Bank of India, Mission Chariali Branch
Business Activity: Ambulance Service
Loan Category: Tarun
Amount Disbursed: Rs. 6 lakhs
His Story:

Dhaneswar used to be a daily-wage driver, earning around Rs. 4,000-5,000 per month. His income was irregular and insufficient to meet his family needs. As fate would have it, he happened to meet Mr. D. Chakravarty, Tezpur RBO's Credit Manager, from whom he learnt about the MUDRA scheme. Without wasting any time, he applied for the loan for doing an ambulance service business.

His loan for Rs. 6 lakh got approved by Mission Chariali branch. Further, he was also financially helped by his landlord Mr. H.K. Borah for depositing the margin money of Rs. 2 lakh with the bank to get the loan. Dhaneswar is now a happy man. With his honesty and good behaviour, he is successfully operating his ambulance service. He nets a minimum monthly income of Rs. 30,000 and is able to take care of his parents and family.

Today, Dhaneswar not only maintains a good financial discipline towards his loan account, he is also repaying his landlord in lumpsum on a monthly basis.

□

5

New Infrastructure for New India

Infrastructure is key to ease of living. Good and modern infrastructure not only improves the quality of life of people, but also contributes to all-round economic growth and development. Good roads, extensive railways network, usable and clean waterways, large ports, increased air connectivity, access to electricity and the Internet are some of the infrastructure resources intrinsic to the well-being of a country and its citizens. Dr. B.R. Ambedkar wanted all of these for the people of India so that their quality of life would improve.

After taking office, the Prime Minister Narendra Modi's government embarked on an unprecedented infrastructure push. The rationale behind this was simple. To cite an example, when PM Modi came into power, he observed that it was a shame that even after nearly seven decades of Independence, India still had villages without electricity. His government's focus was, therefore, to undertake rapid electrification of villages and ensure electricity reached every household. After all, no aspirational country, which is also the fastest growing economy, can still have parts of its rural areas unelectrified in the 21st century!

If behind so many of India's new ideas, innovations and opportunities lie its tier-2 and tier-3 cities, could such places still suffer poor-quality roads, lack of air connectivity, slow internet, etc.? How could e-governance and farmer-friendly services become a reality without Internet in India's villages?

These are just a few of the concerns that would have

mattered to Dr. Babasaheb Ambedkar that the Modi government has sought to answer. Dr. Babasaheb Ambedkar's views on infrastructure stemmed directly from his belief in the necessity of industrialisation in India, the role industrialisation had to play not only in India's rapid development, but also in lifting Indians out of poverty. In a world-view like Dr. Babasaheb Ambedkar's, therefore, primacy would undoubtedly be given to building sound and enduring infrastructure.

The Modi government has been ensuring the expansion of basic infrastructure necessities, like electricity, roads, rail and air connectivity, etc. But above and beyond that, it has also been building next-gen infrastructure that takes into account the needs of the future. To cite a few examples, we can think of the Bullet Train, or the scope and expanse of Digital India, or even the Prime Minister's emphasis on Artificial Intelligence to make life easier. After all, ease of living follows from easy access to sound infrastructure.

Electricity to Every Village

In the reconstruction that began even as World War II raged, Dr. Babasaheb Ambedkar played a key role as the Labour Member in the Viceroy's Executive Council. His role in setting up the Central Technical Power Board, which later came to be called the Central Electricity Authority, is well known. But he was also behind foundational concepts, such as the grid system in electricity production and transmission, or the idea of regional rather than local development in electricity. He had laid emphasis on two operative words: 'cheap' and 'abundant', with regard to electricity when he had asked:

"Why do we want cheap and abundant electricity in India? The answer is that without cheap and abundant electricity, no effort for the industrialisation of India can succeed... why is industrialisation necessary? ...we want industrialisation in India as the surest means to rescue the people from the eternal cycle of

poverty in which they are caught."[117]

Electricity, thus, is no perk or privilege. It is a necessity without which progress and economic uplift cannot happen.

PM Modi's approach to this necessity is best captured in his own words:

"It is important for us to understand what life is like without electricity. When electricity will reach these households, only then their fortunes will shine... New India requires an energy framework that works on the principle of equity, efficiency and sustainability."[118]

While racing towards achieving 100% village electrification, the Government of India focused on achieving electrification of all un-electrified households in the country. As such, PM Modi not only set an ambitious target for electrifying villages under the Deendayal Upadhyaya Gram Jyoti Yojana (DDUGJY), but also went beyond that to electrify all households with the SAUBHAGYA scheme.

In December 2014, Deendayal Upadhyaya Gram Jyoti Yojana (DDUGJY), with a total investment of Rs. 43,033 crore was launched with the following objectives:

(i) Village electrification.
(ii) Providing access to households.
(iii) Feeder separation.
(iv) Strengthening of sub-transmission and distribution network.
(v) Metering.

In addition, Grameen Vidyutikaran (GARV) App was launched to monitor village electrification in the country. The app worked as a catalyst in expediting electrification with a real-time feedback mechanism.

When PM Modi came into power in 2014, 18,374 villages were in darkness. Though the work on rural electrification was ongoing, the pace kept on declining from 2009-10 as it became increasingly difficult to reach the villages situated in the remote corners of the country or those with tough terrain. In 2014-15, the speed shot up, with the number of villages electrified rising from 1,405 in 2014-15 to 7,108 in 2015-16. By 2018, all villages had been electrified.[119]

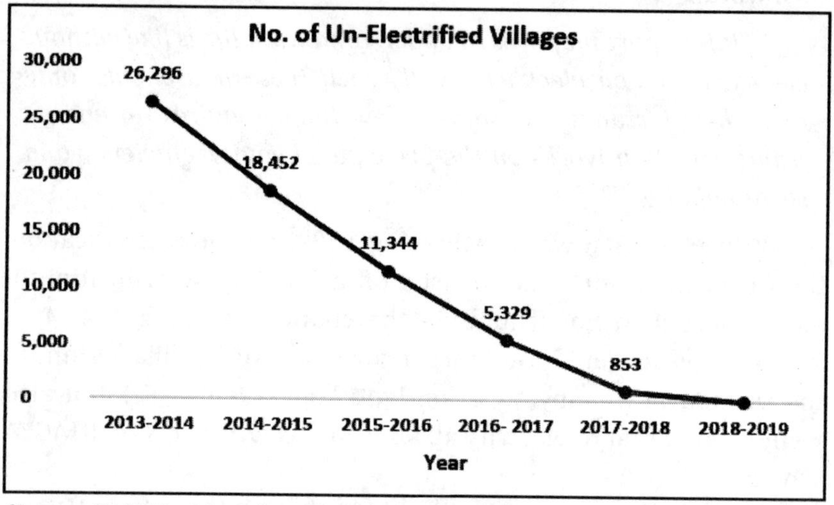

(Source: GARV Dashboard)

However, the Prime Minister had already set a higher bar, ensuring electricity for the poorest of the poorat very affordable rates. Therefore, in September 2017, Sahaj Bijli Har Ghar Yojana, or SAUBHAGYA was announced. Under SAUBHAGYA, the government focused on achieving complete penetration of those poor households that did not have BPL cards, or were not capable of paying initial connection charges. For houses located in remote villages where grid extension is not possible, solar PV-based stand-alone systems are being provided. SAUBHAGYA covered the cost of all equipment and infrastructure required, e.g. service cable, energy meter, light point with LED bulb, electricity pole, etc. SAUBHAGYA has emerged since then as one of the most celebrated achievements of PM Modi's government.

Under SAUBHAGYA, 2.62 crore poor households were granted electricity connections. Today, 633 out of 637 districts stand saturated in terms of household electrification.[120] The target in fact was achieved 12 days ahead of the target date, which was unique given how projects stood delayed for decades on a stretch. Those who benefited were the most socially and economically vulnerable groups, including the SCs, Adivasis and OBCs who had been suffering due to decades of political neglect and institutional apathy.

On top of that, important reforms have been introduced, such as UDAY, which focuses on the financial health and other problems of distribution companies (discoms). A 360° approach focuses on increasing power generation, strengthening transmission and distribution, adding capacity, building energy efficiency and reducing power loss. As recently as July 2012, northern and eastern India had suffered a power grid failure for two consecutive days, affecting about 30 crore people.[121]The second day's blackout reportedly was the largest in history. Post 2014, the probability of such a scenario occurring has reduced drastically.

Stories of transformation from various corners of the country define the impact electrification has had on faraway villages. With children being able to study even during the night and village-based enterprises and farms getting access to power, change is broad-based. The International Energy Agency (IEA) in its World Energy Outlook Report, 2018 called India a 'star performer' for ensuring complete electrification of villages.[122] India's rank on World Bank's Ease of Doing Business 2020–'Getting Electricity' has seen excellent rating with the country scoring 89.4 out of 100.[123] Energy deficit reduced to 0.7% in FY20 from 4.2% in FY14.[124]

Connectivity: Roads, Waterways, Ports, Railways, Civil Aviation, Digital India and New Age Infrastructure

The transformation, not mere improvement of life in the villages, as in towns and cities, directly connects Dr. Babasaheb Ambedkar and PM Modi. Just like Dr. Babasaheb Ambedkar, the

Prime Minister understood very early the need for large-scale transformative development in infrastructure to boost industry and economy; thereby, redefining Indian lives, especially among the poorer sections of society. Being a champion of urbanisation, Dr. Babasaheb Ambedkar advocated Indians to move out of villages to urban cities and break the shackles of social depravity or exclusion. Today, even as India is rapidly urbanising, transformation is happening in villages as well, making way for what is called the 'rurban' landscape. This involves not only new-age infrastructure, like optical fibre, but something as fundamental as roads, waterways, railways and airways.

ROADS

Roads play a vital role in not merely connecting cities, but ushering in all-round development and subsequently impacting the lives of millions. Life becomes easy for a villager or a farmer with access to good and pucca roads, which connect his home to the market and give him access to essential services. For children going to school every morning, a road allows them to commute safely. Movement of freight across the country on seamless and wide highways is crucial for trade and economic development. Roads are actually pathways to prosperity that is being realised at an unprecedented scale.

Highways and Bharatmala

Taking a cue from the Vajpayee government that realised the vision of connecting India's four corners under the Golden Quadrilateral project, the Modi government has revived the highway sector like no other.

Now road projects are a high priority and highways are being built at a much faster rate. It was factually correct when PM Modi had declared in Parliament that *"The NDA government is building more roads than the previous one. We have given a strong boost to the infrastructure sector across the nation."*[125]

The speed at which national highways are being constructed has doubled. Highway construction in India increased at 17% CAGR between FY16-FY21. India constructed 13,298 km of highways in FY21. In the last seven years, the length of national highways has gone up by more than 50% - from 91,287 km (as on April 2014) to around 1,41,000 km till 2021-end.[126] Despite the pandemic and lockdown, during the financial year 2021-22, around 5,400 km of national highways had been built till December 2021.

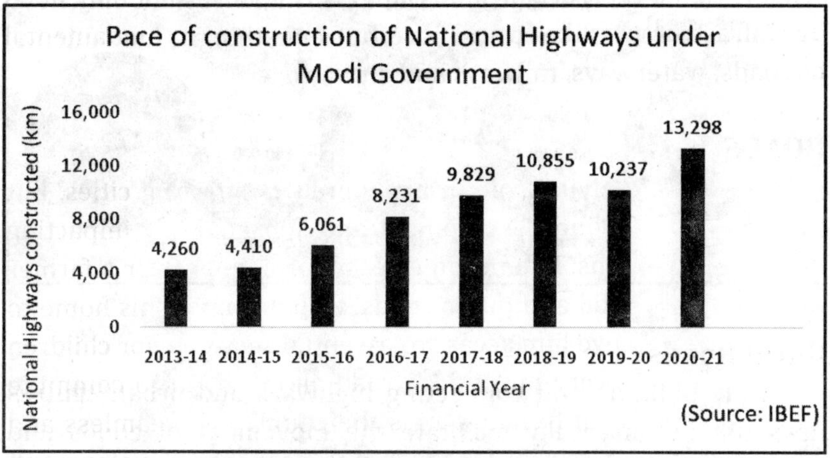

The Bharatmala project, announced in 2017, is an umbrella programme that focusses on optimising the efficiency of road traffic movement by bridging critical infrastructure gaps. Under Bharatmala, special attention is being paid to connectivity needs of backward and tribal areas, areas of economic activity, places of religious and tourist interest, border and coastal areas, and also trade routes linking India with its neighbourhood.

Bharatmala Pariyojana is developing and upgrading 34,800 km of national highways with an outlay of Rs. 5.35 lakh crore from 2017-18 to 2021-22. Along with Bharatmala, other road development projects that cover the north-east as well as the Maoist-affected areas are being implemented over a five-year period at a cost of Rs. 7 lakh crore.

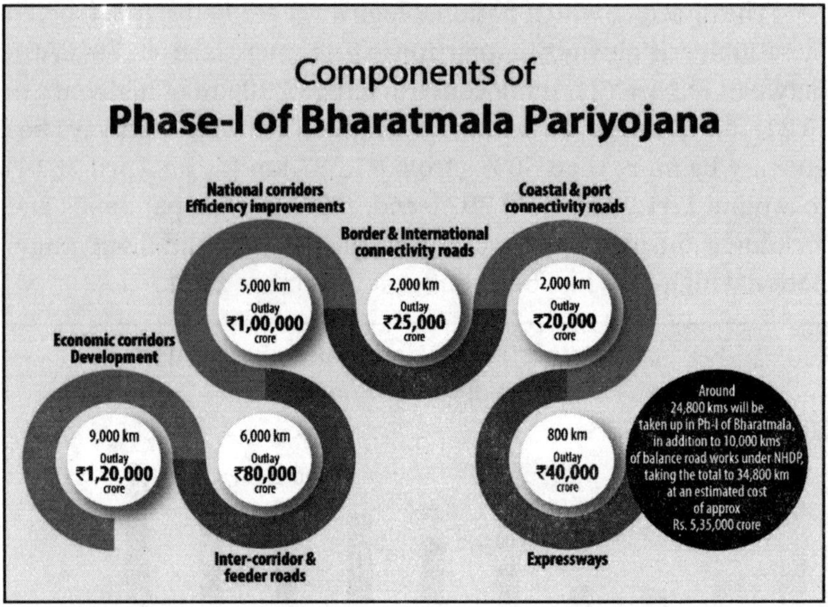

Rural Roads

Only building and connecting highways and urban centres does not automatically facilitate the movement of goods and people, nor economically lift the areas traversed by the big roads. We also need to look at village roads. The Modi government has been constructing rural roads at a much faster pace than earlier, under the Pradhan Mantri Gram Sadak Yojana (PMGSY), knowing that economic development of the village and increase in farmers' incomes cannot happen without such basic infrastructure.

In order to fuel the rural economy, it is essential to connect them with roads. It is one of the outstanding features of the Modi government –the pace at which it has carried out the construction of rural roads. The speed of rural road construction doubled from 69 km per day in 2013-14 to an all-time record of 134 km per day in 2017-18, thanks to which rural road construction reached a massive scale. As a result of this ramp up, by March 2022, rural road connectivity was at more than 99% as against 55% in March

2014.[127] As on March 2022, more than 6.97 lakh km of total road length was completed under PMGSY I, II and III.

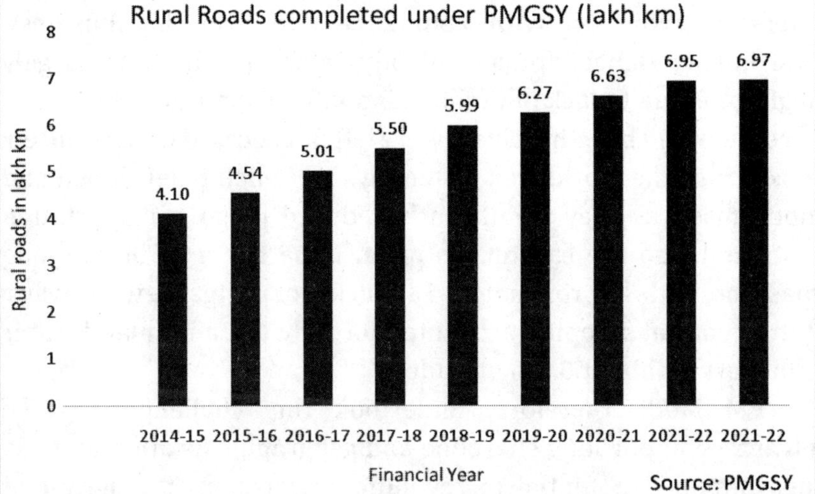

Source: PMGSY

In recent years it was felt that rural connectivity cannot be limited to habitations. For the benefit of the local economy, PMGSY III was expanded and recalibrated to connect other basic facilities as well. This latest phase focuses on upgrading existing road networks that connect habitations to Gramin Agricultural Markets (GrAMs), higher secondary schools and hospitals. Easy and faster movement to and from the food processing centres, mandis and other farmer-related enterprises not only helps in farm production, but also yields many direct and indirect benefits, such as minimising the spoilage of perishable goods like fresh fruits and vegetables, and ensuring adequate remunerative prices for them. Such a facility ultimately leads to a more vibrant agrarian economy and helps the development of the region, creating multiple opportunities. Similarly, affordable and easy access to high schools and higher secondary schools is essential to enable improved access to education centres, while there is a strong positive correlation to improve in health indicators and all-weather roads, underscoring their need.[128]

Waterways and Ports

As a land of rivers, Indian civilisation evolved along river banks. For centuries, Indians have travelled up and down the rivers, carrying on with commerce and everyday business. Post-Independence, India's inland waterways became largely neglected. Due to lack of funding and infrastructural lacunae, our once-busy and bursting rivers were left unused and underutilised. In contrast, the worldover, waterways were being developed and modernised as they significantly reduced cargo transportation costs and also the carbon footprint. India has a 7,500-km-long coastline, with, approximately, 14,500 km of navigable waterways. But its coastal shipping accounted for only 6% and inland water transport for about 0.4% of trade.[129,130].

PM Modi, therefore, undertook this challenge to take advantage of our long shoreline and geographic location and use this untapped potential to revolutionise economic activity and ease of living. The advantages of using our waterways are self-evident. The waterways' development would complement road and highway development and, at the same time, reduce the burden on the latter.

The government began to take initiatives to change things and holistically develop inland and coastal waterways and ports, with several major projects. The government unveiled an exciting new blueprint for rejuvenating and developing the national waterways with the National Waterways Act, 2016. But developing national waterways is not merely a matter of constructing pathways through rivers. The project envisions a waterways future for India through an on-going infrastructural transformation, which will create big employment opportunities directly and indirectly. The Gangetic Plains may emerge as a big beneficiary, but the north-east is also going to reap dividends.[131]

There is another story. On October 22, 2017, PM Modi inaugurated the first phase of the Gogha-Dahej Ro-Ro ferry service in Gujarat. As South Asia's first-of-its kind, state-of-the-art Ro-Ro ferry service, it will speed up transportation between Saurashtra's Bhavnagar city and South Gujarat's Bharuch, revolutionising the two regions socio-economically. It is also a template for similar Ro-Ro ferry services on Indian waterways. The Gogha-Dahej Ro-Ro ferry service also connects waterway development to coastal shipping and port development.

To develop port infrastructure and encourage the growth of Indian tonnage, the government has taken several steps. While cargo traffic and cargo-handling capacity has been steadily increasing at Indian ports, measures have also been taken to improve the performance of Indian ports, including benchmarking of major ports to international standards.

In November 2018, the first multi-modal terminal in Varanasi was inaugurated, marking another milestone in the infrastructure development journey. National Waterways-1 was commissioned allowing heavy cargo movement from Varanasi to Haldia in Kolkata. In November 2019, the first-ever movement of container cargo on Brahmaputra (National Waterway-2) began from Haldia Dock Complex (HDC) to Pandu in Guwahati via Indo-Bangladesh Protocol (IBP) route. It gave fillip to connectivity to north-east India.

To promote inland water transport in the country, a total of 111 waterways (including five existing and 106 new) have been declared as National Waterways (NWs) under the National Waterways Act, 2016. Based on the outcome of techno-economic feasibility and Detailed Project Reports (DPRs) of NWs, 25 NWs have been found viable by Inland Waterways Authority of India (IWAI) for cargo/passenger movement, while developmental activities have been initiated in 13 NWs.[132]

The vision of Dr. Babasaheb Ambedkar to fully capitalise on India's waterways is finally coming to fruition with such mega projects being undertaken on a massive scale.

Sagarmala

Perhaps the biggest port-focused project is Sagarmala– a flagship programme that seeks to harness India's long coastline and navigable waterways as well as our 'strategic location on key international maritime trade routes.'[133] Sagarmala, as PM Modi said, is ushering in not only development of ports, but also port-led development. It encompasses over 802 projects related to the upgrade of port infrastructure with investment of more than Rs. 5.53 lakh crore.[134] As of 6th November, 2021, as many as 172 projects worth of Rs. 88,235 crore stood completed, while another 235 projects worth Rs. 2.17 lakh crore were at various stages of implementation.[135] An additional 137 projects are under development while 235 are under different stages of implementation. Over the years, this will enable the creation of 1 crore direct and indirect jobs.

In December 2021, the Prime Minister launched the Maritime India Vision 2030, which contains the targets to be achieved by the maritime sector over the next decade along with the strategies related to each of the stakeholders of MoPSW.

Indian Railways

The Indian Railways are the arteries of India since pre-Independence days. In connecting a village to a town and in driving the economy, its importance remains undented. If freight moves from one corner of the country to another on railroad networks, so do millions of Indians who travel every day for work or to find work, to get medical treatment, to commute to school, or for leisure. In effect, the Indian Railways are a microcosm of the Indian nation. When Dr. Babasaheb Ambedkar emphasised the need for good infrastructure for industry, development and lifting Indians out of poverty, this significance was not lost on him.

PM Modi has himself said: *"Creating a railway system which is modern and technologically advanced is vital. We are strengthening the railways network across the country."*[136]

Because, when we travel on trains, there are a few basic things we would like to take for granted: Safety, security, relative comfort and reaching our destination on time. The government, therefore, has been implementing an all-round development plan for the Indian Railways. This includes the basic infrastructure, such as broad gauging of tracks, station development, passenger safety and systems upgrade, as well as high-speed rail.[1] By March 2021, 45,881 Route Kilometres (RKM) or 71% of the total broad-gauge network of Indian Railways (on including Konkan Railway) stood electrified. Remarkably, out of this 45,881 RKM, 34% has been electrified only between 2018 and 2021. In fact, since 2014, a record 24,080 RKM has been electrified against electrification of 4,337 RKM during 2007-14.[138] It must also be pointed out that in 2020-21, electrification of 6,015 route kilometres was achieved despite the pandemic.[139]

State-of-the-art infrastructure, like the HSR (Bullet Train) offers India not just a giant technological leap, but a boost to manufacturing and construction. An interesting aspect of it is also skill-development and engineering capacity-building. Once more, if we recall Dr. Babasaheb Ambedkar, he had categorically emphasised skill-development and training our own engineers and personnel, whether at home or abroad.

In October 2019, India's first private train Tejas Express on Lucknow-Delhi route was flagged off, bringing in a paradigm shift in the approach of the government towards railways. Since then, two more such trains, plying on the Mumbai-Karmali and Chennai-Madurai-Egmore route, have been launched.

Today, Indian Railways is among the world's largest rail networks and its route length network is spread over 67,956 km, with 13,169 passenger trains and 8,479 freight trains, plying 23 million travellers and 3 million tonnes (MT) of freight daily from 7,349 stations.[140] In FY2021-22, Indian Railways witnessed the highest ever capital allocation of Rs. 2.15 lakh crore for infrastructure development. Presently, its fleet includes 1,768 mail/express trains, 5,626 sub-urban and 3,634 passenger trains.

For the first time, special 1,806 Kisan Rails are carrying around 5.9 lakh tonnes of agricultural products across on 153 routes. During the Covid pandemic, Indian Railways ran around 900 Oxygen Express Trains to deliver oxygen in the shortest possible time across the country. In fact, the Oxygen Train even made a special stop in Bangladesh! Moreover, over 4,000 coaches were converted into quarantine/isolation facilities to meet the growing demand for health facilities at the time. In every sense, the Indian Railways proved how it was the backbone of India![141]

Civil Aviation

At the launch of the first UDAN flight on 26th April, 2017, Prime Minister Modi declared: *"My dream was to see a person who wears a hawai chappal fly on the hawai jahaz."*

Perhaps nothing demonstrates India's efforts at combining economic growth with spreading out the benefits of that growth than civil aviation. Expansion of civil aviation infrastructure, increase in number of flights and airports do not just add to economic potential by creating jobs, but also enable ease of doing business. It also adds to the ease of living and forms an essential portion of the aspirations of an emerging big economy. That is why, the government has been striving to not only build a strong civil aviation infrastructure, but also ensure that more and more people are able to access it.

India is well on its way to becoming the world's third-largest air travel market by 2024[142] and is already the fastest growing aviation market in the sub-continent.Even in a pandemic-affected phase, the aviation industry has been able to hold strong, with December 2021 seeing a 49% growth in domestic Route Passenger Kilometres (RPKs), much higher than the global average growth rate of 34.7%.[143]

Behind this growth, there have been policy interventions. For example, the National Civil Aviation Policy (NCAP-2016) is the first comprehensive policy for the growth of India's aviation ecosystem. UDAN was launched in October 2016 to make flying accessible and affordable for everybody and in regionally-important cities. A first-of-its-kind scheme to boost regional connectivity through a market-based mechanism, UDAN caps passenger fare at Rs. 2,500 for an hour-long flight.

Out of a total of 449 airports and airstrips located throughout India till December 2021,[144] Airport Authority of India owns 136 airports,[145]- a bump-up from just 64 airports in 2014.[146] Of these, 130 airports are operational.[147]

Newer modes of air transportation have been introduced under UDAN including seaplanes, helicopters and flights via smaller aircraft. UDAN is helping airline operators to develop sustainable business models and, at the same time, provide start-up and scale-up opportunities to small regional airlines. It has facilitated increase in demand and growth for profitable routes by providing the middle class the opportunity to travel in comfort and reduced travel time at affordable prices. A large number of first-time flyers have been able to take to the skies due to UDAN.[148]

A special Krishi UDAN scheme was launched in 2020 to help improve value realization, especially in the north-east and tribal districts by seamlessly integrating agri-harvesting and air transportation in a cost-effective and time-bound air transportation system. It enhances the share of Indian carriers in domestic and international air freight for transportation of agri-produce. The scheme is being implemented at 25 airports from the north-east, hilly and tribal regions and 28 airports from other parts of the country.[149]

As global travel came to a standstill due to spread of the Covid pandemic in 2020, India's civil aviation industry undertook upon itself a new role. Ministry of Civil Aviation launched 'Lifeline UDAN' on March, 26, 2020, to ensure a steady supply of essentials as well as medical equipment, PPEs, test kits, etc. to all parts of the country. For this purpose, the ministry established Lifeline UDAN mechanism to match the requirements of states/UTs, various ministries, etc. with special flight plans. Lifeline UDAN has played a big role in not only speedily transporting medical supplies, but also personnel, health professionals, and later, even oxygen and Covid vaccines to the remote regions during this critical time of emergency.

The Vande Bharat Mission (VBM) was a unique initiative undertaken to bring home lakhs of stranded and distressed Indian nationals in various parts of the world due to the Covid pandemic. The mission involved a massive operation organised by the Government of India to evacuate Indian nationals by air, sea and land routes. The VBM also helped individuals of various nationalities stuck in India to return to their respective countries. Then GoI-owned Air India group emerged as the backbone of the VBM while some private Indian carriers participated in the exercise as well. By the sheer number of passengers and countries covered, it became the biggest evacuation exercise by any civilian authority in the world.

Under the VBM, more than 2,17,000 flights were operated till October 2021, facilitating over 1.83 crore passengers.[150]Air India/ Air India Express covered more than 50 countries; even such countries where they did not fly in the normal course.[151]

Gati Shakti

PM Modi launched the Gati Shakti–National Master Plan in October 2021, heralding a new chapter in governance. Gati Shakti is a digital platform that will bring together 16 ministries, including railways and roadways, for integrated planning and coordinated implementation of infrastructure connectivity projects. The master plan will incorporate the infrastructure schemes, like Bharatmala, Sagarmala, inland waterways, dry/ land ports, UDAN, etc. as well as economic zones, like textile clusters, pharmaceutical clusters, defence corridors, electronic parks, industrial corridors, fishing clusters, agri-zones to improve connectivity and make Indian business more competitive.

The multi-modal connectivity will provide integrated and seamless network for movement of people, goods and services from one mode of transport to another and within the country. It will also facilitate the last-mile connectivity of infrastructure and also reduce the travel time for people. Gati Shakti will also leverage technology, including spatial planning tools with ISRO imagery developed by BiSAG-N.

The Gati Shakti Cargo Terminal Policy will fast track the approvals and ease of establishing cargo terminals to increase the freight loading share of the Indian Railways. Work on the multi-modal logistics parks (MMLPs) gained momentum in 2021, with tenders invited for two MMLP projects at Nagpur and Chennai.

Digital India

As an economy, India is rapidly becoming digitally empowered. Digital empowerment is not merely simplifying processes, but also ensuring transparency and quality of services. A powerful example of this is how mobile and e-banking are bringing about financial inclusion of all households in India through Jan-Dhan Yojana. At the same time, farmers are learning about judicious use of chemical fertilisers through Soil Health Cards integrated with Digital India. The Swachh Bharat App is integral to Swachh Bharat Abhiyan, which has turned into a citizens' movement across India. Again, Unified Mobile Application for New-Age Governance (UMANG) is a key e-governance initiative to provide a single-point access to all government services. SVAMITVA digitises property cards of rural landholders, thus reducing chances of dispute or even cheating.

Examples of how Digital India is transforming lives and the economy could go on, but the essence of this revolution can be summed up in PM Modi's own words: *"I dream of a Digital India where the netizen is an empowered citizen."*[152]

However, a primary factor behind the increasing digitalisation of the Indian socio-economy is the laying of optical fibre cable (OFC). In connecting and integrating rural India with the digital world, the growth of the optical fibre network must be noted. The government has laid down a plan to connect all the 2,6 lakh gram panchayats in the country by utilising existing fibres of PSUs (BSNL, Railtel and Power Grid) and laying incremental fibre to connect to gram panchayats wherever necessary. A Special Purpose Vehicle (SPV), Bharat Broadband Network Limited (BBNL) was incorporated to execute and operate the infrastructure created under the Bharat Net Project.

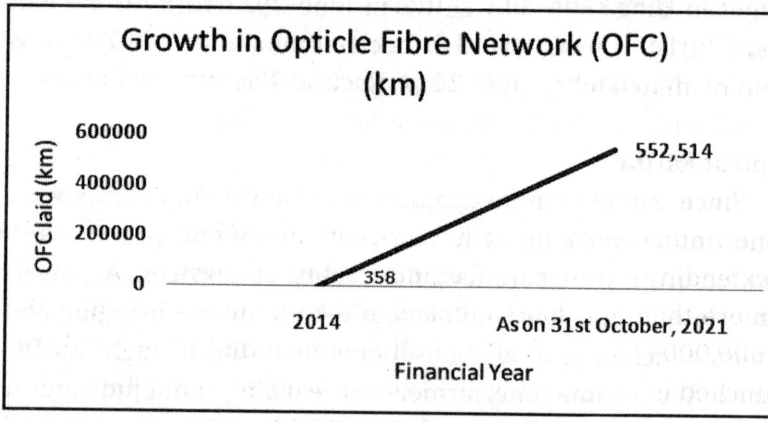

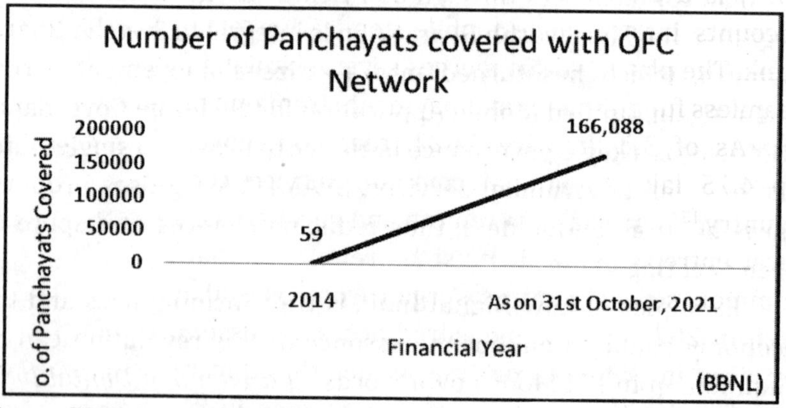

(Source: BBNL Annual Report[153])

Meantime, growing popularity of Internet across the entire spectrum of the country has seen big advances in its usage. Smart devices have become a part of our daily lives, whether in the hands of children for education or games; or in government and private offices, connecting with the world; or even in basic day-to-day functions. Internet connections jumped from just over 25 crore in March 2014 to over 83 crore in June 2021, registering a growth of 231%. Broadband connections rose from 6.1 crore in March 2014 to 79 crore in June 2021, growing by about 1,200%. Average monthly data consumption per wireless data subscriber increased by 22,605% to 14 GB in June 2021 from 61.66 MB in March 2014.[154] This has also been accompanied by an overall trend of affordability– if in 2014, Rs. 268.97 was the average cost per subscriber for 1GB wireless data,[155] in September 2021 this stood at Rs. 9.53,[156] i.e. 28 times lesser.

Since 2014, the government led by PM Modi has left no stone unturned to digitally empower every citizen, whether it is extending corruption-free direct benefit transfer of benefits to more than 100 crore citizens, providing Internet connectivity to 600,000+ villages, or digitally empowering citizens of India. Launched in 2016 with just 21 banks, Unified Payments Interface (UPI) is a digital interface that brings together multiple bank accounts into a single mobile application of any participating bank. The platform also merges several banking features to allow seamless fund transfer and payments from one point.

As of 31st January, 2022, the Modi government had set up 4.75 lakh functional common service centres across the country,[157] especially in remote and rural areas, creating village-level entrepreneurs. It must be reiterated that the number of common service centres surged from 64,000 in 2014 to 4.75 lakh in 2022. This has ensured access to essential government services in fields as diverse as health, education, agriculture, social and financial inclusion for citizens in rural and remote areas. In another major achievement, the government has now made provision for linking of electoral roll data withthe Aadhaar ecosystem. This curbs the menace of multiple enrolment of the same voters in different places.

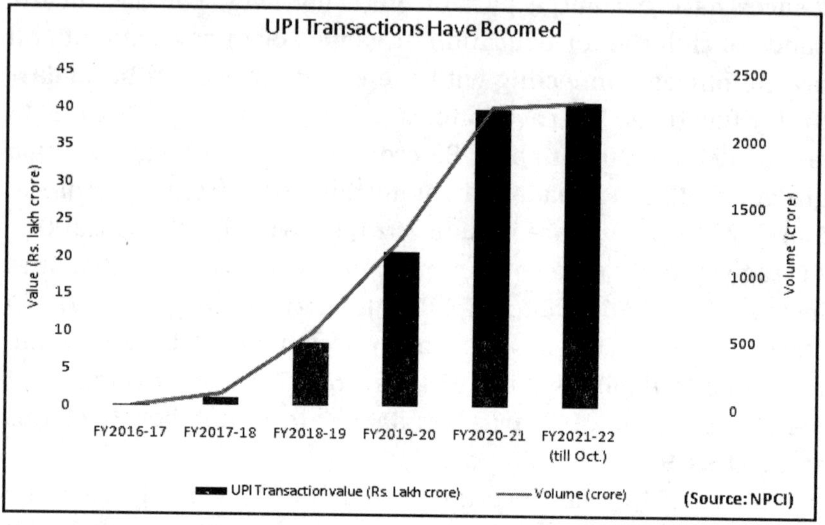

Digital India is the umbrella that covers all. Not only is it banking the unbanked, but it is also helping to make the economy a less-cash one. Today, people can book train tickets or transfer money in a matter of minutes while sitting at home. A woman in distress can make an emergency call or send a message to the police in an instant, thanks to a facility like the Himmat App. The area covered by the Digital India umbrella, indeed, includes even climate-friendly, energy-saving LED lamps to building cities with 'smart' solutions. In fulfilment of Dr. Babasaheb Ambedkar's wish for an empowered citizenry with an enhanced quality of life, no better and rounded example can perhaps be cited.

New-age Infrastructure

Modi government is constantly working towards bringing in reforms in all sectors. This zeal to modernise India to be at par with the rest of the world has opened avenues never existing before! This has also resulted in creation of new industries and infrastructure.

With radical advancements in transport and telecom technology, was the advent of drones in the Indian space. A little-known technology that is in fact gaining all-round acceptance, the government saw the need to regulate the operation of drones, to promote the manufacturing of drones in India under Atmanirbhar Bharat, and to facilitate training of drone operators. As a result, the drone policy was prepared and subsequently simplified. A Digital Sky Platform (DSP) was launched to cover the entire range of activities, like online registration, approval of flight path, post flight analysis, etc. The move will greatly benefit sectors including transportation, agriculture, defence, law enforcement, etc.

Major reforms have been undertaken in the telecom sector as well to address multiple issues including liquidity crunch, connectivity issues, infrastructure upgrade, etc. Up to nine structural and five procedural reforms have been introduced. As a result of these reforms, Foreign Direct Investment (FDI) in telecom sector has risen by around 150% in 2014-2021 from Rs. 62,386 crore in 2002 to 2014 to Rs. 1.55 lakh crore during 2014-2021. There is a spurt in infrastructure upgradation activity and the results are already visible. The number of mobile base transceiver stations (BTS) increased from 8 lakh in 2014 to 23 lakh in 2021, growing by 187 %. The number of mobile towers increased from 4 lakh in 2014 to 6.6 lakh in 2021, a growth of 65%.[158]

Another step that will go a long way in putting India on the global map is the new Geospatial Data Guidelines introduced by the Modi government. With the arrival of publicly available geospatial services, a lot of geospatial data is being freely exchanged in India and across the world. These guidelines will give an equal chance to both public and private entities, and ultimately benefit many sectors of the economy. Locally available maps and geospatial data will also help in improved planning and management of resources. Industries, such as fisheries, deep sea mining and offshore oil and gas that make up a large section of India's blue economy, will be greatly benefitted as the reforms will have a direct impact on the proposed 'Deep Ocean Mission' to explore India's rich cache of minerals, energy and marine diversity.

National Infrastructure Pipeline and National Monetisation Pipeline

A major paradigm shift has now been incorporated into policy making by the government. Through initiatives like the National Infrastructure Pipeline (NIP) and the National Monetisation Pipeline (NMP), an integrated approach towards building and managing infrastructure has arisen.

National Infrastructure Pipeline is an ambitious effort of PM Modi's government. A plan that identifies how Rs. 111 lakh crore of projects that are needed to ensure a $5 trillion economy and ease of living for all citizens was much needed. NIP has emerged as a first-of-its-kind, whole-of-government exercise and covers all infrastructure sub- sectors, including MSMEs working in infrastructure sector, as identified through a Harmonised Master List of Infrastructure Sub-sectors.[159] Aiming to build this infrastructure between 2020 and 2025 across the country, NIP touches upon more than 9,000 projects covering 34 sub-sectors.

Of course, building infrastructure also needs to be complemented with managing it while maximising its value realisation to generate money for building new infrastructure. In this regard, the National Monetisation Pipeline has emerged as a novel way of approaching the situation. As a key means for sustainable infrastructure financing,[160] the NMP approach has already generated traction and interest, with the private sector in particular expressing its desire to be part of the new India story like never before.

New-Age Space Reforms

India is the land of great scientists, like Dr. A.P.J. Abdul Kalam and Dr. Homi J. Bhabha who laid the foundation of the country's space and nuclear programme. While ISRO is doing great work in India's space programme; it is still dependent upon Western nations for a lot of technological inputs. Keeping in mind the growing popularity of ISRO in helping other nations with their space programmes, and also the potential of the country to become self-reliant in the sector, PM Modi asked why we were not doing much to boost our capabilities. This gave birth to the idea to open up the sector to private players.

The government, through regulatory reforms, has opened up the space sector to provide level playing field for private companies to use Indian space infrastructure. This will bring in greater investments in technology development and acquisition, capacity building and space exploration. Valuable Indian talent that was, till now, migrating to the Western world to pursue a career, can now contribute towards India's space aspirations. Furthermore, our space technology will now be available for commercial demand and supply of space assets and services, such as imaging, communication transponders, satellites, launch services, etc. This is a big step in leading India towards creating atmanirbharta in the space sector.

Conclusion

The Modi government has been able to give shape and body to Dr. Babasaheb Ambedkar's vision in terms of both the scale and kind of development India needs. The infrastructure, thus built, had to be accessible to all and transform the lives of all, be it in the village or the city. Whether we are looking at village electrification and rural roads or highways and affordable air travel, from the poor to the middle class, from the farmer to the industrialist, everybody is witnessing a qualitative transformation of their life.

□

6

Urbanisation: Powering Social and Economic Mobility

"Cities are not only growth centres. Our cities have strength and capacity to mitigate poverty."[161]

—Prime Minister Narendra Modi

With these words, Prime Minister Narendra Modi laid out his government's commitment towards developing our urban centres as inclusive spaces with the objective to alleviate poverty. The vision towards greater urbanisation is in consonance with the firm conviction of Dr. B.R. Ambedkar, who saw urbanisation as a panacea to social and economic inequality.

A votary of urbanisation, Dr. Babasaheb Ambedkar emphasised on shifting the populace from villages to urban centres. He had a clear vision of an egalitarian society, seeped in ideals of equal opportunity and dignified living for all. He had a strong conviction that the urban centres can break the silos of identity and allow each individual to soar on his own merit. He envisioned India's salvation in greater urbanisation.

He pushed for industries to grow and towns to revive as they were the modern tools for the development of the poorest of the poor. However, despite the assertion by one of the most visionary leaders of modern India, governance inertia did not allow growth of urban centres beyond the colonial legacy already built. The growth centres remained few, attracting a large influx of people from villages and small towns in the hope of breaking the clutches of poverty for a brighter tomorrow.

Laxity in developing urban India to meet the growing demands of an aspirational India led to haphazard growth of the urban clusters. The unwarranted pressure on a handful of cities caused ballooning of urban infrastructure. Lack of basic facilities of water and sanitation, electricity and cheap public transport meant deprivation and destitution of lakhs of migrants. There soon emerged a new class of poor, called urban poor, who mostly worked as daily-wage workers, lived in slum dwellings and earned the bare minimum for survival. However, their contribution to the economic growth of the cities was unparalleled and, unfortunately, unrecognised.

The nature of inequality changed, but inequality remained. The lack of forward planning to accommodate the demands of a growing economy had led to decaying of existing cities, which were envisioned to be growth engines.

The difference between haves and have-nots is starker in urban settings, seen in the spatial segregation of homes. Between burgeoning high rises, a vast cluster of slums would emerge. The double-digit inflation and skyrocketing property prices had ensured that the poor remained trapped in the cycle of poverty.

Therefore, the vision foreseen by Dr. Babasaheb Ambedkar of creating a land of equal opportunity that leads to dissolution of divisions remained gravely unfulfilled.

New Model of Inclusive Urbanisation

As per the Census 2011, 37.71 crore Indians comprising 31.16% of the country's population resided in urban areas. This number was set to rise to about 60 crore by 2031[162] as more and more people moved to the cities for better economic opportunities. In villages, agriculture still remains a primary source of income. The agriculture sector had a share of 20.2% in Gross Value Addition (GVA) to the economy in 2021,[163] with high levels of disguised unemployment, leading to inadequate utilisation of the human resource. For India to achieve higher economic growth, it is important that more urban centres are developed to unleash India's growth potential.

The possibilities of upward mobility have proven to be a potent driver for people from small towns and villages to move to cities. Unable to bear the cost of living, they reside in slums, which seem to be easy entry points to a new life. The Census 2011 report revealed that 17.4% of India's families lived in slums in conditions unfit for human habitation. Usually, such dwellings are dilapidated, overcrowded, dark and dingy, without proper sanitation. In the slum homes surveyed, one-third of the slum homes did not have an indoor toilet, while 64% of such units were not connected to any sewerage system.[164]

Lack of basic amenities and security severely restricts the growth trajectory of a daily-wage earner. Though many of them toil hard, day in and day out, to provide their children the education and facilities they never enjoyed; yet they are trapped in a spiral which does not allow them to alleviate their lives in any sense. Therefore, inequalities continue to exist over generations, even when the landscape has changed.

But PM Modi and his government understand the hardships faced by the majority of people who migrate to cities in search of a better life. Its policies of inclusive urban development manifest its commitment to provide institutional support to the marginalised to ease their lives and help them achieve their dreams. A rickshawalla, a street vendor, a house-help, if not for oneself, but for his or her next generation, can aspire to enlarge choices and attain a better standard of living.

With the PM Modi's government in power, the policy framework has transformed. Bringing urban planning back in focus, there have been strident efforts to not only upgrade the existing urban infrastructure, but also develop new cities and townships to accommodate the rising number of people moving to urban areas.

Following the adage of 'Sabka Saath, Sabka Vikas, Sabka Vishwas and Sabka Prayaas', the government has made inclusiveness and cohesion focal points of urban planning. Deficit in affordable housing, access to sanitation and clean water had marginalised the migrant populace in cities and offered limited opportunity for economic and social mobility. Setting target-based goals towards provision of a holistic model of urban development has hastened the urban transformation.

Sustainable Cities

In pursuit of urban rejuvenation and growth, the Modi government has launched bottom-up model of urban planning and implementation. The Smart Cities Mission and Atal Mission for Rejuvenation & Urban Transformation (AMRUT) are meant to infuse energy, effort and resources in enhancing a city's productivity and give a new lease of life to the deteriorating infrastructure.

The Smart Cities Mission is conceptualised to meet the demands arising out of expanding economy and decentralised growth by creating more centres of economic activity. These projects are not only expected to streamline the basic infrastructure of the cities, but also make them livable for the citizens. The broad objectives of the mission include sustainable urban planning and development, management of urban affairs with citizen participation, area-based development, resilience to climate change, natural disasters, etc., and technology-based solutions for better governance and infrastructure management. These smart cities are expected to create a domino effect and further accelerate the pace of development in the nearby regions. As on February 2022, 6,939 projects worth about Rs. 1.9 lakh crore had been tendered and of this work, orders have been issued for 6,301 projects worth Rs. 1.65 lakh crore, while 3,577 projects worth Rs. 60,073 crore have been completed.[165]

Easing people's day-to-day lives by building the foundation of smart cities on the agenda of digital governance has far-reaching effects on the standard of living for the most vulnerable sections of the society. For them, forgoing a day's work to fill government forms would often prove to be a costly affair. Many times, the sheer bureaucratic hassles would discourage them to avail the services. Ensuring government provisioning on click of a button has deepened citizen trust and engagement.

Further, making our urban centres environment-friendly is the need of the hour. Those with limited resources are the most affected in times of natural disasters or climate change. With disaster-resilient infrastructure, people living in the cities are well prepared for any eventuality.

Under AMRUT, the government has removed bureaucratic bottlenecks that hindered the process of urban development. By introducing a single-window clearance system, many projects have been green-lighted in a timely manner. AMRUT aims to make urban areas more habitable and inclusive. It focusses on items that constitute basic amenities critical to the quality of life. From ensuring household access to assured supply of water and creating green and open spaces, the scheme covers a wide spectrum of services. A total of 500 cities are being targeted for urban reforms based on PPP model, which will directly benefit 2 crore households. As of January 2022, nearly 4,000 projects had been completed, while another 1,800 projects were cleared for action.[166]

This large-scale urban infrastructural development and transformation has caught the world's attention as it is looking towards India for enhanced investment opportunities. Many leading economies have signed pacts with India to lead the development of smart cities. According to UNCTAD's (UN Conference on Trade and Development) World Investment Report 2021, India attracted $64 billion FDI inflows, thanks to the schemes like AMRUT.[167]

Improvement in standard of living has been the driving force of the government's urban policy. In a first in 2018, the Modi government brought out the Ease of Living Index (EoLI) of 111 cities that include smart cities, state capitals and cities with one million-plus population, wherein livability standards with 78 indicators in 15 categories were used for measuring institutional, social, economic and physical aspects that affect the quality of life. The index works as a feedback mechanism to assist cities to assess their progress and correct course for more effective implementation of various urban development schemes.

Similar to the EoLI index, a Municipal Performance Index (MPI) was also launched to examine the sectoral performance of 111 municipalities across five verticals– Services, Finance, Policy, Technology and Governance– which comprise 20 sectors and 100 indicators. The two indices provide an assessment tool that evaluates the quality of life and the impact of various initiatives for urban development. This encourages all cities to move towards an 'outcome-based' approach to urban planning and management and promote healthy competition among cities.

Urban renewal and growth are not only meant to build cities for the future, but also ensure that the baggage of social backwardness does not continue to hold the marginalised from writing a new chapter of economic and social empowerment in the urban centres. The cities need to become a thriving and accommodating space for people, irrespective of where they come from; only then can we realise the vision of a new India.

Housing for All

A house for practical purposes is a marker of security. Around the concrete structure, people build their lives and their dreams and even plan for their future generations. With real estate prices rising, owning a house had largely become a luxury, pushing millions to live in slums. Considering that the number of people living in slums is increasing with increased migration, the UN Sustainable Development Goals (SDG) call on national governments to make cities and human settlement inclusive, safe, resilient and sustainable. It entails ensuring access to adequate, safe and affordable housing and basic services and upgradation of slums.

In India, the situation requires targeted redressal. As per Census 2011, over a third of India's slum population lived in its 46 million-plus cities. Of the metros, Mumbai has the highest proportion of slum-dwelling households (41.3% of its population). Kolkata is next at nearly 30% with Chennai not far behind. Delhi has 14.6% of its households living in slums. In such a scenario, implementation of government's mission of 'Housing for All' becomes a much-needed intervention in balancing the housing deficit.

The government aims to provide low-cost, affordable homes with water connection, toilet facilities and 24X7 electricity supply to meet the demands of the growing urban poor by 2022. Under the scheme, the government has extended tax incentives for affordable housing to builders and home buyers and credit-linked interest subsidy under Pradhan Mantri Awas Yojana (PMAY) to home seekers. The scheme is being implemented in 4,427 cities.

PMAY(U) adopts a demand-driven approach wherein the housing shortage is decided, based on demand assessment by states/Union Territories. The scheme started off with four verticals– In-situ Slum Redevelopment; Credit Linked Subsidy Scheme (CLSS); Affordable Housing in Partnership; and Beneficiary-led Individual House Construction/ Enhancement.[168] Since then, the scheme has also been expanded to incorporate Affordable Rental Housing Complexes (ARHCs) to cater to migrant labour in urban centres by utilising existing government-funded vacant houses and constructing, operating and maintaining ARHCs on vacant land in public-private partnership mode.

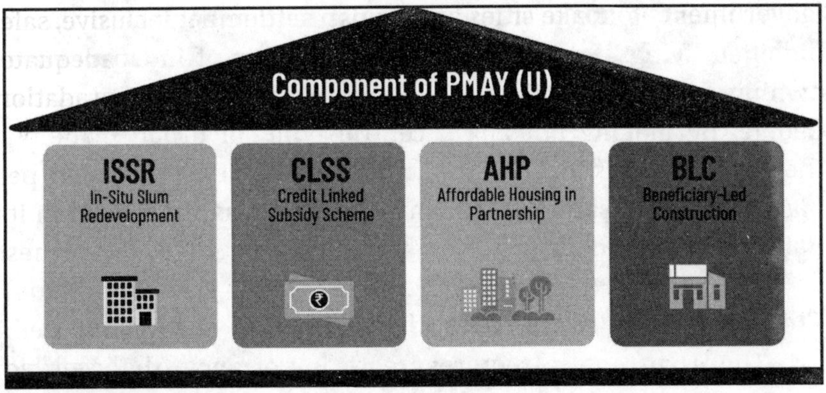

Till December 2021, the Ministry of Housing and Urban Affairs had sanctioned 1.14 crore houses under Pradhan Mantri Awas Yojana (Urban), of which 53.4 lakh had been completed. Rs. 1.8 lakh crore had been committed by the government of which Rs. 1.2 lakh crore has been released. A key feature of the scheme is that it promotes women empowerment by giving preference to women as sole or joint owners of houses. Also, preference is given to differently abled persons, senior citizens, SCs, STs, OBCs, minority, single women, transgender and other weaker and vulnerable sections of the society. Interest subsidy of Rs. 1.24 lakh crore on housing loans has been credited directly to beneficiaries under the Credit-Linked Subsidy Scheme (CLSS), making it easy for even low- and lower-middle income groups to have a home of their own. Similarly, a total of 88,236 existing government-funded vacant houses were made available for conversion to ARHCs for rental accommodation for poor migrant workers till 29th July, 2021.[169]

In the words of PM Modi:

"A house is a turning point in the lives of poor, leading towards a better life and the government's effort was to not just provide a house, but to provide the right environment to live life to the fullest."[170]

A house is the first and foremost requirement to ensure a dignified living. However, even after 70 years of Independence, owning a house remains out of reach for the majority of the people. By making housing a central point of urban planning, the government is fortifying sustainability of cities, making them places for actualisation of human possibilities, as conceived by Dr. Babasaheb Ambedkar.

Clean Cities for a Thriving Citizenry

The urban renewal requires greater importance to be accorded to cleanliness and sanitation. Unhygienic living conditions are the primary cause of the spread of diseases. The massive health burden impacts the lives of poorer sections of society the most. As per UNICEF, unsafe drinking water, poor hygienic conditions and inadequate sanitation are the leading causes of high diarrhoea and under-five mortality caused by pneumonia, neonatal disorders and malnutrition. These health problems faced during childhood tend to affect children throughout their life span. However, these are easily preventable by ensuring sanitation facilities, access to safe drinking water and awareness about various hygienic practices. In the light of this, the PM Modi's government made the cleanliness mission a critical governance agenda in pursuance of a healthy and happy nation.

Launched in 2014 by the PM Modi, the Swachh Bharat Mission aimed to achieve universal sanitation coverage and make India open defecation-free by 2019 to coincide with the 150th birth anniversary of Mahatma Gandhi. The mission's objectives were also to eradicate manual scavenging, effect behavioral change in healthy sanitation practices and generate awareness about sanitation and its linkage with public health. It has two sub-missions– SBM-Urban (SBM-U) and SBM Gramin (SBM-G). Rural (Gramin) India is now declared open-defecation free. The SBM-U focusses on making urban India free from open defecation and achieving 100% scientific management of municipal solid waste in 4,041 statutory towns.

A glimpse into the performance parameters shows the positive results (as on 23rd March, 2022) Swachh Bharat Mission-Urban has produced:[171]

- 4,371 cities have been declared open defecation-free.
- 62.6 lakh household toilets were constructed against a target of 9 lakh[58].
- 6.2 lakh community/public toilets (CT/PT) were constructed against the target of 5 lakh.
- Under Solid Waste Management (SWM), over 1 lakh tonnes/day of waste was processed against 1.4 lakh tonnes/day of waste generated.
- 100% door-to-door waste collection was achieved in 86,972 Wards.

The cleanliness mission is based on the model of janbhagidari, i.e. people's participation. It uses the concept of the common good to channelise the energies of one and all towards a common goal and encourages people to take collective responsibility of their communities and cities. In Dr. Babasaheb Ambedkar's vision, the Swachh Bharat Mission is a precursor to an equitable and dignified living. It makes each and every one a stakeholder in its implementation, ensuring that it positively impacts the most vulnerable sections of the society.

Low-cost Urban Living

The daily-wage earners, who barely manage to make ends meet, find it extremely difficult to save for the future. In the era of double-digit inflation prior to 2014, day-to-day living became a costly affair. In the absence of any institutional support, if any of the family members would have fallen sick, the cost of treatment and medicines would force the household to raise a loan with their personal belongings as collateral.

In the Modi era, double-digit inflation has become a thing of the past. With inflation under control and Goods and Services Tax

(GST) in place, prices of essential commodities have substantially come down. In June 2017, India's retail inflation had hit a record low of 1.54%, lowest since 1999. The money saved on essentials has given poorest of the poor enough breathing room to save for their future.

In the case of medical exigencies, a universal health care coverage plan, Ayushman Bharat, has been put in place that provides health insurance to crores of households in the country. The government has been setting up Health & Wellness Centres (HWCs) to deliver comprehensive primary health care, free of cost to all. With a target to set up 1.5 lakh HWCs till the year 2022, the government has already exceeded this target. Presently, there are 76,663 Health & Wellness Centres, 3,998 Urban Primary Health Centres, 21,081 Primary Health Centres, and 51,584 Sub-Health Centres spread across the country.[172]

Pradhan Mantri Jan Arogya Yojana (PMJAY) is the largest health insurance scheme for the poor in the world that provides a health cover of Rs. 5 lakh per family for secondary and tertiary care hospitalization. The scheme covers over 10 crore poor and vulnerable families (approximately 50 crore beneficiaries) that form the bottom 40% of the population. Services include approx. 1,393 procedures covering all the costs related to treatment, drugs, diagnostic services, physician's fees, room charges, surgeon charges, OT & ICU charges, etc. Up till December 2021, 2.6 crore hospital admissions had taken place under the scheme. Of the Ayushman cards issued, approximately11.60 crore were PMJAY cards and 5.85 crore state cards.

In September 2021, PM Modi launched Ayushman Bharat Digital Mission, an online platform that connects the digital health solutions of hospitals across the country with each other. Every citizen will now get a digital health ID and their health record will be digitally recorded. This facility is connecting thousands of Indians living in far-flung parts of the country every day with doctors of big hospitals across cities while sitting at home.

A novel initiative to set up a network of retail pharmacies

Affordable Medicines & Reliable Implants for Treatment (AMRIT) has been undertaken across the country. These pharmacies sell more than 5,200 drugs, stents, implants, surgical disposables and other consumables at discounts of up to 50% on maximum retail price (MRP). There are 221 AMRIT pharmacies that provide generic and life-saving branded drugs under one roof, thus helping millions from running place-to-place to buy these medicines. As on 15th December, 2021, around 2.71 crore patients had made purchases from AMRIT pharmacies, where drugs worth Rs. 3,952 crore (MRP) were sold at discounted rates.

Janaushadhi Kendras make quality generic medicines available at affordable prices to help reduce out-of-pocket expenses of the poor towards healthcare. Prices of Janaushadhi medicines are 50-90% cheaper than branded medicines sold in market. As on 15th December, 2021, about 8,578 Janaushadhi outlets were functional across the country. The government has set a target to increase their number to 10,000 by March 2024.

The long-overdue interventions in the health sector have laid down a safety net for the poor, thus removing the single biggest hurdle that severely restricts their choices and derails their forward journey into the mainstream.

Augmenting Public Transport

Urbanisation is an incomplete process if it does not address challenges related to public transport. A city can neither grow nor expand, nor can it create lively centres if connectivity issues, especially related to transport, are not being addressed. This has been a key area of focus for the Modi government.

Be it the fastest-built Kanpur Metro or the soon-to-see trial of Rapid Rail between Delhi and Meerut, urban mass transit projects have been growing swiftly. Nearly 27 cities today have Metro rails under construction or operational, touching a network length cumulatively of 791 km.[173] Similarly, buses are becoming important. In Budget 2021-22, the government had announced a

Rs. 18,000-crore fund to procure 20,000 buses for Indian cities to augment public bus services.[174]

Urbanisation with Preservation

Taking a departure from an earlier conception of urban development, the Modi government is conceiving urbanisation through a preservatory approach that aims to safeguard the unique identity of every city while equipping it with modern amenities. With Heritage City Development and Augmentation Yojana (HRIDAY), the government aims to not only preserve India's rich cultural heritage, but to also fully utilise its tourism potential. The scheme entails revitalising the urban infrastructure of our heritage cities while carefully preserving and nurturing its inherent soul.

Similarly, Syama Prasad Mookerjee RURBAN Mission follows the vision of modernising our villages and turning them into self-sustaining economic centres, without compromising on the essence of rural community life. The aim is to bridge the widening rural-urban divide, in terms of technology, economy and provision of essential services and stimulate economic development to mitigate poverty and unemployment in rural areas.

Under the Pilgrimage Rejuvenation & Spiritual Augmentation Drive (PRASHAD) scheme, focus is on developing pilgrimage sites across India to provide memorable religious tourism experience. For tapping the potential of pilgrimage tourism, the government has decided to focus on all-round development of select sights, integrate such pilgrimage destinations in a sustainable manner, and at the same time, create awareness among local communities about the importance of tourism as a reliable source of income.

Over 40 sites across 26 states are being developed under the scheme andthese include Kamakhya in Assam, Parashuram Kund in Arunachal Pradesh, Somnath and Dwarka in Gujarat, Katra and Hazratbal in Jammu & Kashmir, etc. So far, UP and Uttarakhand together have nearly 25% of the total allocation of approximately

Rs. 1,200 crore. This has led to the creation of amenities like last mile connectivity, information centres, ATMs, transport, lighting, parking, drinking water, toilets, cloak rooms, waiting rooms, craft bazars, telecom facilities and Internet connectivity. As a result of the development activity and the subsequent influx of tourists, government expects new jobs to be created at the local level and locals will get a chance to showcase arts, crafts, cuisine, etc.

Till a few years back, there was a feeling of individualism and lack of unity among the people of India. This was because of the policy of 'divide and rule' followed by some state governments and also by the ruling party in the Centre. But all that changed in 2015 with the launch of the 'Ek Bharat Shreshtha Bharat' programme by the Modi government. Under the programme, the Central Government is trying to promote the spirit of national integration between the people of the country. Every state/UT is paired with another for a year, during which it carries out regular interactions in the fields of language, literature, cuisine, festivals, cultural events, tourism, etc. This not only helps to bring the people from different parts of the country together but also plays an important role towards nation building. EBSB also encourages the development of tourism across the nation, helping citizens explore new places and get a first-hand experience of the natural beauty and rich cultural heritage that India has to offer.

In the same vein, the Modi government wants the urban planning paradigm to reimagine itself within India. To this end, Budget 2022-23 announced plans for the modernisation of building bye-laws, Town Planning Schemes (TPS), while expressing the intent to implement Transit Oriented Development (TOD).[175] To this end, a high-level committee of reputed urban planners, urban economists and institutions is being formed that will present recommendations on urban sector policies, capacity building, planning, implementation and governance to steer a paradigm change. This has been a marked shift as it recognises the fact that the country's economic potential, including livelihood opportunities for the demographic dividend cannot be achieved if urban planning continues with a business-as-usual approach.[176]

Conclusion

The call to the socially and economically marginalised to be part of urban growth story was made by Dr. Babasaheb Ambedkar, considering the disparities that existed in traditional settings. The cities were not only to be the mainstay of industrial advancement, but were to also serve as a window of opportunity for those who aspired for a higher standard of living.

Today, urbanisation and infrastructural growth is taking place at an unprecedented pace and scale. The same has further given rise to a new set of skills and jobs with which our citizens are being equipped and empowered to script their own journey. People, irrespective of where they come from, are able to push their boundaries. The Modi government is strengthening their resolve by removing clouds of uncertainty and providing them the security of home, income and health.

The new India vision that PM Modi has laid out for the country is not an abstract concept; it is well-rooted in the holistic model of development that Dr. Babasaheb Ambedkar espoused. Under the leadership of PM Modi, the government has instilled in its governance a futuristic zeal that opens up more possibilities for people to fulfil their dreams.

"Salvation of whole of India lies in greater urbanisation."[177]

— Dr. B.R. Ambedkar

□

This picture is from the late 1980s, when Narendra Modi had recently entered the BJP. Remember, this was a time when parties claiming Dr. B.R. Ambedkar's legacy had not made any dent on national politics. It shows Modi's lifelong commitment to Dr. B.R. Ambedkar's values.

Narendra Modi, as Gujarat's Chief Minister, unveils a portrait of Dr. B.R. Ambedkar. CM Modi's work on water management and conservation, a domain close to Dr. B.R. Ambedkar's heart, was noted nationally and internationally.

Gujarat's astonishing sustainable but rapid urbanisation would've made Dr. B.R. Ambedkar, a votary of urbanisation, proud. Here, CM Modi garlands a statue of Dr. B.R. Ambedkar at the stone laying ceremony for Dr. Ambedkar Bhavan, held on 15th August, 2003.

Narendra Modi's admiration for Dr. B.R. Ambedkar and his ideals has been a constant feature for long. Here, Modi, as Chief Minister of Gujarat in 2006, lights a lamp in front of Dr. B.R. Ambedkar's photo on his punyatithi at the Dr. Ambedakar Bhavan Lokarpan.

In 2010, CM Modi leads a unique tribute to mark the 60th anniversary of the adoption of the Constitution. The Samvidhan Gaurav Yatra began from a statue of Dr. B.R. Ambedkar. The imagery of a giant replica of the Constitution atop an elephant while the Chief Minister and his Ministers walk beside it speaks volumes.

In Gujarat, be it empowerment of women, disadvantaged communities or industrial development, CM Modi implemented the vision of Dr. B.R. Ambedkar in letter and spirit.

Celebrating a glorious life: In 2015, PM Modi leads the National Committee for Celebration of the 125th Birth Anniversary of Dr. B.R. Ambedkar. From laying the foundation stone of Dr. Ambedkar International Centre to the celebration of Constitution Day for the first time ever, many initiatives were seen.

During the 125th birth anniversary year of Dr. B.R. Ambedkar, PM Modi unveils two commemorative coins. PM Modi threw light on lesser-known facets of Dr. B.R. Ambedkar's life such as his thoughts on Economics, Finance Commission and RBI.

Memorial for a maker of modern India: In 2015, PM Modi facilitates an agreement for transfer of land near Chaityabhoomi, Mumbai for the construction of a memorial for Dr. B.R. Ambedkar, at the place where his final rites were performed.

In 2015, the 125th birth anniversary year of Dr. B.R. Ambedkar, PM Modi pays floral tributes while laying the foundation stone of the Dr. Ambedkar International Centre in New Delhi. This project was conceived decades ago but neglected. PM Modi's government ensured completion by 2017, in just about two years!

The Dr. Ambedkar National Memorial at 26 Alipur Road, Delhi, was inaugurated by PM Modi on April 13, 2018. This is where Dr. B.R. Ambedkar lived. The memorial is built in the form of a book, uses static and dynamic media, audio-visual content, and multimedia to provide an immersive experience into Dr. B.R. Ambedkar's life and work.

The Dr. Ambedkar International Centre, a 'Centre of Excellence' for studies, research, analysis, and policy formulation in the field of socio-economic transformation, was inaugurated on December 7, 2017 in New Delhi. Designed as a fusion of Buddhist and modern architecture, the Centre inspires young people to follow the ideals of Dr. B.R. Ambedkar.

Serving the poorest and the most disadvantaged was a cause close to Dr. B.R. Ambedkar's heart. At the Conference on Transformation of Aspirational Districts, held in 2018, aimed at uplifting India's most backward districts, PM Modi pays tributes to Dr. B.R. Ambedkar.

When it comes to pay a true tribute to Dr. B.R. Ambedkar both in symbolic gestures and in concrete implementation of his ideals, PM Modi has been at the forefront. Here, he is seen at Dr. B.R. Ambedkar's Asthi Kalash Pushparpan in Lucknow in 2016.

If there is one word that jumps out of Dr. B.R. Ambedkar's life as the key to overcoming all odds, it is education. At the 6th Convocation of Dr. Ambedkar University in Lucknow, 2016, PM Modi pays his respects to Dr. B.R. Ambedkar.

As a lasting tribute to Dr. B.R. Ambedkar, PM Modi developed the Panch Teerth—five sites related to Dr. B.R. Ambedkar's life. Here, at Mhow, the birth place of Dr. B.R. Ambedkar, PM Modi pays his respects, 2016.

At Chaityabhoomi in Mumbai, PM Modi lays the foundation stone of Dr. B.R. Ambedkar Memorial, 2015. This is part of the Panch Teerth—five sites related to Dr. B.R. Ambedkar's life, developed by PM Modi.

PM Modi inaugurates the Ambedkar Memorial in London in 2015, at the house where Dr. B.R. Ambedkar stayed. This is part of the Panch Teerth—five sites related to Dr. B.R. Ambedkar's life, developed by PM Modi.

PM Modi pays tribute to Dr. B.R. Ambedkar at Deekshabhoomi in Nagpur, 2017. This is part of the Panch Teerth—five sites related to Dr. B.R. Ambedkar's life, developed by PM Modi.

At Mahaparinirvan Sthal in Delhi, PM Modi pays respects to Dr. B.R. Ambedkar. This is part of the Panch Teerth—five sites related to Dr. B.R. Ambedkar's life, developed by PM Modi.

7

Jal Se Hi Jeevan: How Drinking Water is Transforming Lives

The role of drinking water in the lives of human beings cannot be emphasised enough. Jal or water is the very giver of life (jeevan) to countless beings, including mankind. None perhaps understood this better than Dr. B.R. Ambedkar, who also saw access to drinking water as a fundamental right in his own life and that of countless others. This issue remained close to heart throughout his life. On the day he took diksha and adopted the Buddhist way of life in 1956, Dr. Babasaheb Ambedkar had recalled how water was denied to him because of his social status.[178]

"I could not even have water to drink in the school. I spent many days without water in the school."

Dr. Babasaheb Ambedkar was determined to ensure that he challenged this situation head-on through his life. Water, after all, was about the fundamental and basic human rights. During the 1927 Mahad satyagraha, he had led thousands of Dalits to drink water from the Chavadar Tank. Despite the Mahad municipality changing laws to open the Chavadar Tank to untouchables, there was opposition from some sections of society.[179] At that time, leading the mass movement, he had been categorical in the reasons for this daring effort:[180]

"It is not as if drinking the water of the Chavadar Lake will make us immortal. We have survived well enough all these days without drinking it. We are not going to the Chavadar Lake

merely to drink its water. We are going to the Lake to assert that we too are human beings like others. It must be clear that this meeting has been called to set up the norm of equality."

With the breaking down of barriers through social and political reforms in India, Dr. Babasaheb Ambedkar had made a major contribution to India. However, that was not all. As a member of the Viceroy's Executive Council responsible for labour, power and irrigation portfolios between 1942 and 1946, he played a crucial role in framing the objectives and strategies for a water policy. In this capacity, he used his farsightedness and astute hold on water dynamics in India to take some bold and innovative steps. The present-day Central Water Commission and the Central Electricity Authority were originally conceptualised as the Central Waterways, Irrigation and Navigation Commission (CWINC). And it was Dr. Babasaheb Ambedkar and his team in the Labour Department who were behind the institutionalisation of these bodies in the year 1945.

Dr. Babasaheb Ambedkar, as a member of the Linlithgow government, also focused on improving water supplies in cities and towns. With his control on the Public Works Department, one of the tasks he pursued was the issue of water supply to the city of Delhi during the summers. He recalled, once in 1952 his shock on how the government of the day and its bureaucracy was loathe to take steps in this regard:[181]

"I was then discussing the construction of a barrage over Yamuna in order to provide water to the city of Delhi in summer, because it goes dry in summer, I told my Secretary, who was a European by name Priar. And I said, 'Mr. Priar look here, this is what the Secretary to the Governor General has said to me. Do you think we can do something?' What do you think was his reply? His reply was 'Sir, we must not do any such thing at all'."

Dr. Babasaheb Ambedkar foresaw the criticality of water management and conservation in safeguarding interests of the vast majority of the Indian population. Considering a large part of India and the world are standing at the edge of a water crisis, it requires the active participation of all stakeholders to pool in resources, effort and energy to address this issue.

It took a long time for governments in Independent India to wake up to the vision of Dr. Babasaheb Ambedkar and see the immense untapped potential in our water resources. The Modi government has been leading from the front to fulfil the dream of Dr. Babasaheb Ambedkar to not just conserve water, but to use it in the most effective way to propel the country towards development. He is truly the architect of the water policy in India and this government is committed to turning his vision into a reality.

Is it any wonder then that the man who has worked hard to walk in his footsteps, PM Modi is focused on working on this critical issue? Taking inspiration from Dr. Babasaheb Ambedkar, PM Modi has sought to take a wholesome, rounded approach to the issue of water access to the masses. From resource management to last mile tap connectivity, there is no aspect that has not seen PM Modi's personal touch. Having emerged from a backdrop of discrimination, and emerging from a state that historically witnessed difficulties of drinking water, it is no surprise that this subject holds so much importance for the Prime Minister. Having seen it up close and personal, he has sought to do his bit to improve people's lives:[182]

> *"It is a fact that today almost half of the houses in India do not have drinking water. People have to struggle to get drinking water. Mothers and sisters have to travel 2, 3, 5 km carrying a load of water on their heads. A large part of their lives is spent in struggling for water. Therefore, this government has decided to emphasise upon a special task and that is - to ensure availability of water in every house."*

Jal Jeevan Mission– A Promise being Fulfilled

If Dr. Babasaheb Ambedkar had to face the indignity of being denied drinking water due to social evils, even a century later, crores of Indians, especially the poor, have had to face lack of clean drinking water due to continuous government apathy. Till 2014, successive Central Governments failed in providing clean drinking water to crores of Indians. Climate change has also severely impacted groundwater level in the country and led to many rivers becoming seasonal. As a result, women, especially in rural areas and remote places, were forced to trek for miles to get water for their daily needs.

PM Modi launched the 'Jal Jeevan Mission' in 2019 to provide safe drinking water to all houses in rural India by 2024. Under the 'Har Ghar Jal' scheme, the government is working on providing tap water supply to every rural household in the country. Jal Jeevan Mission is not just a scheme for PM Modi. Inspired by the vision of Dr. Babasaheb Ambedkar who saw it as essential to dignified living, PM Modi has made the scheme about people improving their lives and delivering empowerment.

Up till 15th August, 2019, only 16% (3.2 crore) rural households had tap water connections. This is what India had achieved in seven decades of Independence. However, since the launch of PM Modi's initiative, over 6 crore tap water connections have been provided in a little over two years! This is an indicator of the pace and scale of work that is being done.

A number of states, such as Haryana, Goa, Telangana and Union Territories like Andaman & Nicobar Islands, Daman, Diu, Dadra and Nagar Haveli, and Puducherry have already achieved 100% household tap connections with clean running water. Additionally, states like Punjab (99.36%), Gujarat (93.77%), Himachal Pradesh (92.79%), Bihar (90.60%) and Sikkim (83.08%) are fast approaching universal tap connection availability.[183]

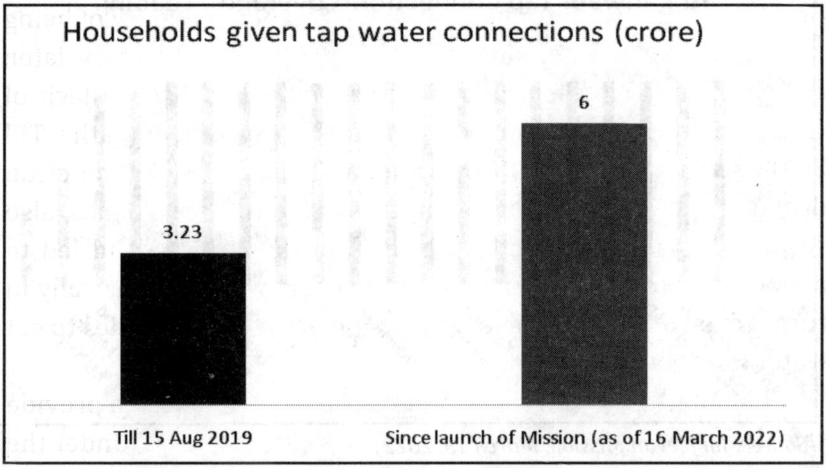

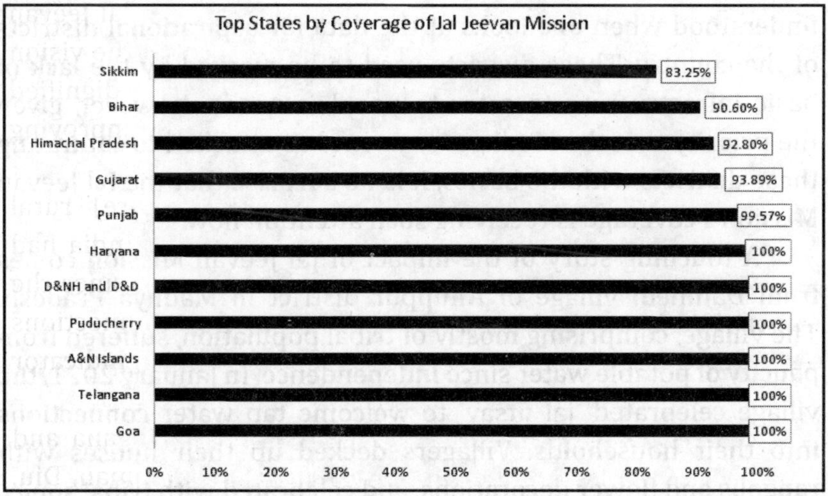

(Source: Jal Jeevan Mission, 15th March, 2022)

Thanks to the Jal Jeevan Mission, today 1.3 lakh villages across the country boast of 100% functional household tap connections. The scheme has also benefitted schools, anganwadis, gram panchayats and community health care centres in rural India as they now have access to clean tap water. Already, 20 states and Union Territories have managed to cross 90% coverage, with 16 of these achieving 100% tap water connection coverage.[184]

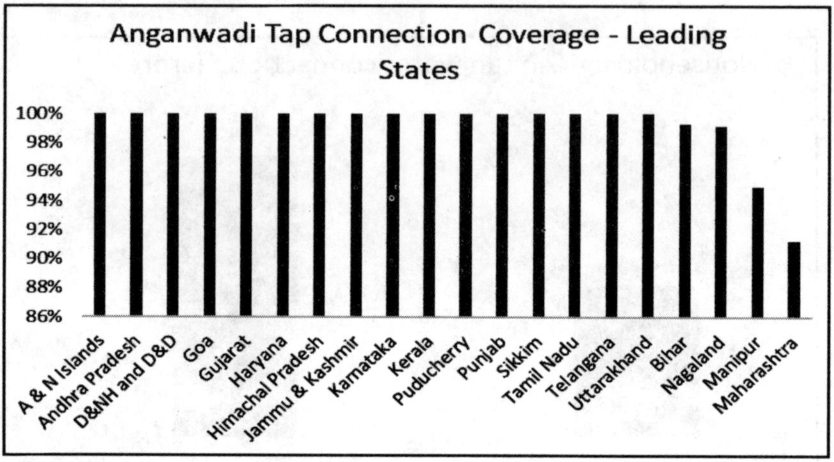

(Source: Jal Jeevan Mission, March 15, 2022)

The nature of the effort being put in can perhaps be best understood when one looks at the data for aspirational districts of the country. These districts used to be marked by the lack of basic infrastructure to cater to people's needs. However, given the priority that the Modi government has attached to saturating these districts with the basics, it is no surprise that the Jal Jeevan Mission's coverage is receiving such attention now.

A touching story of the impact of Jal Jeevan Mission comes from Damhedi village of Anuppur district in Madhya Pradesh. The village, comprising mostly of tribal population, suffered from paucity of potable water since Independence. In January 2021, the village celebrated 'jal utsav' to welcome tap water connections into their households. Villagers decked up their houses with rangolis and flower decorations, and celebrated with tribal songs, dance and music, even as women worshipped the tap.[185]

Another success story of the scheme comes from Leh. Here, officials worked hard to provide tap connections with running water despite the difficult terrain. With freezing temperatures round the year, special insulated pipes were carried across challenging terrain to 12 villages to give them 24X7 piped water.

CASE STUDY–Jal Jeevan Mission Transforms Kamsing Village, West Jaintia Hills in Meghalaya[186]

Kamsing village in Meghalaya's West Jaintia Hills is a peaceful community of only 22 families. Kamsing is located on the banks of River Myntdu, which is also their only source of water and transportation. This river flows through several adjoining villages, making the water unfit for drinking, cooking, or cleaning. Being accessible only through a boat has further exacerbated a host of problems, especially during the summer, when water inflow is at its highest.

The women and children usually take care of fetching water from the river and are forced to make numerous journeys throughout the day. However, with the implementation of Jal Jeevan Mission, the state government got the opportunity to relieve them from the drudgery and ensure safe water for all, in partnership with the local members. The water provided through the mission is safe and sufficient to meet every individual's needs because now every household has access to afunctional tap water connection.

The community members have expressed their satisfaction with their new-found comfort of living and are happy at having easy access to abundant clean water for domestic purposes and storage– a luxury they never enjoyed before. Pas Swer, a mother, shares that her children now have more time to study in the morning and evening, which previously would have been the time they spent on fetching water. Sawan Swer, another woman, mentioned that they are now able to give more to their businesses like betel-nut cultivation.

Community Involvement, a Pillar of Jal Jeevan Mission

Jal Jeevan Mission is all about 'making water everyone's business', with active participation from self-help groups, NGOs, community-based organisations, etc. A major component of the scheme is community involvement. Every village has to prepare a Village Action Plan focusing on drinking water sources, water supply systems, grey water reuse, and operation and maintenance of these systems for long-term and regular tap water supply in every home. A massive training and skilling programme is being undertaken to boost skill development at community level in villages, whether it is plumbers, pump operators, public health engineers, etc. to ensure service delivery.

A key aspect of the scheme is the formation of Village Water & Sanitation Committees (VWSCs)/Pani Samitis that own the water supply systems, operate and maintain them to ensure assured water supply to every home. Notably, the VWSCs/ Pani Samitis are required to have 50% representation of women with proportionate representation from weaker sections as well, thus empowering the community to act as change agents to bring drinking water security in their villages.[187]

Take the example of G. Kala, a mother of two children, who is the only female pump operator in Vallam village of Vellore district, Tamil Nadu. Sharing her experience, she says, *"It is not just a man's bastion. It is the women who is most affected by non-availability of water. When we can do other works then why not a skilled job. I have earned love and respect from my people in this profession."*[188]

Surveillance of water quality being a key element for the success of the scheme, the government has pushed for community involvement in this as well. At least five persons in every village, preferably women, are trained on using field test kitsfor testing the water quality. Drinking water quality-testing laboratories have been opened to general public so that they can check the quality of their drinking water samples after paying nominal charges. With samples regularly collected from villages and checked for quality in laboratories, water quality is maintained at all times.

Noreen Afzal Lone, a water analyst from Rajouri district of J&K, shares, *"After completing my post-graduation from Jammu University, I joined the laboratory. Earlier, the water samples were collected from the water source by the junior engineer and lab technicians. Since we have organised a number of workshops in the villages to sensitise the public, a number of people now visit us with water samples to check for E. coli, bacteria and turbidity in water, especially during rainy season."*[189]

Every year, a nation-wide functionality assessment survey is carried out in each district by a third-party agency. Based on performance of states/UTs on criteria such as high functionality of tap water connections, incentive grants are provided. Meantime, states/UTs are to provide sensor-based IoT solutions to VWSCs/ Pani Samitis to measure and monitor water supply. The Pani Samiti of each village is trained to use a visual dashboard, which is designed in their local dialect. It helps them to proactively monitor groundwater level and build source-strengthening structures.

The scheme also seeks to create the local infrastructure for rainwater harvesting, groundwater recharge and management of household waste water for reuse in agriculture. This is a departure from the past, when the various requirements were seen in isolation and not in sync.

Ending Drudgery, Empowering Women

For the longest time, Indian women have had to spend their time engaged in household chores while men laboured to earn an income. Foraging for fuel, searching for drinking water and managing the household responsibilities were considered 'womanly' affairs. Even today, women in rural India and also in the urban poor belts, lead the same life of drudgery, investing hours of their daily time in futile exercises that go unnoticed by society.

Imagine the scenario: A mother of three children is walking all alone in the forest or woodland to forage for fuel wood, or towards a stream to get water to drink and enable basic chores of the house. Sometimes, the children also need to be taken along just so that sufficient quantities can be collected. But the price and plight of this effort never got acknowledged. Worse, such a hard life was sought to be romanticised by the political and intellectual class, instead of ensuring that women wouldn't have to endure such drudgery in the first place.

Over the decades, experts who followed the situation for varying reasons had essentially come to the conclusion that in many parts of the country, women had literally reached the end of their 'carrying capacities'. In the arid and semi-arid parts of the country and in the hill and mountain villages, women were seen spending as much as five to 10 hours every day on just collecting fuel and fodder. Deforestation and climate change made it worse, affecting everything else in their lives. For instance, it was observed that in western Uttar Pradesh, even pregnant women were working up to 14 hours a day, and then forced to re-start work just hours after delivering the child.[190]

The answers to these challenges were known to everyone: A tap connection that gives water; and a gas cylinder that could prevent women from the foraging exercise, benefit their health besides providing quality time for themselves and families. These basic amenities should have reached them long ago. However, the lack of priority attached to the labour put in by them to raise and support a family through their lifetime by previous administrations seems to be the only explanation for the status quo till 2014.

Providing good quality piped water has been a boon for women and young girls. They no longer have to walk miles to collect water and carry back heavy vessels. Access to clean water in households has also resulted in healthier families as they no longer fall ill due to water-borne diseases and this has improved their overall quality of life. A large number of young girls had to drop out of school to help their mothers in doing household tasks, including getting water. The scheme has ensured that many such girls can now go back to school and continue with their education.

> "With tap water connections at home, women have time for themselves. I am working on engaging women in gainful economic activity so that they are financially independent. Jal Jeevan Mission has opened a new vista of women empowerment."
>
> **Kulwinder**
> **Sarpanch, Memha Bhagwana village,**
> **Bhatinda district, Punjab**[191]

Fund Allocation under 15th Finance Commission

The 15th Finance Commission has recommended an allocation of Rs. 2.3 lakh crore to rural local bodies for the period 2021-22 to 2025-26, out of which, 40% is basic grant and the remaining 60% is tied to (a) drinking water, rainwater harvesting, water recycling, and (b) sanitation and maintenance of the ODF status. Allocating funds to continue building upon the achievements in drinking water and sanitation in rural India will help in further cementing the work done till now and positively contribute towards public health and improved quality of life.

Year-wise Allocation of Tied Grant for Water Supply & Sanitation Services[192]

YEAR	TIED GRANT (Amount in Rs. crore)		
	Water	Sanitation	Total
2021-22	13,470	13,470	26,940
2022-23	13,954	13,954	27,908
2023-24	14,106	14,106	28,212
2024-25	14,940	14,940	29,880
2025-26	14,572	14,572	29,114
Total	71,042	71,042	1,42,084

Tapping Urban India under AMRUT

Similar to the focus on rural water supply, urban water supply has remained a big focus area. The Atal Mission for Rejuvenation and Urban Transformation (AMRUT), that was launched in 2015, in selected 500 cities and towns across the country, had a tap connection with assured supply of water in every household as one of its key objectives. Under the AMRUT mission, out of the total plan size of Rs. 77,640 crore, Rs. 39,010 crore (50%) has been allocated to water supply sector only.[193] The success of the mission can be gauged by the fact that as of 15th March, 2022, nearly 1,351 water supply projects worth Rs. 42,400 crore had been taken up, of which 834 projects worth Rs. 14,049 crore stand completed. Against the target to provide 1.39 crore tap connections in 500 AMRUT cities to achieve universal water supply, 1.26 crore new tap connections, or 90% coverage had been provided so far under AMRUT and in convergence with other schemes.

To ensure the balance also gets covered, the Government of India launched AMRUT 2.0 on 1st October, 2021 for a period of five years (FY 2021-22 to 2025-26), with the objective of providing universal coverage of water supply through functional household tap connections in all statutory towns in the country. AMRUT 2.0, also called Jal Jeevan Mission (Urban)[194] focuses on covering the gap of 2.68 crore urban households that did not have a tap connection as of February 2021[195] while making cities water secure through recycle/reuse of treated sewage, rejuvenation of water bodies and water conservation.

Addressing Water Resource Management Holistically

The PM Modi government's past eight years are a reflection of a holistic approach to water management. Using technology, harnessing resources and ensuring maturity in management has meant that results have poured out in many ways.

India ranks third globally, after China and USA, with 5,334 large dams in operation and about 411 dams under construction. In addition, there are several thousand smaller dams. These dams are vital for ensuring the water security of the country. The Modi government approved the externally-aided Dam Rehabilitation and Improvement Project (DRIP) Phase II and Phase III in October 2020. 19 states and three Central agencies are involved. The Budget outlay is Rs. 10,211 crore for a period of 10 years, to be implemented in two phases, thus showing foresight and vision.[196]

The Central Water Commission (CWC) has been working on various projects that contribute to better management of the multipurpose hydro projects. In-house sedimentation assessment studies of 12 reservoirs is currently underway. Moreover, the work of Indian dam authorities towards preservation has ensured that four historical irrigation structures of India won the 'World Heritage Irrigation Structure Award (WHIS)' of ICID in 2021. These four reservoirs– Dhukwan Weir, UP; and Grand Anicut, Veeranam Tank, and Kalingarayan Anicut in Tamil Nadu– stand testament to the approach taken towards their management.

The number of reservoirs under the monitoring of Central Water Commission has increased to 133, while the monitoring of 477 glacial lakes and water bodies, having size greater than 50 hectare in the Indian Himalayan region using satellite remote sensing, has been completed for the year 2021. Moreover, during the year 2021, three new Flood Forecasting Stations (1 Level and 2 Inflow) have been added in Rajasthan and Madhya Pradesh states.

Focus is not restricted to surface waters alone. Groundwater has been a key area of focus. Under the Ground Water Management & Regulation scheme, the Central Water Ground Board (CGWB) has taken up National Project on Aquifer Management (NAQUIM) studies for aquifer mapping and management plan formulation. During 2021, aquifer maps and management plans were developed for more than 3.7 lakh square km area under the aquifer mapping programme. CGWB has also initiated high-resolution mapping of aquifers using modern heli-borne geophysical survey in parts of the arid areas spread over Rajasthan, Gujarat and Haryana states.

Realising the need for availability of reliable and up-to-date water data for efficient management of water resources of the country, the government has recently established the National Water Informatics Centre. The Centre serves as a repository of water resources data storage, collation, management and dissemination. Data on water resources and related issues, like rainfall, river water levels and discharge, groundwater levels, reservoir levels, water quality, etc. are disseminated through a GIS-enabled public platform to the public.

In order to respond to the water-related challenges, the Modi government, in its second term, announced the establishment of dedicated machinery for the cause. The Ministry of Jal Shakti was formed, integrating different ministries and departments dealing with water-related issues. The government is aiming for multiple targets, including ensuring water security, conservation and management, especially in the water-stressed districts of India.

River Rejuvenation for Efficient Resource Utilisation

Dr. Babasaheb Ambedkar had rightly called water as 'wealth', which needed to be optimally harnessed. There is an entire economy around major water resources and every civilisational advent has been around large rivers.

In India, River Ganga is a lifeline for millions and a source of sustenance for almost the entire northern plains. It is the source of employment, sustains agriculture, helps industrial growth and has an unquestioned cultural and spiritual connection with people. Therefore, one of the biggest projects that the government has undertaken is to rejuvenate the river and promote peripheral development of all cities and villages, which depend on it. The project was so central to the vision plan of the Modi government that the Ministry of Jal Shakti was also renamed to include Ganga rejuvenation in it (Department of Water Resources, River Development & Ganga Rejuvenation).

Under the Namami Gange programme, a total of 366 projects have already been sanctioned[197] for activities like sewage infrastructure, ghats and crematoria development, river-front development, river surface cleaning, institutional development, biodiversity conservation, afforestation, rural sanitation, and public participation. Of these, 187 projects have been completed. Cleanliness of River Ganga and the surrounding areas is a priority of the government. After a survey of 1,109 grossly polluting industries in 2017, 333 industries were closed down.[198] For river surface cleaning, 11 trash skimmers have been deployed at major cities, including Haridwar, Kolkata, Patna, Allahabad and Varanasi. 4,465 villages on the banks of the Ganga have become open defecation-free and more than 10 lakh individual household toilets have been constructed.[199] The government has also reached out to countries like Australia, UK, Germany, Finland and Israel to get the best technology for rejuvenating the river.

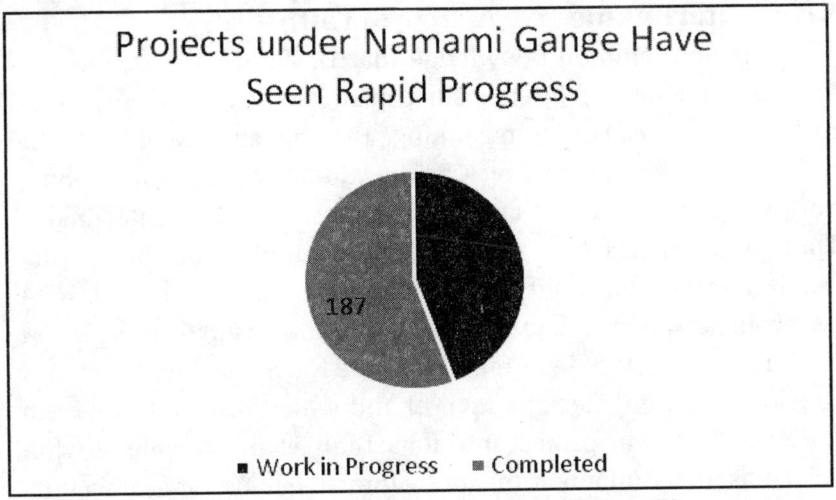

(Source: National Mission for Clean Ganga, 31st December, 2021)[200]

With the Ganga getting its life force back, the people of the belt are also benefitting through improved economic opportunities, hygiene and institutional development. However, PM Modi is not one to rest on his laurels. Instead, he has expanded the scope of attention by including 13 more rivers into the fold of the efforts. Detailed Project Reports (DPRs) on the rejuvenation of 13 major rivers through forestry interventions have been released recently, laying out the approach they want to take that is sustainable.[201]

These 13 rivers for which DPRs were released are Jhelum, Chenab, Ravi, Beas, Sutlej, Yamuna, Brahmaputra, Luni, Narmada, Godavari, Mahanadi, Krishna, and Cauvery. These 13 rivers collectively cover a total basin area of 18.90 lakh square km that represents 57.45% of the geographical area of the country. Their length including 202 tributaries within the delineated riverscapes, is 42,830 km. The proposed interventions in the 13 riverscapes would help in groundwater recharge to the extent of 18,898.9 lakh cubic metres per year, and reduction in sedimentation to the tune of 64.83 lakh cubic metres per year, while generating 344 million man-days of employment through planned activities.

River-Interlinking– An Article of Faith

It is not common knowledge that Dr. Babasaheb Ambedkar had even spoken of inter-basin transfer of water. It is what is today known as river-interlinking. He had suggested that the water from the rivers like Krishna, Godavari and Tapi should not go waste to the sea and these rivers should be interlinked. Though Dr. Babasaheb Ambedkar could not fulfil this dream in his lifetime, his bold idea was picked up by the first NDA government under Prime Minister Atal Bihari Vajpayee. Now, PM Modi is bringing it to fruition. In fact, the Narmada Canal, which is considered an engineering marvel and which brings water from the Sardar Sarovar project into Rajasthan, is an example of what Dr. Babasaheb Ambedkar meant by inter-basin transfer of water.

The river-interlinking project is an ambitious initiative taken up by the government as it will be vital in securing the future of citizens against both droughts and floods. Budget 2022-23 stands out in this regard for its ambitious announcement of the Ken-Betwa interlinking project. The project, with an estimated cost of Rs. 44,605 crore, aims to provide irrigation benefits to 9.08 lakh hectare of farmers' lands and drinking water supply for 62 lakh people, among other benefits. Allocations of Rs. 4,300 crore in RE 2021-22 and Rs. 1,400 crore in 2022-23 have been made for this project.[202] Further, draft DPRs of five river links– Damanganga-Pinjal, Par-Tapi-Narmada, Godavari-Krishna, Krishna-Pennar and Pennar-Cauvery– stand finalisedand await consensus among beneficiary states for implementation.

In March 2021, the Union Ministry of Jal Shakti came together with Madhya Pradesh and Uttar Pradesh states to implement the first major centrally-driven river interlinking project in the country–Ken-Betwa inter-linking of rivers project. The project, proposed to be implemented over eight years, will be a milestone in inter-state co-operation to carry water from areas that have surplus to drought-prone and water-deficit areas, through the interlinking of rivers.

This project involves transfer of water from the Ken to the Betwa river through the construction of Daudhan Dam and a canal linking the two rivers, the Lower Orr Project, Kotha Barrage and Bina Complex Multipurpose Project. The project will provide an annual irrigation of 10.62 lakh hectare, drinking water supply to a population of about 62 lakh and also generate 103 MW of hydropower and 27 MW solar power. The project will be of great benefit to the water-starved Bundelkhand region and will provide enormous benefits to the districts of Panna, Tikamgarh, Chhatarpur, Sagar, Damoh, Datia, Vidisha, Shivpuri and Raisen in Madhya Pradesh and Banda, Mahoba, Jhansi and Lalitpur of Uttar Pradesh.[203]

Further, Budget 2022-23 highlighted how draft Detailed Project Reports (DPRs) had been readied for five more projects and consensus among beneficiary states is awaited. The new proposed river-linking projects– Damanganga-Pinjal, Par-Tapi-Narmada, Godavari-Krishna, Krishna-Pennar and Pennar-Cauvery– will go a long way in easing the problem of water shortage in remote and arid parts of the country.[204]

What was unthinkable has been made possible in India. As

20th century initiatives get fulfilled in the 21st century, PM Modi has been laying the foundations for an India that can reach the sky as it does not have to worry about the 'bijli, sadak, pani' basics anymore. The foundation stone of empowerment– the aim of Dr. Babasaheb Ambedkar's life and work– is finally being acknowledged through efforts of the Modi government in the ways that he had envisioned.

□

8

Waterways as Pathways of Development

"Today is the 125th birth anniversary of a great son of India who also lived and worked in Mumbai. I am referring to Dr. B.R. Ambedkar, who was the architect of our Constitution. He is also the architect of the water and river navigation policy in India. I also wish and pray that his wisdom continues to guide us in our efforts towards nation-building."

— Prime Minister Narendra Modi[205]

In the year 2016, the Modi government declared that the birthday of Dr. B.R. Ambedkar would henceforth be celebrated as 'Water Day' in India. It has taken a period of 60 years after the death of Dr. Babasaheb Ambedkar for a government to acknowledge his towering contribution towards laying the roadmap for the country's water policy. Like his views on most other issues, he thought way ahead of his time and had worked towards an all-India policy for the management of the water resources in an efficient manner.

In a conference on the development of Odisha's rivers, Dr. Babasaheb Ambedkar expressed his view about conservation and use of water resources. He was in clear disagreement with the remedies suggested by the committees. He said:

"With all respect to the members of these committees, I am sorry to say that they did not bring the right approach to bear

on the problem. They were influenced by the idea that water in excessive quantity was an evil, that when water comes in excessive quantity, what needs to be done is to let it run into the sea in an orderly flow. Both these views... are now regarded as grave misconceptions, as positively dangerous from the point of view of the good of the people."[206]

A research work by the Central Water Commission summarised Dr. Babasaheb Ambedkar's statement, stating:

"Man suffers more from lack of water than from excess of it, Ambedkar said. Not only was nature niggardly in the amount of water it gave, it was also erratic in its distribution, altering between drought and storm. But this could not alter the fact that water was wealth. Water being the wealth of the people and its distribution being uncertain, the correct approach was not to complain against nature, but to conserve water."[207]

Dr. Babasaheb Ambedkar clearly saw water as wealth and understood that this huge resource needs to be conserved and harnessed. The above quote also helps us understand how Dr. Babasaheb Ambedkar differed from other thinkers of his age in conceptualising water as a resource. Since excess water and not lack of it was considered the major problem, policies around water always focused on flood control. Dr. Babasaheb Ambedkar challenged that vision.

There were three core areas that he stressed upon when he envisaged optimisation of water resources. These were: development of irrigation, development of waterways and hydro-electric power. He found these three areas absolutely necessary and basic to both agricultural and industrial development of the country. Irrigation would directly impact food supply and would permanently alter the prosperity of region. Electricity was fundamental to infrastructure creationas it would propel further industrialisation. And development of waterways for navigation purposes would generate more jobs as well as take away the pressure on railways.

"It is not far from the truth to say that so far there has been an absence of a positive all-India policy for the development of waterways. And there has not been enough realisation that our policy for waterways must be multipurpose policy as to include provision for irrigation, electrification and navigation."[208]

—Dr. B.R. Ambedkar

But this vision also created a situation between the Centre and the provinces because of water being a subject of shared resources. Implementation of projects could involve more than one province and hence, a new water policy would be required to smoothly oversee such projects. He believed that the establishment of a River Valley Authority was the best way to proceed with work on inter-state rivers. He also felt that there was a need for a strong central body, which would provide technical expertise and advisory support to manage a waterways policy between provinces and settle any disputes that may arise. He had anticipated the possibility of clashes in the sharing of water between states and advocated the creation of a River Valley Authority to oversee the Centre and state issues on irrigation and hydropower. Dr. Babasaheb Ambedkar was also the proponent of developing river valley projects, including the bigger projects on Mahanadi, Damodar and Sone rivers.

Waterways and Navigation Infrastructure

Dr. Babasaheb Ambedkar was prescient in the way he had envisaged the role of waterways for rapid development. He believed that simply damming rivers for prevention of floods were an ineffective use of river water. It should instead be harnessed for irrigation, power and navigation purposes. He was a very vocal proponent of using the waterways for navigation and believed that the development of Railways had drawn away the attention from the possibilities that waterways provided. He also felt that, traditionally, water-based navigation in India was dominant and had lost that space gradually. It was an untapped potential which could be further explored. The quote below illustrates the fact that Dr. Babasaheb Ambedkar could also see how the development of waterways for navigation could be made cost-effective:

> *"I am not quite happy about this victory of railways over canals. Much more annoying is the opinion of supporters of railways that canals must go because they do not pay without knowing that if the canals do not pay, it is not because they cannot pay, but because their capacity to pay has been terribly mutilated by leaving them uncompleted."*[209]

Dr. Babasaheb Ambedkar believed that efficient development of waterways would become a source of upliftment for the poverty-stricken people of the country as it would generate employment. During his time, inland waterways were overshadowed by the Indian Railways, and since it was a provincial subject, the role of the Centre was limited. The condition of the waterways themselves had deteriorated, as no measures were being taken to improve the navigability of rivers. Therefore, Dr. Babasaheb Ambedkar was keen to work towards the construction of new artificial waterways, improvement of existing waterways, increased use of steamers, tugs and barges and meeting the competition from other forms of transport.

In the year 2017, Prime Minister Narendra Modi inaugurated the Ro-Ro Ferry services from Ghogha in Bhavnagar district to Dahej in Bharuch district of Gujarat. This Rs. 615-crore project, was not just the first such project in India, but also the first such project in South Asia. This was a direct translation of the dream that Dr. Babasaheb Ambedkar had. The ferry services reduced the distance of 310 km between the two towns to 30 km, and the journey could be completed in an hour. The waterways would generate new jobs and bring in economic development for the region.

In the same event, PM Modi lamented the fact that, since Independence, very little had been done for the development of water navigation in India. He said that in other developed countries water transport accounts for up to 30% of the transport services, but, the apathy of the previous governments had made it negligible in India.[210] Guided by the vision of Dr. Babasaheb Ambedkar, the present government has made rapid strides in the development of waterways in the country.

In the year 2016, the government brought in the National Waterways Act after which, 111 new inland waterways with a total length of 20,275 km were declared as National Waterways (NWs) across 24 states. These NWs will be a low-cost, environment-friendly transportation option with the potential to turn the poorest and most populous parts of the country into a thriving logistics hub.

Based on the techno-economic feasibility and Detailed Project Reports (DPRs), Inland Waterways Authority of India (IWAI) has identified 25 NWs for cargo/passenger movement. Development activities have been initiated in 13 of these since then.[211] It has been reported that cargo movement through National Waterways, and coastal waterways having linkage with NWs, have registered a growth of more than 2.76 times since the Modi government came to power. While the growth rate of Inland Water Transport (IWT) on National Waterways from 2009-10 to 2013-14 was 1.5%, the growth rate increased to 13.5% in 2020-21.[212]

The government has also introduced a number of initiatives to boost traffic on the National Waterways, such as revision of levy and collection of fees, enhanced regional trade using IWT model, standard operating procedures for facilitating the stakeholders to use inland water transport and access the information related to NWs and Ro-Ro/Ro-Pax service for National Waterways, which was inaugurated by PM Modi in February 2021.[213]

The Parliament passed the Inland Vessels Bill, 2021 that will replace an over 100 years-old Act to usher in a new era for inland water transport. The reformist bill provides an opportunity to tap into the potential of the NWs by bringing in uniform standards and regulations, while preserving the legislations passed by state governments. The bill is expected to play a big role in improving ease of doing business.

In 2018, the Modi government, with the support of the World Bank, initiated India's first multi-modal terminal on River Ganga under the Jal Marg Vikas project. In the first phase of the project, the stretch of the river between Varanasi and Haldia was developed for navigation of cargo vessels weighing up to 1,500-2,000 tonnes. The project, spread across Uttar Pradesh, Bihar, Jharkhand and West Bengal, is expected to be completed by March 2023 at a total cost of Rs. 5,369 crore. Large-scale infrastructure development, like multi-modal and inter-modal terminals, Roll on-Roll off (Ro-Ro) facilities, ferry services, navigation aids, etc. are part of the project, which will lead to 46,000 direct employment generation and around 84,000 indirect employment via the vessel construction industry.[214] Also, the ambitious project of developing the Brahmaputra as a national waterway, that holds the potential to transform the entire north-east, has started, with the commencement of the dredging work.[215]

Dr. Babasaheb Ambedkar had talked about how logistics using waterways could be made cost-effective and the current government is aiming for just that. Cargo from U.P. and Bihar states used to take long land routes to reach ports in Maharashtra and Gujarat; now it can be easily and cheaply ferried on water and directed towards Haldia and Kolkata instead.

When the Modi government was formed, India's logistics sector was highly fragmented, making it more expensive and complex. The sector accounted for 14% of the GDP, which the government aims to bring down to 10% to make Indian goods globally competitive.[216] In developed countries, the logistics costs account for 7-8% of the GDP.

Staying true to Dr. Babasaheb Ambedkar's vision, our National Waterways will be able to give a wider market access to the farmers along such belts and also allow industries and manufacturing units to get a better shot at seamless transportation of goods. The possibilities are endless when all the identified waterways become functional.

The rapid development of waterways in India is a fulfilment of Dr. Babasaheb Ambedkar's vision and a gradual progression towards more inclusive development of making India a 'green economy'.

Development of Irrigation

Dr. Babasaheb Ambedkar was a strong proponent of more capital expenditure on agriculture to offset the damage from smaller landholdings. His economic thoughts were clear on the fact that agriculture was pressured by population and the most sustainable way of addressing this was to push for rapid industrialisation. But agriculture could still be made more productive by expending more capital and capital goods, while reducing the input labour. Irrigation, in his view, was one such large-scale capital investment that needed to be made to spur agricultural growth. Since agriculture remained the mainstay of the larger population, it would also directly benefit the poor and oppressed sections.

Dr. Babasaheb Ambedkar was the proponent of projects like the Damodar Valley project, the Hirakud project and the Sone project, which were aimed at not just flood control, but to serve multiple purposes, primary being irrigation. He saw improved irrigation not just as a means of addressing famine conditions in many areas, but also as a way of uniting provinces through the well-conceived usage of shared water resources. After his detailed study of poverty in Odisha, Dr. Babasaheb Ambedkar had concluded that the state had not been able to harness and optimise the use of its abundant natural water wealth, which resulted in its deprivation. He saw dams as multi-purpose projects, which could result in regional prosperity.

With the passage of time, Dr. Babasaheb Ambedkar's vision of capital influx into agriculture has seen fulfilment and multiple large irrigation projects have been established. However, water access for irrigation did continue to be a problem. After decades of inaction by previous governments, PM Modi inaugurated the Sardar Sarovar project in Gujarat in September 2017. This project aims to *"provide drinking water to 131 urban centres and 9,633 villages (53% of total 18,144 villages in Gujarat) and irrigation facilities for 18.54 hectare of land, covering 3,112 villages in 15 districts."*[217] Also, delayed projects, like the Saryu Nahar Pariyojana, that had languished for more than four decades,[218] and the Renukaji Dam[219] have managed to see the light of day, bringing much relief to the lives of farmers across large parts of India.

Irrigation had been an issue close to PM Modi even when he was the Chief Minister of Gujarat. Gujarat, as a water-starved state, saw a turn-around under his watch, where farmers could get easy access to irrigation. One of his flagship schemes, 'Sujalam Suphalam' was introduced nearly 10 years back in 2007 and brought water to 10 water-starved districts of the state and 1.2 lakh hectares of land. The focus on irrigation continues in his new role as Prime Minister of India.

The Dam Rehabilitation and Improvement Project, with loan assistance from the World Bank for rehabilitation and improvement of about 198 dams in seven states (Jharkhand, Karnataka, Kerala, Madhya Pradesh, Odisha, Tamil Nadu and Uttarakhand), was accelerated[220] and institutional strengthening of Central Water Commission (CWC) and other implementing agencies was undertaken. Even after 70 years of Independence, there were 112 districts in the country, which had less than 20% irrigation coverage. The government implemented the National Ground Water Management Improvement Scheme in collaboration with the World Bank to address these situations in a time-bound manner.

Pradhan Mantri Krishi Sinchayee Yojana (PMKSY)

The most important irrigation scheme brought in by the Modi government is the Pradhan Mantri Krishi Sinchayee Yojana (PMKSY), which was conceived by bringing together a number of ongoing schemes, viz. Accelerated Irrigation Benefit Programme (AIBP) of the Ministry of Water Resources; River Development & Ganga Rejuvenation (MoWR, RD & GR); Integrated Watershed Management Programme (IWMP) of Department of Land Resources (DoLR); and the On Farm Water Management (OFWM) of Department of Agriculture and Cooperation (DAC).

Working on the principle of 'more crop, per drop', this scheme is looking to expand the cultivable area under assured irrigation and help improve on-farm water use efficiency. 'Per drop-more crop' is an idea, which PM Modi had also used when he was the CM of Gujarat, wherein he promoted micro-irrigation through both drip and sprinkler. The micro-irrigation scheme of PMKSY is seeing a lot of traction among farmers and has a high adoption rate.

Staying true to the vision of Dr. Babasaheb Ambedkar, PMKSY is not just about ensuring water access for irrigation, but also in helping conserve water as wealth through the adoption of precision irrigation, recharge of aquifers and sustainable water conservation techniques.

A total of 69.44 lakh hectares of land had been irrigated under the scheme during 2013-14 and up till March 2021.[221] In order to conserve water and remove the barriers associated with acquiring land, the government is focussing more on drip irrigation and irrigation through pipelines. In 2013-14, the area covered under micro-irrigation was only 4.32 lakh hectares. In comparison, in 2020-21, the area covered was 9.38 lakh hectares!

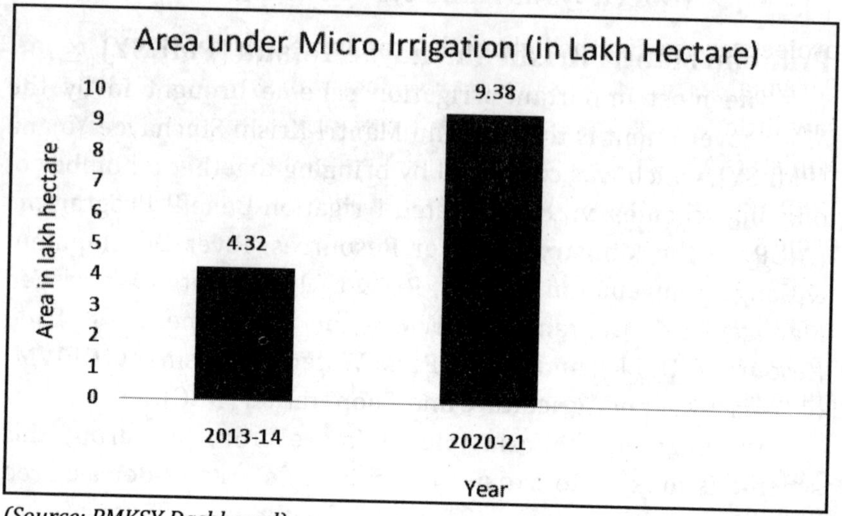

(Source: PMKSY Dashboard)

A number of innovative measures have been planned under PMKSY for 2021-26 to improve implementation and maximise benefits up to 22 lakh farmers. In addition to a central support worth Rs. 37,454 crore to states, an amount of Rs. 20,434 crore has been set aside for debt servicing of loans taken for irrigation development during PMKSY 2016-21.

In addition to that, Accelerated Irrigation Benefit Programme (AIBP), Har Khet ko Paani (HKKP) and Watershed Development components will be continued during 2021-26.

Accelerated Irrigation Benefit Programme (AIBP) is a flagship programme that gives financial support to irrigation projects. Against an estimated irrigation potential of 76.03 lakh hectare, up to 63.85 lakh hectare had been created till 31st March, 2021. A total of 46 out of 99 projects had been completed. Now a further target of 13.88 lakh hectare has been set for 2021-26.

The AIBP programme of the PM Modi's government was a conscious effort to expedite projects that had been pending for decades for a variety of reasons– approvals, land acquisition, clearances and what not. A great example of how delayed irrigation projects are seeing the light of day can be seen in the Saryu Nahar Pariyojana project. This project, which was first conceived in 1978, saw little to no progress despite the nation witnessing 12 Prime Ministers and 15 Chief Ministers.[222] The budget in turn ballooned from the initial Rs. 100 crore to Rs. 10,000 crore. However, the project was taken up head-on in 2017, and was finished in less than five years.[223]

Apart from completing 60 ongoing projects, including 30.23 lakh hectare under Command Area Development & Water Management (CADWM), additional projects will be taken up. This scheme focusses on enhancing physical access to water on farm to expand cultivable area. Between 2016 up to March 2021, funds amounting to Rs. 2,747 crore were released for 76 projects against a progress reported by states of 14.96 lakh hectare.

Har Khet Ko Pani (HKKP) aims to increase access to irrigation water on the farm and help in expanding the cultivable area. Under HKKP, activities such as surface minor irrigation and repair-renovation-restoration of water bodies is targeted to provide up to 4.5 lakh hectare irrigation. The scheme is designed especially for small and marginal farmers with priority given to SC/ST and women farmers. Groundwater irrigation facilities are created through dug wells, dug-cum-bore wells, tubewells, etc. So far, 15 projects in 12 states have been approved. Till December 2021, Rs. 458 crore was given as Central assistance to 10 states. More than 22,500 irrigation wells have been constructed, benefiting nearly 36,000 small and marginal farmers.

Watershed Development scheme focuses on development of rain-fed areas for soil and water conservation, regeneration of groundwater, arresting runoff and promoting extension activities related to water harvesting and management. The approved Watershed Development component of Department of Land Resources is looking to complete sanctioned projects covering 49.5 lakh hectare rain-fed/degraded lands. This will bring in up to 2.5 lakh hectare land under protective irrigation between 2021-

26. A specific provision for development of spring-sheds has also been included in the programme.

Under the Repair, Renovation and Restoration (RRR) of Water Bodies scheme, since the 12th Plan onwards, a total of 2,218 schemes have been initiated at an estimated cost of Rs. 1,910 crore. Target irrigation potential restoration of these schemes is estimated to be 1.888 lakh hectare, out of which 1.319 lakh hectare was restored till March 2021.

'Catch the rain' campaign, with a tagline–'catch the rain– when it falls, where it falls'– encourages building rain-water harvesting structures (RWHS) suitable to the climatic conditions and soil composition, to catch the rains with active participation from people. Drives have been undertaken to make water harvesting pits, rooftop RWHS, check dams, etc.; removal of encroachments and de-silting of tanks to increase their storage capacity; removal of obstructions in the channels which bring water to them from the catchment areas; repairs of step-wells; and use of defunct bore wells to put the water back into aquifers. Boosting groundwater level plays an important role towards boosting the irrigation potential of an area through natural means.

□

9

Education: The Great Social Leveller

"The object of primary education is to see that every child that enters the portals of a primary school does leave it only at a stage when it becomes literate throughout the rest of his life"

— Dr. B.R. Ambedkar[224]

"If anyone found the antidote for all social ills, it is Babasaheb. There are many people who realised there are problems. Some people also made efforts to remove social ills. However, if anyone provided a permanent solution, that was Babasaheb. What was his solution? He gave just this message to society: Get educated. The solution of all problems lies in education. Once you get educated, you can look injustice in the eye and fight it. None can humiliate you. None can insult you saying you are untouchable. His life's message was to generate an inner power to take on injustice and win. Rather than focussing merely on the outer shell, Dr. Babasaheb Ambedkar showed us a way to awaken our inner power."

— Prime Minister Narendra Modi[225]

Education is one of the edifices on which a civilisation itself rests. Across geographies, cultures, languages and religions, all successful civilisations had high regard for education and the educated.

A pithy and popular Sanskrit verse goes:

स्वगृहेपूज्यतेमूर्खः स्वग्रामेपूज्यतेप्रभुः ।
स्वदेशेपूज्यतेराजाविद्वान्सर्वत्रपूज्यते ॥

(A fool is respected only in his own home, a landlord/headman is respected in his own village and a king is respected in his own kingdom. A learned man, however, is respected and honoured everywhere.)

In the history of modern India, if one's personality symbolises education itself and stands for the infinite possibilities for self-development and societal transformation that education offers, it is Dr. B.R. Ambedkar. From a poor, underprivileged and socially discriminated background to charting the course of destiny of the nation of a billion, Dr. Babasaheb Ambedkar's story is truly inspirational and at the core of his soaring achievements lies his constant thirst for knowledge.

Dr. Babasaheb Ambedkar himself wasn't oblivious to this perspective. In fact, he said:

"Coming as I do from the lowest order of the Hindu society; I know what is the value of education. The problem of raising the lower order is deemed to be economic. This is a great mistake. The problem of raising the lower order in India is not to feed them, to clothe them and to make them serve the higher classes as the ancient ideal of this country. The problem of the lower order is to remove from them that inferiority complex, which has stunted their growth and made them slaves to others, to create in them the consciousness of the significance of their lives for themselves and for the country, of which they have been cruelly robbed of the existing social order. Nothing can achieve this purpose except the spread of higher education. This is in my opinion the panacea of our social troubles."[226]

This is both the perfect synopsis and the perfect prescription. Education is not merely about literacy, although literacy is the first step towards education. Access to good education for those from socially underprivileged backgrounds is the key– not only to material prosperity, but also to give boost to social self-esteem. Education gives the deprived a language with which to comprehend the world, to understand the opportunities out there, to make the world aware of the tremendous human potential in them and to carve out a unique niche. Healing the scars of oppression and poverty can happen fastest through education that opens up a world of opportunities.

A classic patronage-based system would keep the underprivileged in poverty and dispense small favours now and then, thus establishing a relationship of necessity that never allows the poor and deprived to truly grow. However, education is disruptive. The transformation that it brings in is often irreversible. It is highly unlikely that a well-educated son of a daily-wage labourer will go back to the drudgery of daily labour. Not only will the boy chase much bigger dreams, but he will also take his family and, more importantly, help others in his circle access better opportunities.

This, in essence, is the story of Dr. Babasaheb Ambedkar himself. Not only did he improve his own material conditions, but he also took along the whole nation on a path of irreversible transformation– something that will be known in history as an act of unleashing the power of millions of people in one go.

Reforming Education through a National Policy

A big hurdle in imparting quality education and making it accessible to the poor of the country was the disparity in the very system in place. Education being a State subject, PM Modi's vision of realising Dr. Babasaheb Ambedkar's dream of providing education to the poorest of the poor expressed itself in the form of a National Educational Policy (NEP). The landmark NEP 2020 prioritises the needs of the 21st-century India by bringing path-breaking changes to an education system put in place in 1986, with the objective to make the youth 'future ready'.

NEP 2020 has been formulated after an unprecedented process of consultation that involved nearly over 2 lakh suggestions from 2.5 lakh gram panchayats, 6,600 Blocks, 6,000 ULBs and 676 districts. The primary focus of NEP is to provide universalisation of education from pre-school to secondary level by 2030. Close to 2 crore out-of-school children are expected to re-enter the mainstream through an open school system. Similarly, the GEP in higher education is expected to be raised to 50% by 2035 with the addition of 3.5 crore seats in higher education. NEP also aims to establish Multidisciplinary Education and Research Universities (MERUs), at par with IITs and IIMs as models of best multidisciplinary education of global standards in the country. Also, with the focus on learning in mother tongue, emphasis is being put on ensuring a fundamental understanding of concepts.

Key features of the NEP across various Categories[227]

School Education	Higher Education
• Focuses on universal reach of school education by 2030 with 100% Gross Enrollment Ratio (GER). • Emphasis on early childhood care and education. • New curricular structure of 5+3+3+4 instead of the existing 10+2. • National Mission on Foundational Literacy & Numeracy to achieve literacy and numeracy. • Flexibility in the selection of subjects with no clear separation among the disciplines of art, science and vocational education. • Improvement in the curriculum for school education and pedagogy for promoting creative thinking and 21st-century skills among learners. • Gender Inclusion Fund for promoting education for girls. • Beginning of vocational education from Class VI, including internship.	• Gross enrolment ratio in higher education including vocational education to be increased to 50% by 2035. • 3.50 crore new seats to be added to higher education Institutions. • Emphasis on flexible curriculum with creative combinations of subjects. • Vocational education to be integrated with mainstream education. • Multiple entry and exit will be allowed with appropriate certification. • Setting up of Academic Bank of Credit for digitally storing academic credits so that these can be counted and transferred towards the final degree earned. • The National Research Foundation will be created as an apex body for fostering a strong research culture and building research capacity in higher education.

• NCERT will develop a new and comprehensive national curriculum framework. • Recommendation for multilingualism and three-language formula. • 360 degree holistic report card for an improved evaluation. • Provision for equal and inclusive education. • Provision for the recruitment and professional growth of teachers.	• Affiliation of colleges to be phased out in 15 years. • Multidisciplinary Education & Research Universities (MERUs) at par with IITs, IIMs, to be set up. • National Mission for Mentoring to be set up. • Focus on internationalisation of education. • Setting up of an Indian Institute of Translation & Interpretation, National Institute for Pali, Persian and Prakrit language, strengthening of Sanskrit and all language departments in the higher education institutions. • Open and distance education, online and digital education to be promoted. • Provision for professional growth of faculties. • Focus on internationalisation of education.

Many other things have been changed for the better when one compares to the previous education policy. Earlier, the emphasis was on marks obtained in the examination rather than on learning; in contrast, NEP 2020 pursues improvement in school curriculum for emphasis on creative thinking. From little focus on vocational courses, there is a refreshing change of focus on the same.

The old education policy had no provision for multiple entry and exit. This compelled a student seeking a break from studies before completion of the course to remain stuck, as there was no credit for the education he had acquired thus far. NEP has done away with it, by allowing multiple entry and exit for learners. This enables them to continue their studies as per their convenience. Also, foreign institutions will now be able to open campuses more easily, enabling quality exposure to students.

Primary and Secondary Education

Primary education must take precedence in both capacity creation and delivery, for education to truly spread. Only with students accessing primary education can they be expected to move up the ladder for higher education. Avery glaring error that policy-making in education has made in India since the time of Independence is chasing the glamour of higher education before putting the basics of primary education in place.

Even during his time, Dr. Babasaheb Ambedkar had taken cognisance of the fact that primary education was facing challenges. He said:

> *"The object of primary education is to see that every child that enters the portals of a primary school does leave it only at a stage when it becomes literate throughout the rest of his life. But if we take the statistics, we find that out of every hundred children that enter a primary school only 18 reach the fourth standard, the rest of them, that is to say, 82 out of every 100 replace into the state of illiteracy. The government should spend sufficient amount of money so that every child who enters a primary school reaches the fourth standard."*[228]

Samagra Shiksha is a Central Government integrated scheme that aims for all children to have equal access to quality education in an inclusive classroom environment, irrespective of their diverse background, multilingual needs, different academic abilities, etc. The scheme has been revamped and aligned with the recommendations of NEP 2020. Samagra Shiksha is now providing support for major NEP recommendations, such as emphasis on foundational literacy and numeracy; provision for Holistic Progress Card (HPC); capacity building of teachers; bag-less days and internships; separate stipend for girl child with special needs; expansion of schooling facilities including residential hostels, Kasturba Gandhi Balika Vidyalayas and vocational education, etc. The scheme has been extended from 2021-22 to 2025-26.[229]

SARTHAQ, or Students & Teachers Holistic Advancement through Quality Education programme is an initiative of the Department of School Education and Literacy. Under this initiative, an implementation plan has been proposed, keeping in mind the concurrent nature of education. States and UTs have been given the flexibility to adapt and modify the plan as per their needs and requirements. The plan lays down the roadmap for implementation of NEP over the next 10 years.

Vidya Pravesh is a three-month play-based school preparation module, developed by NCERT for all Grade 1 students with or without preschool education. The idea is to get all children Grade I ready till universal provisioning of quality preschool education is achieved. Vidya Pravesh was launched in July 2021 to be adapted or adopted by states/UTs as per their need. Also, the National Initiative for Proficiency in Reading with Understanding and Numeracy (NIPUN Bharat) programme was launched in 2021 as part of a larger exercise to ensure that every child in the country attains Foundational Literacy and Numeracy (FLN) by the end of Grade 3. The goals and objectives are required to be achieved by all government and private schools so that universal acquisition of FLN skills can be achieved.

In a landmark initiative, the Government of India in its Budget speech of 2021-22, announced plans to strengthen more than 15,000 schools across the country to include all components of the National Education Policy, 2020. These 'exemplar schools' will play the role of mentoring other schools in their regions to achieve the ideals of the National Education Policy.

In India, there is a big number of children toget an opportunity to go to school either due to lack of such facilities in their area, or because their poor parents cannot afford the cost of schooling.

Dr. Babasaheb Ambedkar also repeatedly highlighted the plight of such children and professed the need to include them into the education system at all costs. Unfortunately, the onset of Covid pandemic has added to the problem with many students belonging to poor households dropping out of school due to their parents losing their jobs or migrating back to villages. Fortunately, NEP 2020 has been designed, keeping in mind the needs of such children also.

NCERT has developed a bridge course for 'Out of School

Children' (OoSC) studying in special training centres for age group from six to 14 years. The course bridges the learning gaps and help children to be mainstreamed in regular school. Adapting to the unique situation, NCERT developed an 'Alternative Academic Calendar' (ACC) for all the stages of school education to help students of all classes to continue receiving education at home through social media tools, radio, television, etc. Provision has been made to allow children of migrant labourers to get admission into schools without any documents.

With Covid-19 negatively impacting the education of children across the spectrum, special attention has been given to developing social media tools and integration of Information & Communication Technology into the existing system. The government hopes to utilise such tools to prevent a large number of poor students from dropping out of the education system. Till December 2021, ICT Labs had been approved in 1.15 lakh schools and smart classrooms in 58,499 schools across the country.

An integrated teacher training programme, National Initiative for School Heads and Teacher's Holistic Development (NISHTHA)-1.0, 2.0, and 3.0 has also been introduced for different stages of school education. Under the programme, teachers, principals and other stakeholders are imparted training with focus on improving the quality of school education.

Padhe Bharat Badhe Bharat

This is a unique initiative to inculcate the reading habit among students of all ages. School libraries are being revamped and provided with books through a special library grant (Samagra Shiksha) to government schools. An outlay of Rs. 630 crore for the year 2020-21 and an outlay of Rs. 716 crore for 2021-22 have been approved so far. The old guidelines on library grants were also revised in 2021 to put stress on reading as a whole, apart from development of libraries and procurement of library books. The guidelines were framed, based on recommendations under NEP.

Khele India Khile India

PM Modi has always encouraged sporting activity among the children and youth of India as part of a holistic growth experience for the future generation. To this end, the 'Khele India, Khile India' focuses upon providing grants for sports and physical education. The sports and physical education component has been introduced for the first time to encourage sports, physical activities, yoga, co-curricular activities, etc. Government schools can access the sports grant of Rs. 5,000 for primary schools, Rs. 10,000 for upper primary schools and up to Rs 25,000 for secondary/senior secondary schools. The government has issued guidelines to states and UTs to ensure proper utilisation of the sports grant. They have also been advised to encourage schools to include traditional and regional games.

FIT India Campaign

This movement is an initiative very close to the heart of PM Modi himself. While launching the movement in 2019, he said: *"Today lifestyle diseases are on a rise in India, affecting even the young. Cases of diabetes and hypertension is on the rise and even common among children in India. But small lifestyle changes when introduced early in life can become lifelong habits, thus helping to prevent these lifestyle diseases. 'Fit India Movement' is an effort to bring these small lifestyle changes".*[230] The mission of the movement is to encourage people to incorporate behavioural changes and move towards a more physically active lifestyle.

Schools play a very big role in the 'Fit India' movement. They are encouraged to celebrate FIT India School Week to give a chance to all students to step out of their classrooms and enjoy sports activities. In the two years since its launch and till the onset of Covid-induced lockdown, schools all over the country participated in the Fit India movement. In 2019, a total of 14,000 events were orgainsed across schools. However, this number jumped to an astounding 4.3 lakh events in 2020.[231] Meantime, the

Department of Sports has prepared a ranking system according to the resources available in the schools– Fit India Star Rating– to make it a people's movement. As on December 2021, 4.45 lakh schools were awarded Fit India Flag; 43,074 schools had applied for 3 Stars Rating, and 13,008 schools applied for 5 Stars rating. The Fit India Freedom Run encourages schools across the country to participate in large numbers. In 2021, the Fit India Quiz was launched for schools to spread awareness about fitness among students.

Making Higher Education Accessible

A highly educated scholar of law, economics and political science; someone who had earned doctorates from the Columbia University and London School of Economics; Chairman of the Drafting Committee of one of the most exhaustive constitutions of the world; and a high quality public intellectual, Dr. Babasaheb Ambedkar's name was synonymous with academic excellence. On the subject of higher education and its role in bringing equality to society, Dr. Babasaheb Ambedkar observed:

> *"Education is something which ought to be brought within the reach of everyone...the policy, therefore, ought to be to make higher education as cheap to the lower classes as it can possibly be made. If all these communities are to be brought to the level of equality, then the only remedy is to adopt the principle of equality and to give favoured treatment to those who are below level."*[232]

His stress on making higher education as inexpensive as possible for the lower classes is based on the principles of social justice and empowerment. To give an example, in the year 2016, when the Standing Committee of IIT Council recommended a three-fold hike in the fees for education in the IITs, the proposed hike was denied by the Modi government. However, there was a smaller increase in the fees so as to make more funds available for better facilities; but, interests of the socially and economically weaker sections were protected. SC/ST and Divyang students got a complete waiver; students categorised as 'most economically backward' received a full remission of fee; and the students categorised as 'other economically backward' received a remission of 66% of the fee. Interest-free loans were made available to all students. These measures stem from a worldview that higher education should actually help in easing the burden of the poor and the marginalised by opening up new vistas of socio-economic mobility rather than being a burden by itself.

Additionally, with the expansion of the network of the Eklavya Model Residential Schools (EMRSs) with increased funding is also being pursued aggressively, with the intent of bringing these schools at par with Navodaya Vidyalayas. A total of 740 EMRSs are to be sanctioned by 2022, in addition to the 632 EMRSs sanctioned till August 2021. A total of 367 EMRSs are already functional with 85,232 students.[233]

Autonomy with Accountability

Academic excellence grows with the setting up of a culture of valuing it and giving it institutional impetus– something that the PM Modi-led government has been appreciated for doing. A domain in which the government has made bold and reformist moves, higher education in India has received unprecedented importance across fields of study.

In a historic and unprecedented decision, the government, in March 2018, enhanced the autonomy of about 63 higher educational institutions that have maintained high standards of academic excellence. PM Modi has understood the link between incentive, performance and autonomy. If there are incentives to excel, the desire to excel only becomes more intense and performance improves. With the improvement of performance comes well-deserved autonomy, which helps the institution access better resources to excel more.

The National Institutional Ranking Framework (NIRF) was launched in September 2015. It ranks institutions based on objective and verifiable criteria. Not only has it been made available separately for streams, such as engineering, management, pharma, architecture, humanities, law and others; it has also been applied to universities as a whole. More than 4,500 institutions participated in the exercise, making it the highest participatory ranking exercise in the world.

Introducing a liberalised regime in the higher education sector by emphasising on the link between autonomy and quality is a reform that reinforces the virtuous cycle of excellence, leading to more autonomy and vice versa. The granting of autonomy to institutions that excel is also a mark of the humility of a government that understands that it is not omniscient and quality can be decentralised.

The freedom to start new courses, more off-campus centres, skill development courses, research parks and any other new academic programmes is a key part of this autonomy. These institutions also have the freedom to hire foreign faculty, enrol foreign students, give better incentive-based monetary compensation to the faculty and also enter into academic collaborations.

The Indian Institutes of Management Act, 2017 (also known as IIM Act), that was enacted by the Modi government, is another example of commitment towards excellence and autonomy in higher educational institutions. Indian Institutes of Management are the nation's foremost institutions in imparting world-class education in management. Run on globally benchmarked processes of education and training in management, the IIMs are spoken of highly across the world.

There are some important transformations that the IIM Act ushers in. Earlier the IIMs were societies, and, hence, not authorised to award degrees. They were awarding post-graduate diplomas and fellow programmes that were treated as equivalent to Master of Business Administration and Ph.D, respectively. However, in the global arena, such terminological equivalences are not universally acceptable. The IIM Act ensured that the IIMs were declared as Institutions of national importance, enabling them to grant degrees to their students. Apart from authority to grant degrees, the Act provides for complete autonomy to the institutions, combined with adequate accountability. Greater participation of experts and alumni in the Board is another important feature.

Ensuring that the ultimate aim of enabling socio-economic empowerment through higher education is fulfilled, the presence of women and members from Scheduled Castes and Scheduled Tribes in the Board has been mandated. The Act also provides for periodic review of the performance of institutions by independent agencies and placing the results of the same on the public domain. Thus, while unshackling institutions from bureaucratic inertia, the Modi government has ensured there is no free pass and a culture of accountability fosters along with autonomy.

Similarly, the decision on the creation of a National Medical Commission and its autonomous Boards will steer medical education towards a transparent, qualitative and accountable system. The basic change that has happened is that the Regulator is now 'selected' on merit, as opposed to an 'elected' Regulator. Men and women with impeccable integrity, professionalism, experience and stature have been now placed at the helm to steer the medical education reforms further. The Boards in turn, namely Under-Graduate Medical Education Board, Post-Graduate Medical Education Board, Medical Assessment & Rating Board and Ethics & Medical Registration Board will oversee UG/ PG education, accreditation and assessment and the matters related to ethics and professional conduct of doctors.[234]

Capacity Addition

Quality and capacity matter, especially in higher education. The Modi government has been cognizant with the importance of more institutions that can impart quality higher education. In just a single year in 2016, setting up of several new higher education institutes was approved or expedited.[235] This included:

- 7 new IITs
- 7 new IIMs
- 1 new NIT
- 2 new IISERs
- 14 new IITs (fully operational)
- 4 central universities
- 14 new AIIMS

Capacity addition has been significant even in the number of seats. For example, in medical education, when the Modi government came to power in 2014, there were 82,000 undergraduate seats. By 2021, there were 1.48 lakh undergraduate seats, as the Modi government increased the seat number by 80%. This was possible with the huge increment in the number of medical colleges, from 387 in 2014 to 596 in 2021.[236]

With the objective of creating 10,000 MBBS seats in government colleges in the country, the government is implementing the Centrally-sponsored scheme for upgradation of existing state/Central government medical colleges to increase MBBS seats. Already 48 colleges in 15 states have been approved for increase of 3,325 seats with Rs. 6,719 crore released as Central share.[237] This initiative is being undertaken in two phases:

- Phase-I was launched during the 11th Plan period with the objective to strengthen and upgrade state/Central government medical colleges to create new PG seats. A total of 72 government colleges have been approved to increase 4,058 PG seats for which funds worth Rs. 1,049 crore have been released.
- The objective of Phase-II is to create 4,000 PG seats. A total of 16 government medical colleges have been approved under the scheme for increasing 1,741 PG seats till date and funds to the tune of Rs. 694 crore have been released for the same.

Setting the Basics Right

General apathy towards the state of public schools affects the poor and marginalised severely since they cannot always be expected to afford private schools. Even among the poor, girls were affected much more than boys due to the grievous lack of even basic facilities, such as toilets. The question of toilets in schools and their impact on education may seem slightly misplaced. However, the absence of toilets, especially separate toilets for girls, is seen to have a negative impact on access to education because it pushes up the girl dropout rate.

PM Modi, in his experience as the Chief Minister of Gujarat, had dealt with the problem of girls dropping out from school closely and ushered in a major turnaround. No wonder that he spoke about this and announced an action plan in his first Independence Day speech as Prime Minister. He said:

> *"All schools in the country should have toilets with separate toilets for girls. Only then, our daughters will not be compelled to leave schools midway. I appeal to parliamentarians to utilise their MPLAD funds for constructing toilets in schools. The government will utilise its budget for providing toilets. I urge the corporate sector also to give priority to the provision of toilets in schools through the expenditure under corporate social responsibility. The target to finish this in one year from today. With the help of state governments, this is possible. On the next Independence Day, we should be in a position to proclaim that there is no school in India without separate toilets for boys and girls."*[238]

The signal that the Prime Minister sent by speaking about toilets for girls in schools from the ramparts of the Red Fort inspired the administration to shake off inertia. As a result, the Swachh Vidyalaya mission to build toilets in all schools and separate toilets for girls was launched.

A culture of setting targets publicly was also ushered, something that was refreshing to a nation accustomed to broken promises. But could an activity of such a scale be completed in a year? The next year, on Independence Day, from the Red Fort, he described the speed and scale of the achievement:

"I had announced that we would build separate toilets for boys and girls in all of our schools by today. When we started work as Team India, we realised that there were 2.62 lakh schools, where more than 4.25 lakh toilets were required to be built. This figure was so daunting that any government would think about extending the deadline. But thanks to the resolve of Team India, no one sought any extension. Today, on 15 August, I salute Team India for honouring our tricolour by leaving no stone unturned to realise our dream and almost achieving our target."[239]

On educating the girl child, while infrastructural impetus goes a long way, mindset changes also play a role. On this front, PM Modi has successfully been able to make the motto of 'Beti Bachao Beti Padhao' famous and well-accepted across the nation. There is an unprecedented level of enthusiasm and pride being seen in furthering the education of girls and in correcting earlier societal neglect.

The government is implementing various welfare schemes that provide incentives for girls' education. Under the Samagra Shiksha, there is a provision of Kasturba Gandhi Balika Vidyalayas (KGBVs). KGBVs are residential schools from class VI to XII for girls belonging to disadvantaged groups, such as SC/ST, OBC, minority and BPL. A total of 5,726 KGBVs have been sanctioned in the country of which 5,010 KGBVs are functional with the enrolment of 6.54 lakh girls. Today, nearly 50% of students studying in schools across the country are girls (12.7 crore girls against 13.7 crore boys).[240]

The Centrally-sponsored National Scheme of Incentive to Girls for Secondary Education (NSIGSE) was launched in May 2008 to give incentives to girl students enrolled in Class IX and reduce drop out of girls belonging to SC/ST communities in secondary schools. The scheme has provision of gender segregated toilets in all schools, self-defence training from Classes VI to XII, and stipend to Divyang girls from Classes I to XII.

Another scheme, the National Means-cum-Merit Scholarship Scheme (NMMSS), is also under implementation since 2008 to award scholarships to meritorious students, including girls, of EWS to arrest their drop-out at Class VIII. Under the scheme, 1 lakh fresh scholarships of Rs. 12,000 per annum per student are awarded to select students of Class IX every year and are renewed in Classes X to XII. However, the Modi government felt several inadequacies in the manner and functioning of the scheme, which failed to achieve its primary objective to the desired extent.

Therefore, upon assuming power, this became a major focus point. Under the Modi government, there has been a remarkable jump in the percentage of girls receiving scholarships which helps them continue with their education and realise their dreams. While the percentage of girls receiving scholarships in 2014-15 stood at 32.9%, this jumped up to 52.8% in 2021-22.[241]

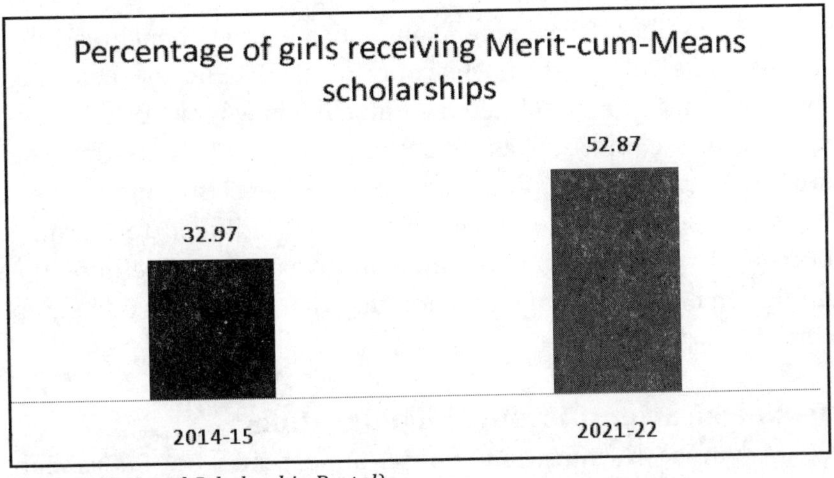

(Source: National Scholarship Portal)

From Outlays to Outcomes

The Right to Education Act that emanated directly from the Directive Principles of State Policy incorporated in the Indian Constitution by Dr. Babasaheb Ambedkar began as an answer to the problem of access to education. However, increasingly it was seen as an instrument that focussed too much on administrative matters, such as buildings, infrastructure, pupil-teacher ratios, working days and hours, prohibition of screening procedures, prohibition of capitation fees and cracking down on private tuitions by teachers. There was very little focus on the actual quality of education that was being provided.

Another common and rightful criticism of the prevalent schooling education system in India, as some have succinctly pointed out, is the focus on outlays rather than outcomes. Budgets, outlays and spending on education are important, but they acquire complete meaning only when there are outcomes delivered. This move from emphasis on mere outlays to emphasis on outcomes, from mere administrative focus to qualitative focus, from mere declaration of a right to actual fruitful realisation of it, has been initiated by the Modi government through its programme on codifying learning outcomes.

Well-defined learning outcomes are benchmarking mechanisms to assess the learning level of children. Learning outcomes have been defined as a matrix of two verticals– class-specific and subject-specific– as guidelines to ensure that the students acquire the appropriate learning level specific to their class and subject. Assessment of students is linked to learning outcomes, thus stressing on the qualitative aspect of defining the minimum benchmark of education that the schools have to equip a student with.

Technical, Scientific and Skill Education

An area of education whose importance Dr. Babasaheb Ambedkar often stressed upon was technical education. As the Labour Member of the Viceroy's Executive Council, Dr. Babasaheb Ambedkar pioneered skill development in the government sector by setting up the Skill Development Programme post the Second World War. The significance he attached to the effort can be gauged in the statement he made while addressing the Technical Training Scheme Advisory Committee in Calcutta:

"No plan for the future development of the country can be deemed to be complete which does not provide for technical and scientific training. This is the age of Machine and it is only those countries in which technical and scientific training has risen to the highest pitch that will survive in the struggle that will commence when the war is over, for maintaining decent standards of living for their people. The Government of India is not oblivious to these considerations and would like to see the Technical Training Scheme not only maintained, but extended all over the country and become a permanent part of the country's educational system."[242]

A large part of the work of the Technical Training Scheme that Dr. Babasaheb Ambedkar spoke about consisted of technical, skill-specific training and development. On skill development, the Modi government has taken a holistic approach, connecting human resource with employability, making this dispensation a pioneer in reforming the sector.

Skill Development and Training

As per a government report *"54% of India's population is below 25 years of age and over 62% of the population is the working age group. Yet, only 4.69% of the Indian population has undergone formal skills training. By 2025, almost one in five of the world's working age population (18.3%) will be Indian. Recent skill gap reports suggest that over 10.9 crore incremental human resources will be required in India alone, across 24 key sectors by the year 2022. 93% of India's workers work in the unorganised sector and acquire skills through informal channels and lack formal certification."*[243]

These are mind-boggling numbers that show both the opportunities and challenges for India if we can find a way to empower youth with skills. Skill development, as an empowering tool, was left neglected and underdeveloped. To provide employment for the crores of the youth of India, skill development plays a central role. The Modi government ushered in a paradigm shift in the way the government looks at skill development and makes a policy for it.

The Prime Minister perceptively explained the way to look at skill and knowledge and why skilling is important. He said:

"We must understand the difference between knowledge and skill in today's fast-changing world. There is a huge difference between the two. Knowledge is all about understanding a concept, about understanding the basics of something. For example, knowledge is about knowing how an electric circuit functions. However, skill is all about applying that knowledge into practice in daily life. There are a lot of people who have studied electronics or electrical engineering, but they call an electrician if the fuse burns out. So, skill is about sharpening and applying the knowledge for practical ends. Skill must grow as fast as knowledge is growing."[244]

Guided by such a vision of providing skill-based education to the youth, the Modi government took some important measures. Firstly, it brought skill development under one ministry from the 24 different ministries and departments implementing over 50 related or unrelated skill development programmes. For the first time ever, a comprehensive policy framework on skilling, the National Policy for Skill Development and Entrepreneurship was launched.

The Ministry of Skill Development and Entrepreneurship was created by the Modi government in 2014. Till February 2021, 738 Pradhan Mantri Kaushal Kendras (PMKKs)[245] had been set up across the country.

Dr. Babasaheb Ambedkar also said:

"From the point of raising the economic condition, technical education for the Scheduled Castes is more important than

literary education... It seems to me that the Government of India can do a great deal to improve his lot by enabling him to acquire technical skill which he does not now possess and this can be easily done by introducing a system of apprenticeship for the Scheduled Caste boys in undertakings run or controlled by the Government of India, in which the possibilities of giving such technical training do exist."[246]

Industrial Training Institutes or ITIs, the contemporary avatar of Dr. Babasaheb Ambedkar's Technical Training Scheme, have been brought under the same ministry that handles skill development. Reforms, such as grading and rating of ITIs and increased industry focus in the training, have been brought in. Since inception of the Pradhan Mantri Kaushal Vikas Yojana (PMKVY) in 2015, 1.3 crore candidates have been trained with over 1 crore certified. An additional 1.4 crore people are presently enrolled. A special course for Covid warriors has also been introduced to meet the growing demand for skilled healthcare professionals, under which more than 1.2 lakh people were trained in 2021 alone. The scheme particularly gives an opportunity to the deprived and backward sections, women, transgenders, etc. to refine their skills and find better-paying job opportunities.

On the matter of apprenticeship, the Modi government took steps to increase the adoption of apprenticeship model in India by amending the Apprenticeship Act, 1961, and by launching the National Apprenticeship Promotion Scheme (NAPS). NAPS was launched to increase the engagement of apprenticeship to 50 lakh people by 2020. Since its launch in 2016, 4.3 lakh people got apprenticeship in 9,482 establishments, gaining valuable skills, which resulted in lucrative job offers for many.[247]

Technology, Science and Innovation

As seen from one of Babasaheb's quotes, where he calls it the 'age of the machine', education must also cater to the furtherance of science, technology and innovation. These are the domains that give a nation an edge over others– the more innovative a nation, the stronger its global position is.

PM Modi too has repeatedly stressed upon scientific and technological innovations as boon to a developing nation where scalable and inexpensive solutions need to be developed. His government has institutionalised connecting education with innovation in many ways.

For example, Impacting Research Innovation and Technology (IMPRINT) is an initiative of the government to strengthen research in the premier institutions to solve important problems that impact the nation at large. A set of 10 domains have been identified for the development of innovative interventions:

- Health care technology
- Energy security
- Rural-urban housing design
- Nanotechnology
- Water-river systems
- Advanced materials
- Computer science and Information and Communications Technology
- Manufacturing technology
- Advanced security
- Environment or climate change

Government of India has taken a number of initiatives to enhance investment in R&D as well as to promote and improve the overall research ecosystem in the country. These include Uchchatar Avishkar Yojana (UAY), which promotes industry-sponsored, outcome-oriented research. Up to 25% of the funds under UAY are contributed by the industry. The IMPRINT programme focusses on socially relevant research in higher educational institutions. During 2018-2019, Rs. 46.3 crore and during 2019-2020, Rs. 47.2 crore was released.[248] Other than that, nine research parks at a total cost of Rs. 775 crores, eight of them being in the Indian Institutes of Technology (IITs) and one in Indian Institute of Science (IISc), have been established. These research parks will propel innovation through incubation and joint research between academia and industry.[249]

In Budget 2018, the Modi government announced a special programme. Called the Prime Minister's Research Fellowship (PMRF), the programme was allocated Rs. 1,650 crore for a period of seven years, beginning from 2018-19. PMRF intends to choose the best graduate or post-graduate students of science and technological streams from certain institutions renowned for technological learning. These students would be offered direct admission to a Ph.D. programme in the IITs or IISc. A handsome fellowship, an attractive research grant and more incentives would be provided. PMRF aims to tap the intelligence of Indian youth to boost indigenous research in cutting edge science and technology domains. This is a key national priority for a rising India and also addresses the shortage of quality faculty in premier educational institutions of the country.

At the school level, NITI Aayog's Atal Innovation Mission is working to cultivate one million children as the innovators of tomorrow. As of December 2021, more than 9,500 ATL labs have been established in 722 districts.[250] These labs are spaces for students between Classes VI to XII to try their hand at scientific and technological innovations. ATLs are equipped with technologies like 3D printers, robotics, sensor technology kits, Internet of Things, miniaturised electronics and more. This sparks the fire of innovation in young minds and opens up possibilities for solutions to India's problems to come from within the student community.

Conclusion

Empowered by education, Dr. Babasaheb Ambedkar made glowing contributions to our democracy. His vision for education was a comprehensive one and even after decades of his passing, his views on the kind of education that the nation needs are as though he had seen the future. This is a tribute to the foresight of the great man.

From higher education to its accessibility, from stress on primary education to the importance of technical and scientific education, the Modi government has taken inspiration from the vision of Babasaheb who personifies the possibilities education opens up and pays tribute to it through its actions.

□

10

Social Empowerment through Development for All

The strongest role that Dr. B.R. Ambedkar played was in addressing the caste-based oppression in India and in redefining the concept of social justice in modern Indian society. Dr. Babasaheb Ambedkar said: *"A just society is that society in which ascending sense of reverence and descending sense of contempt is dissolved into the creation of a compassionate society."*[251]

Dr. Babasaheb Ambedkar was the most vocal champion of the socially disadvantaged castes and communities. He single-handedly brought the nation's attention to the practice of social discrimination on account of the birth-based caste system. Importantly, his mission was not restricted to political power; instead, he wanted even the political order to be based on just social order. Dr. Babasaheb Ambedkar, in his speech before the Constituent Assembly for the passage of the Constitution, said: *"I have completed my work; I wish there should be a sunrise even tomorrow. The new Bharat has got political freedom, but it is yet to raise the sun of social and economic liberty."*[252] He championed the cause of social reforms and gave the call for affirmative action to provide equal opportunities to Dalits and tribals.

Dr. B.R. Ambedkar's Legacy

Dr. Babasaheb Ambedkar's contribution in building the foundation for a modern social order can be seen through three lenses.

First, Dr. Babasaheb Ambedkar systematically initiated the advocacy for social reforms in Indian society. Discarding the age-old norms of caste-based untouchability, he unified and cemented the voice of Dalits, untouchables and women of our society. Inspired by the ideals of equality, liberty and fraternity, he called for equal rights and opportunities of the Scheduled Castes and Tribes.

Explaining the importance of these ideas, Dr. Babasaheb Ambedkar said: *"Political democracy cannot last unless there lies at the base of its social democracy. What does social democracy mean? It means a way of life, which recognises liberty, equality and fraternity as the principles of life."*[253]

He opposed the means of a violent revolution to bring about a social change. Instead, he advocated for educational opportunities, social reform, use of the press and political empowerment as ways to socially consolidate the voice of the depressed classes.

Second, affirmative action was given a whole new life by the writings and political advocacy of Dr. Babasaheb Ambedkar. He believed that a time-bound affirmative action in the form of reservations in educational institutes, jobs and political offices would help overcome the years of social disadvantage. And it is as a result of his efforts that reservations have acted as an important means for bringing forth the historically disadvantaged into the mainstream of the Indian society.

Third, constitutional and legal reforms were used as the ultimate tools for spurring social and economic change. Dr. Babasaheb Ambedkar, who himself belonged to an untouchable caste, went on to become the chief architect of the Indian Constitution, which was nothing short of revolutionary. Though most importantly, he opposed the anarchist methods of revolution to achieve the ideals of social justice.

Contemplating the nature of methods, Dr. Babasaheb Ambedkar said: *"The first thing in my judgement we must do is tohold fast to the constitutional methods of achieving our social and economic objectives. It means we must abandon the bloody methods of revolution. These methods are nothing but the grammar of anarchy and the sooner they are abandoned, the better for us."*[254]

And thus, our Constitution went on to guarantee political, social and economic rights, like the right to equality (Article 14), right against discrimination (Article 15), right to equal opportunity (Article 16), abolition of untouchability (Article 17) and distributive justice (Article 39) amongst many others.

Narendra Modi's Call for Action

Prime Minister Narendra Modi, following the footsteps of Dr. Babasaheb Ambedkar, has given a whole new dimension to the concept of social justice. He is the strongest political advocate for the equality of all castes and classes that the modern political history of India has seen. He sees social justice in the context of empowering the disadvantaged communities, like women, Dalits, backward classes, Divyangs and the poor sections of the society.

PM Modi adds three new dimensions to the application of Dr. Babasaheb Ambedkar's ideals in the current times, which have been discussed below.

Social Empowerment

PM Modi's mantra for addressing social inequities is through the means of social empowerment. He seeks to break the class-consciousness prevalent in most political parties, which treat the SC and ST communities as mere recipients of dole-outs. Instead, he has instituted a spirit of self-confidence, encouraging them to stand on their own feet and, thus, paving the way for social empowerment. The official philosophy of Dalit Indian Chamber of Commerce and Industry (DICCI), 'Be job givers and not job seekers', also supported by current government's initiative for Start Ups India campaign, beautifully sums up the sentiment of the Prime Minister.

Moreover, technology has been cited as the most important

tool for socially empowering backward classes. PM Modi, giving an example of Dr. Babasaheb Ambedkar's dream, says:

"The life mantra of Dr. Babasaheb Ambedkar was 'bahujan hitay, bahujan sukhay' (for the happiness of the masses, for the welfare of masses). He was a messiah for the deprived and the most vulnerable. For them, technology is their biggest strength. It holds the power to empower the poorest of the poor."[255]

To apply the ideals of social empowerment in policy and practice, Antyodaya or 'service to the last wo (man) standing' has been the welfare model adopted by PM Modi. In his own words:

"Antyodaya is integral to our work. We understand the strength of India's poor, reposing faith in the power of the commons."[256]

He goes on to explain:

"How we should support the poor in their fight against poverty and empower them in this arduous effort of theirs. Hence, the meaningfulness of our resources, our schemes and our programmes is in their usefulness to the cause of welfare of the poor."[257]

The most important step taken towards eliminating the caste-based discrimination and the deplorable practice of untouchability has been the launch of Swachh Bharat Abhiyan. Refuting the age-old norms wherein the job of scavenging was unjustly considered to be the duty of a particular community, PM Modi himself picked up the broom to mark the launch of a new era where swachhata is treated as the greatest national duty. A society, which looked down upon the act of cleaning our environment, is now taking pride in picking up a broom and spreading the message of 'swachhata hi Seva'. This campaign, started by PM Modi, is not just a scheme for building toilets, but is a larger behavioural change campaign, which makes each one of us accountable for keeping our surroundings clean. Thus, it's a landmark public campaign, which will go a long way in socially transforming Indian society by addressing the very basis of caste-based discrimination.

In terms of providing special legal support, the Modi government has expanded the scope of protection accorded to the Dalit and tribal community by strengthening the Scheduled Castes & the Scheduled Tribes (Prevention of Atrocities) Act. Cases related to crimes against the weaker sections of the society have been dealt with greater strictness and faster grievance redressal. Even the recent review by the Supreme Court to water down the provisions of the Act was met with a review petition by the government to assure continued protection to the Dalit communities. The ambit of social and legal protection has been expanded even further to set up the constitutional body– the National Commission for Backward Classes (NCBC), while in the area of education, the number of post-matric scholarships for SC-ST students have also increased significantly.

Another noteworthy decision of the government has come in the form of abrogation of Articles 370 and 35A in the Jammu & Kashmir region, seven decades after Independence. People belonging to SC and ST communities were deprived of political reservation in Jammu & Kashmir as provisioned in the special Act for the state. This is historic in terms of protecting the political rights of the SC/ST communities in the region as well as in fulfilling Dr. Babasaheb Ambedkar's vision of democracy and equality.

The Modi government is cognizant of the special requirements of the tribal communities and considers tribal development as one of the most important pillars of social empowerment. Government has already taken various initiatives, like opening of Ekalavya Model Residential School (EMRS) in tribal areas of the country, allocating increased budgets for Tribal Sub-Plans (40 Central ministries have been mandated to earmark Tribal Sub-Plan funds in the range of 4.3% to 17.5% of their total scheme allocation every year for tribal development),[258] online monitoring of Budget allocated specifically for ST communities and, most importantly, increasing the minimum support price for minor forest produce.

A total of 740 EMRSs are to be sanctioned by 2022, in addition to the 632 EMRSs sanctioned till August 2021. As many as 367 EMRSs are already functional with 85,232 students.[259]

Under the Van Dhan Vikas Yojana, the government is economically empowering the tribal community by bringing a large number of minor forest produce (MFP) under this scheme, supporting value addition of the raw produce, providing direct market access by cutting the need for a middle-man, and, even identifying buyers at the local, state and national level to sell the products at market price through TRIFED outlets. Since its launch in 2018, procurement from MFP has gone up from Rs. 30 crore to Rs. 1,843 crore, using government funds across the country. Also, the number of items covered by the MSP for MFP initiative, which used to be 10 in 2013, has now crossed 87,[260] which increases the avenues of earning for tribal forest gatherers otherwise at the mercy of brokers and middlemen. The Van Dhan tribal startups have emerged as a source of employment for tribal gatherers, forest dwellers and the home-bound tribal artisans. Particularly, tribal women have benefitted from the scheme as they now have a chance to be financially independent. Therefore, it can be seen in the manner in which Modi has encouraged the weaker sections of the society to find sustainable solutions based on individual empowerment and government support.

To ensure last mile delivery of government services, the Modi government has used Information and Communications Technology (ICT) in establishing a direct connect between the government and the common citizen. PM Modi explains, *"Technology is an empowering tool for the citizen and an accountability medium for the government. My government fully recognises the huge potential of this tool– Digital India aims to transform the country into a digitally empowered society and knowledge economy."*[261]

Under the banner of Digital India campaign, PM Modi has digitised the working of government. Online filing of applications has become easier and there is greater improvement in the monitoring of the government schemes. Increased beneficiary enrolment through Aadhaar has been achieved, linking Aadhaar to the Jan Dhan Yojana; this in turn has facilitated extensive use of direct benefit transfer. To take the benefits of Digital India to the socially disadvantaged, more than 4.75 lakh common services centres had been set up till February 2022.[262] This has created a new generation of digital entrepreneurs among the poor, marginalised and women of India.

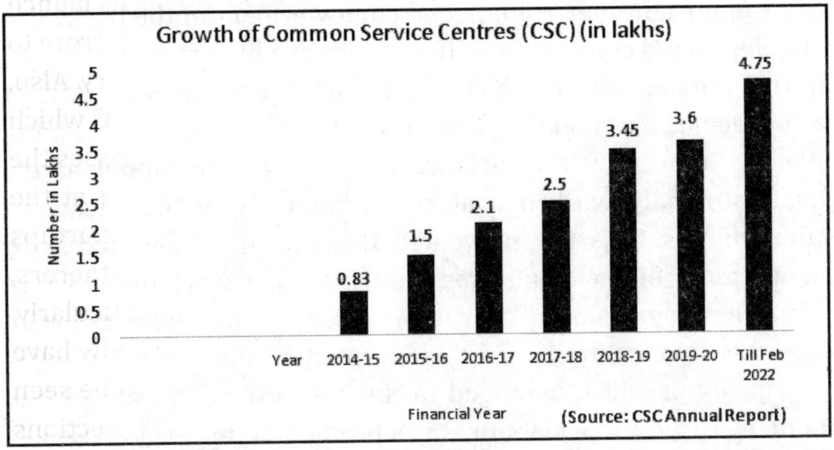

Another relevant aspect of the use of technology in flattening societal hierarchies has been the transformation of India into a cashless economy. Total volume of digital transactions grew from 1,085 crore inFY17 to 5,554 crore in FY21, and had already crossed 3,623 crore by August 2021.[263]

Aware of the need for spreading greater digital literacy in the rural areas, the government has also been implementing the Digital Saksharta Abhiyan (DISHA) to spread the benefits even to the most disadvantaged member of the society.

Economic Empowerment

Dr. Babasaheb Ambedkar's contribution to the Indian banking sector was a monumental one. Few people today remember that the Reserve Bank of India was conceptualised and operationalised based on a proposal outlined by Dr Ambedkar to the Hilton Young Commission, then also known as the Royal Commission on Indian Currency and Finance.[264] Dr. Babasaheb Ambedkar had, in fact, proposed the implementation of an India-centric monetary policy and asked for the formation of a central bank to issue and manage currency through a well-defined monetary policy managed by experts and professionals.

PM Modi believes in economic empowerment as one of the most important means for social empowerment of the backward and depressed communities. If we study the history of how social norms are set, we find that it is, in fact, the economic status of a particular community, which explains its social situation. We all know how the absence of collateral or capital assets has historically worked against the interests of the backward communities. This has prevented them from gaining access to mainstream financial services. Added to that were the woes of moneylending wherein exorbitant interest rates were charged from the poor and relatively uneducated sections of the society, a majority of which belonged to the backward and Dalit castes. In many cases, forced labour was a product of this exploitation. It is this reading of the social problems that PM Modi understands deeply and seeks to uproot the cause of social discrimination, that is, economic inequality.

To promote the economic empowerment of backward communities, financial inclusion through the Jan Dhan Yojana was the first programme implemented by the Modi government. Quoting him, *"Even after 60 years of Independence; even when the banks were nationalised for the poor, 40% people of the country were without a bank account till the 15th of August, 2014; the doors of the banks were not open for the poor. We resolved that we would erase this blot and would provide a solid base to the financial inclusion which is talked about the world over, by integrating the poorest of the poor to the mainstream economic activities; and this is only the beginning."*[265]

Hence, without the requirement of providing collateral or referral, nearly 44.82 crore (as on February 2022),[266] zero balance accounts have been opened since 2014 with the deposits of more than Rs. 1.6 lakh crore. Of these, 29.92 crore accounts were opened in rural and semi-urban areas, while 24.94 crore beneficiaries were reported to be women. This initiative opened the doors of formal banking to the poorest of the poor. In fact, it again has the footprints of Dr. Babasaheb Ambedkar. He not only envisioned empowerment of the most vulnerable but also contributed towards the establishment of the Reserve Bank of India, as a way to serve India's banking sector. The Jan Dhan Yojana is a perfect culmination of the above two visions of Dr. Babasaheb Ambedkar.

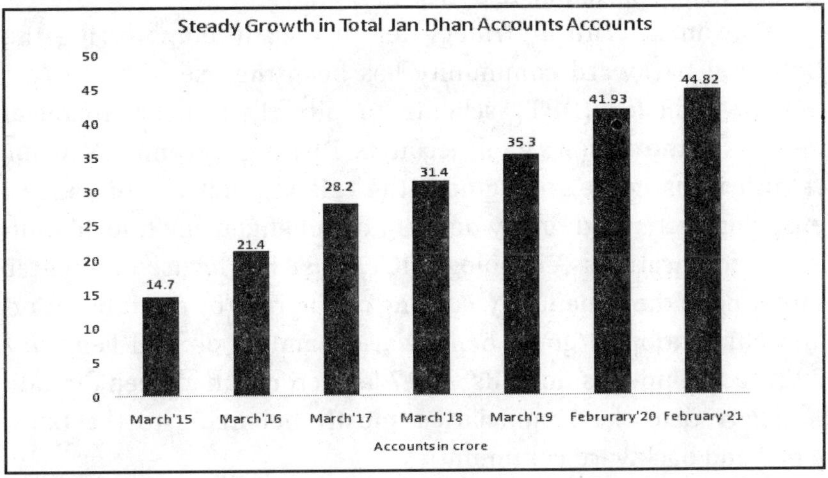

(Source: PMJDY)

Another interesting statistic in this regard is essential to point out the success of the initiative and the social transformation it has ushered. As the latest National Family Health Survey (NFHS) has shown, today, 80.9% women have a bank or savings account that they themselves use.[267] This huge number shows the confidence Jan Dhan accounts has given to India's women, making them realize how they can improve lives through financial inclusion.

Further, in terms of expanding financial inclusion on a massive scale,the Modi government brought forth the BHIM app. It is a biometric payment system app using Aadhaar platform and based on Unified Payment Interface (UPI) to facilitate e-payments directly through a bank. The app, an out and out Indian innovation, was launched on the birth anniversary of Dr. Babasaheb Ambedkar to mark the giant foray in ensuring financial equality. BHIM app can be used on all mobile devices. The digital payments interface saw the number of transactions crossing 1 billion in a month for the first time, in October 2021, marking a significant change in the way India transacts. Since its launch till January 2022, the app registered just over 19 crore downloads.[268] It has caused a paradigm shift by bringing in people who were otherwise averse to technology or unable to access it.

The most critical strategy for financially empowering the Dalit and backward community has been the use of the Direct Benefit Transfer (DBT) scheme to directly transfer financial benefits to the citizen's bank accounts. DBT is government's major reform initiative to re-engineer the existing delivery processes, ensuring better and timely delivery of benefits using Information & Communications Technology (ICT). DBT has focused on better targeting of the beneficiary, curbing of pilferage by de-duplication and elimination of ghost beneficiaries, and so on. Till February 2022, a whopping sum of Rs. 21.47 lakh crore[269] had been directly transferred to the beneficiaries, mostly belonging to the Dalit, tribal and backward communities.

Equal Opportunities to All

PM Modi has expanded the ambit of social equality to include equal opportunities for women, poor and the disabled. He sees social justice to apply to all forms of social discrimination to include gender-based hierarchies, class-based inequalities and for people who are discriminated against on account of physical infirmities. Thus, the scope of social empowerment has been enlarged to cover all the disadvantaged communities with an aim to create a just and equitable order.

Women empowerment or nari shakti has been one of the most important themes in the Modi government. Not only have women leaders been occupying the highest political, defence and service posts; the PM Modi has laid special emphasis on uplifting the social condition of women in the society, both by means of social change and public welfare schemes. Hailing the beginning of 'Beti Bachao Beti Padhao' campaign, PM Modi aims to change the larger mindset of society. This campaign has instilled a renewed enthusiasm in the society for saving the girl-child and promoting the cause of girl and women education. Under Sukanya Samriddhi Yojana, over 2.73 crore accounts have been opened and nearly Rs. 1.19 lakh crore deposited for securing a brighter future for the girl-child (as December 2021).[270]

Healthcare space saw the launch of Pradhan Mantri Surakshit Matritva Abhiyaan which has offered more than 3.02 crore antenatal check-ups, identified more than 25.46 lakh high-risk pregnancies in over 19,215 medical facilities across India, as in November 2021.[271] Further, to prevent malnutrition as an impediment to the health of the mother and the child, the Modi government has to date transferred Rs. 10.244 crore to over 2.5 crore mothers under the Pradhan Mantri Matru Vandana Yojana.[272] And by passing the Maternity Benefit (Amendment) Bill, 2017, India became one of the few countries in the world to offer six months of maternity leave. This was a historic step undertaken by the Modi government to remove the gender disadvantage faced by working mothers in urban areas.

In December 2021, the Modi government took up another historic step. A law was passed in Parliament that formally raised the marriageable age for girls to 21 years.[273] This step was widely appreciatedas it was noted for its sync with the times and the opportunities it creates for seeking higher education and pursuing careers for aspiring Indian women.

As PM Modi says, *"New India can progress only by empowering nari shakti. It is with this thought that the government is taking many progressive steps to facilitate the same. Changes are being made to systems, attitudes and institutions. Recently, the Maternity Benefits Bill has been amended to increase the maternity leave from 12 weeks to 26 weeks. This is a huge leap! Even some of the most developed nations pale in comparison to the maternity benefits in our nation."*[274]

Under the Modi government, a holistic perspective has been taken to qualitatively enhance women's lives. An example of this is the Ujjwala scheme that frees women, especially in the rural areas, from hours of harmful exposure to unclean fuel and poisonous gases. Over 9 crore poor women and their families are living a smoke-free life due to free LPG connections (as on February 2022).[275] Considering the success of the scheme, its ambit has been extended to all poor households in the country. Similarly, under MUDRA collateral-free loans, in terms of number of accounts, women entrepreneurs who secured loans stood at 21.7 crore as on 20th December, 2021.[276]

Economically deprived communities face the dual burden of economic inequality, which, in turn, results in greater social discrimination. More often than not, socially disadvantaged communities overlap with the economically poor strata of society. Hence, lifting the poor out of poverty is equivalent to providing social justice to backward communities. In this context, schemes like Direct Benefit Transfer, collateral-free loans through the MUDRA yojana, providing farmers protection under Pradhan Mantri Fasal Bima Yojana (PMFBY), PM Kisan Samman Nidhi (PM-KISAN), five lakh worth of health cover announced under the national health protection scheme and DAY, the national rural livelihoods mission which seeks to reach out to 8-9 crore rural poor households for organising them into Self-Help Groups (SHGs) are commendable.

The Modi government has given a whole new dimension to

the welfare of persons with disability. While historically persons with disability have been referred to as viklang, which has a very disempowering connotation, PM Modi, instead has given them a new identity of Divyang, meaning the 'divine people'. In fact, an entirely new department was set up solely for the welfare of our Divyang population. Even the name of the Department of Disability Affairs was changed to the Department of Empowerment of Persons with Disabilities to send the message that 'empowerment' would be the key to the policies and programmes for the disadvantaged. The welfare of Divyangs has not been restricted to the word; instead, various new initiatives have been taken for the empowerment of the same.

In a significant move towards the empowerment of the disabled, the Modi government passed the Rights of Persons with Disabilities Bill, 2016, replacing the existing Persons with Disabilities Act, 1995. The new Act increases the reservation provided to Divyangs in the government jobs and also drastically increases the categories of disabilities under its ambit from a mere seven to 21.

In line with the motto of 'Sabka Saath, Sabka Vikas, Sabka Vishwas, Sabka Prayaas', the Modi government has resolved to provide universal accessibility. The government had launched the accessibility campaign called the Sugamya Bharat Abhiyan under which it targeted to make at least 50% of all government buildings in the national capital and all state capitals 'fully accessible' for the disabled. The government, under the 'Sugamya Bharat Abhiyan' has made about 1,000 government buildings and more than 650 railway stations fully accessible to Divyang.[277] A lot of emphasis was laid on education of students suffering from disabilities. A total of 46,000 scholarships have been set aside for Students with Disabilities (SwD) under the pre-matric scholarship scheme and 16,650 under the post-matric scholarship scheme.[278]

There is greater optimism in the governance channels due to the motto of Sabka Saath, Sabka Vikas, Sabka Vishwaas, Sabka

Prayaas reaching people on the ground. The all-round development model that includes social and economic empowerment alongwith equal opportunities presents a remarkable moment to free the nation from the politics of social constructs. In fact, it is giving way for India to pave the way for a larger national construct that is inclusive and progressive and in line with the vision of Dr. Babasaheb Ambedkar.

□

11

Gender Equality: Empowering Women

"Today, nari shakti has shown inner fortitude and self-confidence has made her self-reliant. Not only have women advanced themselves but have also carried the country and society to newer heights. After all, our dream of New India is the one where women are strong and empowered and are equal partners in the development of the country. Today, the country is moving forward from the path of women development to women-led development."

—Prime Minister Narendra Modi[279]

A sense of collectiveness has seeped in our national consciousness. It is an awareness of our role in the building of our nation that is inspiring citizens to join the movement that calls for change and transformation in our governance, discourse, societal norms and even the way we think. The fact that Swachh Bharat received such an enthusiastic response from all quarters of citizenry makes one believe that each one of us are not only pining for change, we are actually getting down to freeing society from years of distortions that had creeped in.

Among the many calls for action made by Prime Minister Narendra Modi, one of the most pertinent has been encouraging discourse on women's participation and their contribution to the development of a nation. The shifting narrative from women development to women-led development is becoming the basis of a new India. Today, the government is working towards a vision where women will not just be seen as beneficiaries of the system; rather, they will be active agents of change and lead the growth story from the front. Women are envisioned as doers, achievers, leaders and, most importantly, equal partners in the resurgence of India. This is the dream with which Dr. B.R. Ambedkar had drafted the Constitution, which is one of the most progressive constitutions around the world in envisaging the role of women as equal and integral to a nation.

The basis of the Constitution, as laid down in the Preamble, is entrenched in the values of justice, liberty, equality and fraternity. These principles, that make the very crux of Indian political thought, stood equally for all, irrespective of class, caste, region, religion or gender classifications. It held a message for the world that women of India would not have to struggle for something that comes as their natural right. This is pertinent in the light of centuries of struggle women had to put in other parts of the world to be allowed suffrage rights.

Hence, India as a nation has always been politically progressive, if one were to follow the Constitution in letter and spirit. For instance, Article 15(1) prohibits discrimination on the grounds of sex. Article 15(3), which allows for positive discrimination of women, is basically affirmative action to help women work towards equality. Article 16(2) says that no citizen will be discriminated against or be ineligible for any employment or office on the grounds of sex. Along with this, Article 39 has multiple provisions to allow women to get an equal opportunity to work and earn a livelihood. Article 39(d) makes the State responsible to secure equal pay for equal work for both men and women. Article 39(e) makes the State ensure that the health and the strength of women workers is not exploited. A large part of the credit goes to the architect of the Constitution, Dr. Babasaheb Ambedkar. In fact, as the first Law Minister of Independent India,

Dr. Babasaheb Ambedkar had pushed hard for the Hindu Code Bill's enactment as law in 1948, which sought to overhaul the status quo and put women on par with men regarding several subjects, including property, divorce and succession.

It would not be an exaggeration to say that Dr. Babasaheb Ambedkar's views on women empowerment have been translated into a grand vision for women-led development. However, if one is to take forward this vision, a thorough analysis of the obstacles faced by women on account of their gender needs to be considered. In the entire life-cycle of a woman, from her childhood to motherhood to old age, there are myriad opportunities for government interventions that may generate positive outcomes, not just for a woman as an individual, but for a society as a whole. From massive financial inclusion of women through Jan Dhan Yojana to improving their lives within their own families through Ujjwala, a number of initiatives are already bearing fruit. From women becoming job creators though the MUDRA yojana to changing mind-sets through Beti Bachao, Beti Padhao (BBBP) programme, the Modi government seems to have been drawn from Dr. Babasaheb Ambedkar's vision.

In order to understand the implications of each step taken in the direction of women empowerment in the last few years, a life-cycle analysis is necessitated.

Protecting and Nurturing the Girl Child

Our nation's biggest misfortune has been the practice of female foeticide that resulted in a skewed sex ratio. Despite years of deterrence, harsh laws and awareness campaigns, the practice continued to exist. In the course of so many years, many governments have put legal sanctions in place, but change is slow because the people's perception of women was not changing fast enough. The Pre-Conception & Pre-Natal Diagnostic Techniques Act (PCPNDT), which criminalises sex determination of an unborn child, was passed in the year 1994. This Act was brought in with the intention to control the declining sex ratio and arrest female foeticide. But, even after a decade and a half after the Act was put in place, Census 2011 figures showed a scary trend of a declining child sex ratio (CSR) at 918 out of 1,000; 244 districts had a CSR of less than the national average.[280]

This indicated that even with the legal sanctions in place, systemic change was not possible without uprooting deep-seated biases. The boy-preference entrenched in the minds of communities across India cannot just be addressed with laws. It was with this understanding that this government started the flagship Beti Bachao, Beti Padhao (BBBP) movement.

In Haryana state, with a heavily skewed child sex ratio, the Prime Minister urged the people to let the girl child live and prosper. In the same vein, a total of 161 intensive districts were identified across the country for advocacy campaigns to change the mind-set of people with a tri-ministerial initiative. At the district level, numerous activities were undertaken to change perceptions. From the celebration of the birth of girls with plantation drives, to rewards and recognitions, the best panchayats registering a change, to the successful 'Selfie with Daughter' campaign spearheaded by the Prime Minister himself, each step in this process was from the book of Dr. Babasaheb Ambedkar, which called for the breaking of stereotypes.

The policy intervention did not completely negate the concerns of the parents, but tried to understand it and provide them with a solution. Like the Sukanya Samriddhi Yojana, which provides the parents with a solution to the financial insecurity that they associate with the girl-child. Under Sukanya Samriddhi Yojana, over 2.73 crore accounts have been opened and nearly

Rs. 1.19 lakh crore deposited for securing a brighter future for the girl-child (till December 2021).[281]

The amount saved under Sukanya Samriddhi can be later used to fund the higher education and the marriage of the girl.

"If a daughter is born, plant five trees in your farm as an occasion of happiness for all and use its produce for the benefit of the girl in the future,"said Prime Minister Modi.

Through the course of just two years, BBBP was able to improve the Sex Ratio at Birth (SRB) in 104 out of 161 districts and institutional deliveries improved in 146 districts. 119 districts reported progress in the first trimester of registration.[282]

As a result, the scheme was extended to 640 districts. Between 2014-15 and 2020-21, the Sex Ratio at Birth (SRB) improved by 19 points, improving from 918 to 937. Out of 640 districts covered under this initiative, 422 districts registered improvement in SRB during 2014-15 to 2018-2019.

Districts with very low SRB in 2014-15 have shown huge improvement after implementation of the scheme, e.g., Mau (Uttar Pradesh) from 694 (2014-15) to 951 (2019-20), Karnal (Haryana) from 758 (2014-15) to 898 (2019-20), Mahendergarh (Haryana) from 791 (2014-15) to 919 (2019-20), Rewari (Haryana) from 803 (2014-15) to 924 (2019-20), and Patiala (Punjab) from 847 (2014-15) to 933 (2019-20).

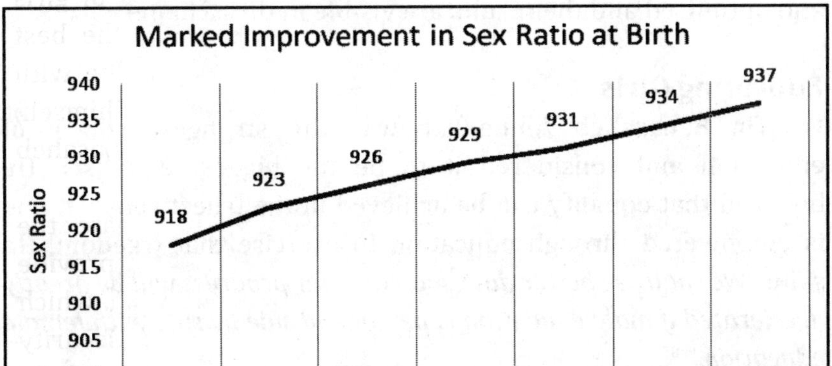

(Source: National Family Health Survey)

Meanwhile, the percentage of 1st Trimester ANC Registration got a boost from 61% in 2014-15 to 71% in 2019-20. Percentage of institutional deliveries has displayed an improving trend from 87% in 2014-15 to 94% in 2019-20. In terms of education, Gross Enrolment Ratio of girls in the schools at secondary level improved from 76 (2014-15) to 78 (2019-20), while the percentage of schools with functional separate toilets for girls increased from 92.1% in 2014-15 to 96.9% in 2019-20.[283]

The BBBP scheme has successfully brought into focus important issues, such as female infanticide, lack of education amongst girls and deprivation of their basic rights and actually brought out solutions through a social behavioural transformation. What's more, it is a fine example of successful engagement of community to defy the age-old biases against the girl-child.

In a massive achievement, India's sex ratio improved in 2021 with 1,020 females to every 1000 males– clocking a female majority for the first time ever.[284] Dr. Babasaheb Ambedkar's understanding of legal sanctions being only as strong as behavioural changes is something that the government has used and optimised and the results are visible in this scheme.

Educating Girls

Dr. Babasaheb Ambedkar was the strongest votary of education and considered it to be the biggest equaliser. He believed that equality can be achieved in the truest sense, if one is empowered through education to exercise that freedom. He said: *"We shall see better days soon and our progress will be greatly accelerated if male education is persuaded side by side with female education."*[285]

Dr. Babasaheb Ambedkar said that children emulate the behaviour of both their parents and, hence, it is important that both men and women need to be educated, bold and fearless to pass across the same attributes to their children. If you theorise Dr. Babasaheb Ambedkar's idea of social justice, education would be the biggest tool that he envisaged.

The BBBP programme puts the education of girls at the centre of discussion. Through the course of the past few years, the Modi government has been able to bring in a change in the mindset of communities regarding the education of girls through enrolment drives and advocacy campaigns. Many district administrations launched their own education drives, like 'Apna bachcha, apna vidyalaya', 'Udaan Initiative' and 'School chalein hum'.

The integrated Centrally-sponsored scheme for school education– Samagra Shiksha was launched in 2018-19. The scheme extends from pre-school to Class XII and aims to ensure inclusive and equitable quality education at all levels of school education without any discrimination on grounds, such as social/ economic standing, gender, etc. Under the scheme a separate stipend is given for girl-child, and especially under CWSN (Children with Special Needs) category.

PM Modi had also discussed the topic of girls' education in his popular 'Mann Ki Baat' programme. External barriers towards girls' education, like lack of toilets in schools was also addressed through programmes, like Swachh Vidyalaya, with a fascinating response to it. In his first ever Independence Day speech as PM Modi declared that he would ensure the construction of separate toilets for girls in every government school in one year. In just a year, the Swachh Vidyalaya programme hasbuilt over 4 lakh such toilets in a bid to bring the dropout rate of girls down.

The National Scheme of Incentive to Girls for Secondary Education (NSIGSE) focusses upon reducing drop-out rate of girls belonging to SC/ST communities in secondary schools. A unique feature of the scheme is the way it addresses almost all reasons responsible for this situation, especially in rural areas– lack of female toilets, fear of safety, etc. Among other perks, girls are given an opportunity to train in self-defence techniques. A special stipend is also made available to Divyang girls.

Girls overall can also secure scholarships of up to Rs. 12,000 under the National Means-cum-Merit Scholarship Scheme (NMMSS).

Between 2014-15 and 2021-22, the percentage of girls getting scholarships has gone up from just under 33% to around 53%. The government is also promoting technical education among girls by providing a tuition fee of up to Rs. 30,000 through the Pragati scholarship. The UDAN scheme is a mentorship programme for girls to transition from school to technical education. Under the Modi government, girls now have equal opportunities to dream and pursue their ambitions through quality education.

PM Modi made an announcement during his Independence Day speech of 2021 that all Sainik Schools will now be open for girls. Following the announcement, more than 350 girls have been admitted and the strength is bound to increase. Transformation of Sainik Schools from all boy schools to co-education has also opened doors of quality training of girl cadets at par with boys.

Dignity within the Family

"Let every girl who marries stand by her husband, claim to be her husband's friend and equal, and refuse to be his slave. I am sure if you follow this advice, you will bring glory and honour to yourselves."[286]

—Dr. B.R. Ambedkar

For Dr. Babasaheb Ambedkar, the quest for equality began within the family. Equality was not just an idea for the wider society, but one which needed to be embedded in each and every action of individuals, both within and outside their families. Dr. Babasaheb Ambedkar did not diminish the position of women in the family and respected their roles as mothers and wives. He advocated the freedom of choice for women and believed that they should not have a master-slave relationship with their husbands and should rather be on friendly terms with them.

One of the most dominant and impactful legacies of Dr. Babasaheb Ambedkar in the domain of women empowerment and legal empowerment was granting Hindu women the right to inherit property. It was not just that– the rights ambit was subsequently extended to a lot of other freedoms pertaining to marriage, succession, guardianship, adoption and maintenance. His efforts also allowed widows to have a share of property, which they were denied earlier. Dr. Babasaheb Ambedkar said: *"On wealth depends Independence and a woman must be very particular to retain her wealth and rights, to help retain her freedom."*[287]

Dr. Babasaheb Ambedkar wanted all women to be equal and was determined to ensure apt conditions in which they could thrive and prosper. Though his work focussed on Hindu women, he could not do much about ameliorating the condition of Muslim women. Dr. Babasaheb Ambedkar was extremely critical of Muslim Personal Law and especially on the plight of Muslim women. On Muslim women and divorce as prescribed in personal laws, Dr. Babasaheb Ambedkar said:

> *"She cannot escape the marriage-tie, however irksome it may be. While she cannot repudiate her marriage, the husband can always do it without having to show any cause."*[288]

Decades have passed, but electoral compulsions fuelled by minority appeasement made political parties turn away from the cause of Muslim women. The debate picked up during the Shah Bano episode, but was brutally thwarted in between. Ever since, no government wanted to take up the contentious issue of rights of Muslim women. Meanwhile, they continued getting oppressed and were subjected to emotional and physical violence, abandonment and penury due to social practices, such as instant triple talaq. Muslim women remained at the mercy of their husbands, who could divorce them by just uttering the word 'talaq' thrice. Dr. Babasaheb Ambedkar's pursuit of social justice hit a roadblock when it came to addressing Muslim Personal Law. Dr. Babasaheb Ambedkar faced many hurdles when a large section of the people were opposed to his reforms. Perhaps, any reformative idea has to go through this rite of passage, but, if the end will help women get that elusive freedom, then it is a fight worth fighting.

After decades, a decisive Modi government took up this cause and passed The Muslim Women (Protection of Rights on Marriage) Act, 2019, criminalising instant triple talaq. It has been a landmark step towards inclusiveness and gender justice. Triple talaq dropped by 82% within one year of passing of the Act. On August 1, 2021, 'Muslim Women Rights Day' was observed across the country to celebrate the enactment of the law. Through this law, the government has strengthened 'self-reliance, self-respect and self-confidence' of the Muslim women of the country and protected their constitutional, fundamental and democratic rights.

Another landmark reform under the Modi government was the proposed amendment to the Prohibition of Child Marriage Act (PCMA), 2006, to raise the legal age of marriage of women from 18 to 21 years in 2021, that seeks to bring uniformity in the marriageable age of men and women. Once approved by the Parliament, the amendment will ensure gender parity and equality. The legal marriageable age of girls is 18 years. Studies have suggested that many girls are forced to drop out of schools and married off by their families, crushing their dreams of creating a bright future for themselves. The government expects that this will help more girls to study further, and even contribute towards the economic growth of the country.

A bold step taken by the Modi government was the removal of Articles 370 and 35A, which were clearly prejudicial to women's empowerment. Both Articles created classes of citizens (A, B and C grade), thus rejecting the idea of equality. Under the law, women and girls of the state were issued a conditional Permanent Resident Certificate (known also as Permanent Hereditary State-subject Certificate) valid only till marriage. If a girl married a non-state subject, she, her husband and also children would lose all rights in the state. Strangely, if a man would marry an outsider, his rights would remain intact and would also extend to the spouse and children. With the abolition of the two Articles in 2019, not only a big roadblock in integrating the Jammu & Kashmir into

India has been overcome; it has ensured justice to the women of the region and empowered them with equal rights.

Ending Drudgery for Women

One common concern visible in most rural households is the drudgery associated with cooking and the collection of firewood. Women spend up to four hours in a day collecting firewood and often have to face uneven terrain and unsafe conditions through all-weather situations. However, it does not end with the unproductivity and the drudgery associated with the long walks. Cooking using firewood has an adverse impact on the health of women because of the smoke and is akin to smoking multiple cigarettes in a day.

The flagship Ujjwala Yojana of the government has provided LPG cylinders to more than 9 crore women across India as on January 2022.[289] The gas cylinders are registered in the names of the women beneficiaries and 35% of these beneficiaries belong to the SC/ST categories. Beneficiaries of the programme have reported not just better health, but have also been saving time, which they are utilising to learn a new skill, indulge in financially productive pursuits, spend on the education of children or simply rest.

Decades after gaining Independence, the political leadership of India failed to provide even basic amenities to millions of Indians. Rural India was particularly neglected and villagers, especially women and young girls, were forced to defecate in fields or secluded areas because they did not have access to toilets. Under Swachh Bharat, the government is on a mission to construct household toilets in rural and urban India. Under Swachh Bharat Mission– Grameen, nearly 10.9 crore toilets have been built, resulting in over 6 lakh villages being declared 'open defecation-free'.[290]The country now boasts of almost 100% rural sanitation coverage due to availability of toilets.

Under Swachh Bharat Mission (urban), over 62 lakh

household toilets and 6 lakh community/public toilets have been constructed. Already 4,371 cities have been declared open defecation-free (ODF). With toilets constructed inside homes, women no longer have to step out at all hours for personal requirements. A simple toilet has given them a chance to lead a life of dignity and safety. What's more, lack of toilets in schools was once a big reason for girls to stop going to school. With toilets constructed in schools, that has changed!

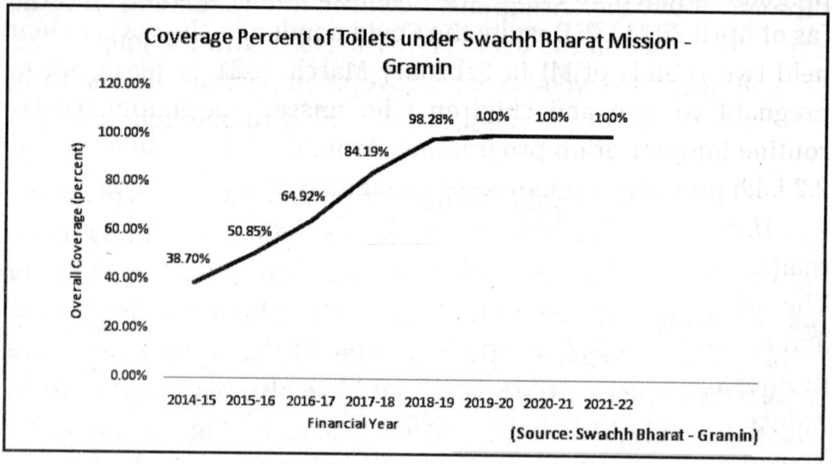

Holistic Healthcare for Women

Empowering mothers amounts to empowering the whole family. The government has laid special and much-needed emphasis on taking forward Dr. Babasaheb Ambedkar's vision of equality for women through adequate health provisions.

The Pradhan Mantri Surakshit Matritva Abhiyan (PMSMA) aims at arresting maternal and neo-natal mortality by providing comprehensive and quality ante-natal care to all pregnant women. More than 12,800 government health facilities across the country conduct free check-ups on the 9th of every month. Adequate check-ups and follow up can lead to much improved health parameters for pregnant women. More than 3.02 crore antenatal check-ups have been so far conducted, and 24.56 lakh high risk pregnancies have been identified under across states/ UTs till beginning of December 2021.[291]

Apart from check-ups, proper vaccination under Mission Indradhanush and cash incentives of Rs. 5,000, in three instalments, for pregnant and lactating mothers under Pradhan Mantri Matru Vandana Yojana are ensuring a safe pregnancy and healthy child. Under Mission Indradhanush nearly 1 crore pregnant women and 3.86 crore children have been immunised (as of April 2021).[292] Despite the Covid pandemic, the government held two rounds of MI in February-March 2021 to reach out to pregnant women and children who missed vaccination under routine immunisation programme. Around 9.5 lakh children and 2.2 lakh pregnant women were vaccinated in these rounds.

Under the Pradhan Mantri Matru Vandana Yojana, more than 2.58 crore women had availed benefits till February 2022.[293] The scheme helps to improve the health of pregnant women and lactating mothers and reduce the impact of malnutrition. It promotes good nutrition, feeding and vaccination practices to reduce infant mortality and malnutrition. Poshan Abhiyaan, also known as the National Nutrition Mission (NNM), was launched in 2018 to tackle the malnutrition problem. The scheme focuses on improving the nutritional condition of adolescents, children, pregnant women and lactating mothers. So far, a total of 10.5 crore beneficiaries have gained from the scheme.

An outcome of all these steps can be seen from the declining maternal and infant mortality rates in the country. The Infant Mortality Rate (IMR) has reduced from 37 per 1,000 live births in 2015 to 30 per 1,000 live births in 2019 at the national Level. The Maternal Mortality Ratio (MMR) has reduced significantly from 130 per 1 lakh live births in 2014-16 to 103 in 2017-19.[294] This 20.7% improvement is a significant achievement of the efforts of the Modi government to address this issue comprehensively.

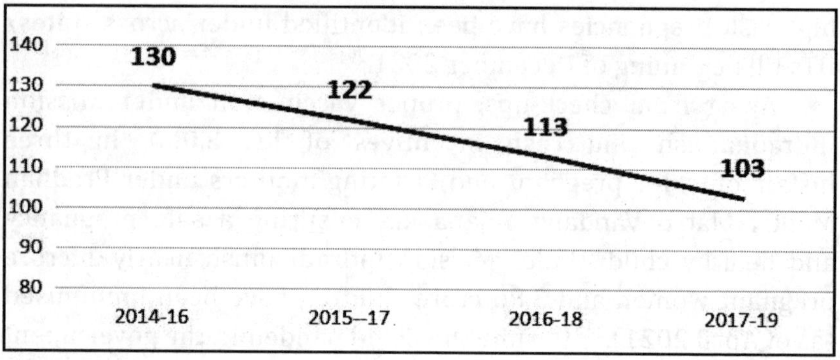

(Source: Registrar General of India)[295]

Economic Empowerment of Women

One of the most significant contributions of Dr. Babasaheb Ambedkar was on providing the necessary and conducive environment for women to enter the workforce. He believed that women cannot truly be liberated unless they are economically uplifted. That is why, he advocated that women by law, should have the equal right to work, right to equal pay and have equal economic rights.

Between 1942 and 1946, as Labour Member in the Viceroy's Executive Council, Dr. Babasaheb Ambedkar passed several progressive legislations relating to better working conditions for women workers. These dealt with casual leave, privilege leave, earned leave, compensation in case of injury and pension. He was the first person to bring in equal pay for equal work, irrespective of gender in the country. In fact, he had ensured that it found place in the Constitution in the Directive Principles (Article 39 (d)).

The stance taken on women working in the mines becomes amply clear when one reads the words of Dr. Babasaheb Ambedkar spoken in February 1944. Addressing the Central Legislative Assembly, Dr. Babasaheb Ambedkar was categorical in spelling out the mistake of previous governments:[296]

"The House will recall that the Government of India had accepted the principle of prohibiting women working

underground long before the Convention came into existence. The matter, so far is my study of it goes, was first debated in the year 1923 when the Government of India brought in a bill for the amendment of the Indian Coal Mines Act. I would like to remind the house that the original purpose of the bill was very limited one. It was a purpose merely to introduce safety measures in coal mines, but when the measurewas taken to the Select Committee, the Select Committee in its judgement thought that the Government of India ought to go forward and take a bold step and claim powers in the Act in order to prohibit the working of women underground. In the Select Committee the Government of India accepted the principle. Not only did the Government of India accept the principle but they framed regulations with the definite and deliberate object of eliminating women labour from working underground."

Economic equality is not possible without financial inclusion. And under the Modi government, the single biggest task of economic integration of women has been their inclusion in banking through the Jan Dhan accounts. By February 2022, 24.98 crore women had bank accounts of their own.[297] This massive financial inclusion meant that women could now get direct payments into their bank accounts for various schemes, like Ujjwala, maternity benefits and even wages under MGNREGA. This is in line with Dr. Babasaheb Ambedkar's vision of economic equality where women do not have to be dependent on others for their social security.

Going a step ahead, the government has enabled women to not just be job seekers, but create jobs on their own, making a sustainable and impactful change in their lives. The Pradhan Mantri MUDRA Yojana was aimed at promoting self-reliance among women by removing the barrier of access to credit and promoting entrepreneurship among them. Though the MUDRA Yojana is open to everyone, about 68% (as of November 2021) of the total borrowers were women entrepreneurs (21.73 crore).[298]

Special incentives of Rs. 2 lakh are given to women entrepreneurs under PM Bhartiya Janaushadhi Pariyojana (PMBJP) to set up Janaushadhi Kendras selling inexpensive generic medicines for the poor.

'Stand Up India' financially empowers women to lead a better life through entrepreneurship. Empowering women and weaker segments of society is an important tool for their uplift and contributes towards the country's economic development. By the end of February 2022, more than 82.5% (1,07,398) accounts with an amount of Rs. 24,626 crore had been sanctioned to women entrepreneurs under the scheme.[299,300] Women have shown great interest in PM Modi's flagship Startup India initiative as well. Up to 46% of the 66,000 odd DPIIT recognised startups have at least one female director.[301]

Maternity Benefit Act

One of the most celebrated contributions of Dr. Babasaheb Ambedkar was the passing of the Mines Maternity Benefit Act, which provided women working in the mines with an eight-week leave for childbirth. But, before that, he had brought in the first-ever instance of maternity leave in the Bombay legislature for factory women workers and a revolutionary attempt at making workplaces more inclusive and equitable. Way back in 1929, Dr. Babasaheb Ambedkar said:

> *"It is in the interest of the nation that the mother ought to get a certain amount of rest during the prenatal period and, also subsequently, and the principle of the Bill is based entirely on that principle..."*[302]

Dr. Babasaheb Ambedkar thought way ahead of his time and that is evident from this piece of legislation. Even today, women are sometimes confronted with the dilemma of choosing between their career and their child. Sometimes, it is due to economic compulsion and sometimes due to job insecurity, but in both the cases it is unfair towards women.

The Modi government has taken forward what was started by Dr. Babasaheb Ambedkar. The new amendment in the Maternity Benefit Act brought in by the government has extended the period of paid maternity leave for new mothers from 12 weeks to 26 weeks. This is a massive relief for women who can take adequate rest and recuperate without the associated financial insecurity. Additionally, there is also the provision of working from home for nursing mothers, which will help women balance personal and professional responsibilities.

The Act also makes it mandatory for organisations having more than 50 members to have a crèche within the office or factory premises for the children of employees. The amended Maternity Benefit Act is much more holistic and inclusive from the previous version as it extends to mothers who have adopted children and the commissioning mothers. This Act makes the workspace more conducive for women and will prevent sudden dropping out of female employees post pregnancy.

The government has also brought in other measures to encourage women to join the formal workforce. The 2018 Budget proposed an amendment to the Employees Provident Fund and Miscellaneous Provisions Act, 1952. The amendment would allow women to take home higher salary by reducing their contribution to EPF to 8% without any change in employer contribution. This would be done for the first three years of their employment.

The Modi government approved the Code on Occupational Safety, Health and Working Conditions Bill, 2019. It seeks to have a uniform threshold for welfare provisions, like creche, canteen, etc. and makes women's consent critical when required to work in night shifts. The Code on Wages Bill has already been passed in August 2019 by the Parliament, ensuring equal minimum wage for men and women workers.

Economic upliftment of women is vital to the strengthening of their social and political position.

Dr. Babasaheb Ambedkar had realised this early on and the government is translating his vision to reality.

Women Leading the Nation

Dr. Babasaheb Ambedkar had famously said: *"I measure the progress of a community by the degree of progress women have achieved."*[303] The discussion on women empowerment is incomplete without considering their political participation, especially in decision-making roles. As an institution that guides the entire nation, the government has a big role to play when it comes to being a role model for the society to emulate. Today, women are scripting their own destiny and with them the destiny of the nation. In the Modi government, women-led development has become a key theme with women taking on leadership roles. In its first term, the government set an example by appointing six women in the Union Council of Ministers. Notably, in his second term, PM Modi appointed 11 women to the Council, which is the highest-ever number in the history of India. Women ministers have been handling important ministries, such as Finance, Corporate Affairs, Women & Child Development, Rural Development, etc. in various capacities.

The same could be seen at the party-level politics. The 17th Lok Sabha has the highest number (78) of elected female MPs and almost half of those are from the BJP. Even at the grassroots level of democracy, in panchayats and at city level, BJP is making a mark in women empowerment with an increasingly higher number of women representing the party, and winning. For example, six out of the 14 BJP-ruled Nagar Nigams in Uttar Pradesh in the year 2018 had women mayors.

Women in Defence

The Modi government has undertaken several initiatives towards boosting the role and presence of women in the Armed Forces. A Permanent Commission (PC) of women officers has been implemented in the Armed Forces. Women officers are serving proudly in various operational theatres of the Indian Army and can aspire to achieve greater glory and shoulder higher ranks and responsibility. PC to women officers in junior batches has also commenced. The National Defence Academy (NDA) will be inducting women cadets from June 2022. A total of 1,700 women soldiers will be inducted into the Corps of Military Police at the rate of 100 women per year (for 17 years). The first batch of women soldiers has successfully completed training and joined their units. This is a major development towards women empowerment in the country.[304]

Indian Army has commenced recruitment of women in the Military Police (MP) too. The first batch of 100 women MP personnel passed out in May 2021 and have been posted to various units. Women officers are being posted on frontline warships, including 'INS Vikramaditya', which has four women officers. A total of 28 women officers are placed across ranks, including as medical officers, on ships and numbers are increasing. In yet another first in the history of naval aviation, the first batch of women naval operations officers were inducted into the rotary wing and joined the helicopter squadron INAS 336 at 'INS Garuda', Kochi in February 2021.

Women officers are representing India overseas as well. The first woman officer was deputed to Maldives as part of operational crew for maiden Dornier deployment in September, 2020. Women officers have also been inducted in Remotely Piloted Aircraft (RPA) stream in 2021 and the first officer is presently undergoing RPA conversion training. First time in the history, Border Roads Organisation (BRO) appointed women officers to command important Road Construction Companies (RCC) along border areas, such as the important Indo-China Road connecting Munisairi-Bughdiar-Milam. On August 30, 2021, Major Aaina Rana took charge as Commanding Officer, 75 RCC in Chamoli, Uttarakhand, to become the first Indian Army engineer officer to command a road construction company. In fact, all three platoon commanders under her, Captain Anjana, AEE (Civ) Ms Bhawana Joshi, and AEE (Civ) Ms Vishnumaya K. have together created the first-ever women RCC.

Indian women are proving that given an opportunity, they can easily assume challenging leadership roles, akin to their male counterparts.

Holistic Development of Women

Legal protection, economic empowerment, social justice and changing mindsets are some of the pillars of Dr. Babasaheb Ambedkar's idea of women empowerment. In his lifetime, through the multiple roles that he had, he gave the women of this country, the hope, the expectation and the vision that they should have towards equality. Through the Constitution, he gave women the tools, the strength and the conviction to fight for their rights. He showed the path, but with time the path got shrouded with inaction. There was a need for someone to clear the air of despondence, find and connect with that progressive vision and lead the nation and its women towards that goal of equality and empowerment.

It seems that the government has finally been able to do that to hold the hand of a resurgent nation and guide it on the path laid down by one of its tallest leaders.

□

12

Team India: Building a Nation

"The basic principle of federalism is that the legislative and executive authority is partitioned between the Centre and the States, not by any law to be made by the Centre, but by the Constitution itself. This is what the Constitution does. The States under our Constitution are in no way dependent upon the Centre for their legislative or executive authority. The Centre and the States are co-equal in this matter"

— Dr. B.R. Ambedkar[305]

"Both the Union and the states are created by the Constitution, both derive their respective authority from the Constitution."

— Dr. B.R. Ambedkar[306]

Dr. B.R. Ambedkar, as the Chairman of the Drafting Committee, incorporated quasi-federal features in the Constitution of India. As a wise democrat, he emphasised, while discussing in the Constituent Assembly, the need of afederal constitution with unitary features. The chapter focusses on various spectrums of federalism, envisioned by Dr. Babasaheb Ambedkar and their relevance in the present context.

Article 1 of the Constitution of India describes India as a 'Union of States'. While submitting the Draft Constitution, Dr. Babasaheb Ambedkar unambiguously stated that although the Constitution may be federal in structure, the committee had preferred the usage of the term 'Union' to indicate two things:

1. The Indian federation is not the result of an agreement among the states.
2. The states have no right to secede from the federation. The federation is a Union because it is indestructible.

To quote him verbatim:[307]

"...the use of the word 'Union' is deliberate. I do not know why the word 'Union' was used in the Canadian Constitution. But I can tell you why the Drafting Committee has used it. The Drafting Committee wanted to make it clear that though India was to be a federation, the Federation was not the result of an agreement by the states to join in a Federation and that the Federation not being the result of an agreement no state has the right to secede from it. The Federation is a Union because it is indestructible. Though the country and the people may be divided into different states for convenience of administration the country is one integral whole, its people a single people living under a single imperium derived from a single source. The Americans had to wage a civil war to establish that the states have no right of secession and that their Federation was indestructible. The Drafting Committee thought that it was better to make it clear at the outset rather than to leave it to speculation or to dispute."

The intellectual depth of Dr. Babasaheb Ambedkar as a brilliant lawyer can be seen in the way he handled opprobrium in the house, regarding incorporation of quasi-federal features in the Constitution. By calling the Centre and states as co-equals in their legislative and executive capacity, he gave credence to the cultural and linguistic diversity of the states in India.

At the same time, he defended the structure against accusations of 'centralisation' by stating the fact that both Centre and the states derive their authority from the Constitution of India. He observed:

"A serious complaint is made on the ground that there is too much centralisation and the states have been reduced to municipalities. It is clear that this view is not only an exaggeration, but it is also founded on a misunderstanding of what exactly the Constitution contrives to do."[308]

According to him, the unitary bias in the Constitution is according to the time and circumstances. This unique feature, according to some constitutional experts, is basically to ensure safeguards and prevent centrifugal tendencies among the states. He observed:

"Yet the Constitution avoids the tight mould of federalism and could be both unitary as well as federal according to the requirements of time and circumstances."[309]

Further, while explaining why the residuary powers including the powers during the times of emergency are being vested in the Centre, Dr. Babasaheb Ambedkar had observed:

"There can be no doubt that in the opinion of the vast majority of the people, the residual loyalty of the citizen in an emergency must be to the Centre and not to the constituent states. For it is only the Centre which can work for a common end and for the general interests of the country as a whole."[310]

Dr. Babasaheb Ambedkar's view of 'question of federalism' in the Constitution, while clearly enunciating the relationship the Centre and the state ought to have, did not, in any way patronise the state or exceed its power. However, he still hinted at the Centre being at the helm and cautioned regional consideration not to supersede national interest.

Cooperative Federalism

"The Draft Constitution is Federal Constitution in as much as it establishes what may be called a dual polity. This dual polity under the proposed Constitution will consist of the Union at the Centre and the states at the periphery, each endowed with

sovereign powers to be exercised in the field assigned to them respectively by the Constitution."

— Dr. B.R. Ambedkar (1948)

Though Dr. Babasaheb Ambedkar did not talk of co-operative federalism specifically, his speeches have an implicit mention of the principle. While explaining the features of the Constitution, during the debates on the floor of the Constituent Assembly, he mentioned that the essence of Indian federalism is characterised by the Central and state polities working together. Indian federation should be seen as independent democratic units of governance (functional autonomy) at the national and state levels.

A strong Centre maintains unity among diversity in the country, while ensuring that no state lags behind in the course of development. The responsibility of taking care of astate financially to ensure its development is taken care of by the Finance Commission, which recommends a formula-based transfer of Union revenues to the states. The recommendation is approved by the Central Government through a reasonable debate in the Parliament.

Prime Minister Narendra Modi, in the same vein as Dr. Babasaheb Ambedkar, believes, in principle, in the mutual working of Central and state governments. He believes that the course of development should not be in isolation, but together; and the Centre and states should together share the fruits of progress. With regard to the usual stresses and tensions in inter-governmental relations between the Centre and states, PM Modi has given a clarion call to the nation to work as a team towards development.

He is of the view that in spite of parties with different ideologies at the helm of affairs in the Centre and states, no state should suffer from resource crunch that could hinder its development path.

"The Centre will join hands with the states in working towards the goal since it is possible only with cooperative federalism, wherein the Centre and states work together."[311]

— Prime Minster Narendra Modi

"Prime Minister and Chief Ministers together make a team... without Team India, Hindustan cannot make progress... country is above any [political] party. Whether it is Rajya Sabha or Lok Sabha, all opinions can be amalgamated for the sake of Team India."[312]

— Prime Minister Narendra Modi

In that spirit, the PM Modi-led government at the Centre has undertaken numerous measures to ensure co-operative federalism among the states and the Centre. Some of the major initiatives are worth mentioning.

Goods and Services Tax

"A consensus on the GST regime will go down in history as a great illustration of co-operative federalism. GST reflects the spirit of one nation, one aspiration, one determination."[313]

— Prime Minister Narendra Modi

The historic Goods and Services Tax was rolled out on 1st July, 2017, post the passage of the 101st Constitutional Amendment Act. The passing of GST was a critical event with respect to the state of fiscal federalism in India. A milestone in the indirect tax reforms in India, GST has subsumed a large number of Central and state taxes. With GST, States and the Centre are trading in a common national market.

In a federal polity like India, a major challenge for any Central Government is to take into confidence the states for a legislation, affecting both the state and the Centre. Unless both governments are in unison, the passage is not possible. The successful passage of GST, therefore, embodies a watershed moment in the history of co-operative federalism in India, wherein all states were taken into confidence, to pass the legislation. The whole process of the rollout of GST had been in discussion for a decade; however, previous Central Governments had failed in building consensus. It was here that the Modi government came forth, addressing the long-standing concerns. Having been a Chief Minister himself, he carried the concerns to the Centre and got issues like revenue loss compensation and tax revenue sharing mechanisms resolved in a manner that satisfied the state governments.

Goods and Services Tax Council, which is a constitutional body (Article 279A), comprises the Union Finance Minister, the Minister of State in charge of Revenue or Finance and the State Finance Ministers to recommend the GST rate, exemption limits among other things. This particular mechanism partially removes the possibility of a discord on different aspects of GST between the Centre and the states, and among the states themselves. The GST Council makes sure that the states are crucial partners in the decision-making.

In the pre-GST regime, states did not have a say in taxes that were exclusively collected, appropriated and levied by the Centre. The decisions in GST Council are taken by a majority of not less than three-fourths of weighted votes cast. Centre has one-third weightage of the total votes cast and all the states together have two-thirds weightage of the total votes cast. So, a major policy decision with regard to GST rates is not possible without the states giving a go ahead. There have been 46 meetings of GST council till September 2021.[314]

Some of the decisions taken by GSTC are as follows:

- The GST has replaced seven Central taxes, which are Central Excise Duty, Central Sales Tax, Purchase Tax, Additional Duties of Excise, Special Additional Duty of Customs, Service Tax and Cess and Surcharges.

- The GST would replace nine state taxes, namely State VAT, Luxury Tax, Entry Tax, Entertainment Tax, and surcharges in relation to goods and services.
- The abolition of various state taxes would facilitate inter-state trade and commerce and would remove cascading effect of taxes.
- The 12% and 18% slabs in the GST structure could be soon merged; thereby Centre and states will be a step closer to the ideal of single standard GST rate.
- The decision taken in the 31st meeting of GSTC of simplifying tax structures, to fasten the pace of states meeting their revenue collection targets.

GST has improved ease of doing business by adopting a purely technology-driven interface, which facilitated transactions worth Rs. 11.3 lakh crore during FY2020-21. GST collection from April to February 2022 stood at Rs. 13.4 lakh crore.[315]

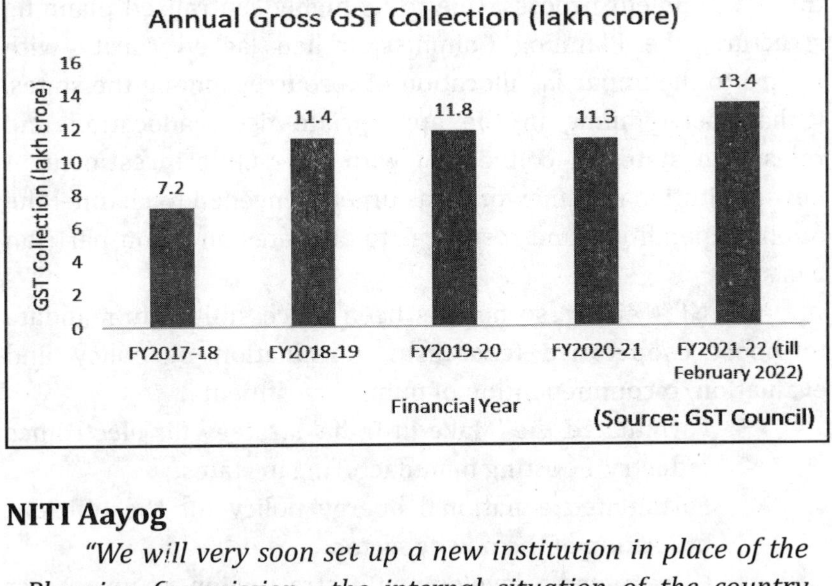

(Source: GST Council)

NITI Aayog

"We will very soon set up a new institution in place of the Planning Commission... the internal situation of the country has changed, global environment has changed... We need an

institution of creative thinking and for optimum utilisation of youth capability."[316]

— Prime Minister Narendra Modi

"Through the NITI Aayog, India will move away from the one-size-fits-all approach and forge a better match between schemes and needs of states."[317]

— Prime Minster Narendra Modi

The National Institution for Transforming India, or NITI Aayog, established on 1st January, 2015, was formed to further the cause of co-operative federalism by evolving a national consensus on developmental goals inspired by the views of all the states. The governing council of the NITI Aayog, consists of Chief Ministers of states, with the Prime Minister as its Chairman.

The NITI Aayog replaced the erstwhile Planning Commission, and came about from the urge to have greater federal inputs in the development process. Due to its highly centralised planning structure, the Planning Commission had lacked clarity with regard to the impartial allocation of resources among the states. It had been failing in the appropriate fiscal allocation and release to states in connection with the public investment. A new institutional framework was urgently needed to channel the public expenditure and resources to all states on a non-partisan basis.

The NITI Aayog, so far, has been successful in its mandate to boost cooperative federalism, formulation of policy and evaluation/recommendation of public investments:

- Formulated the 'Make in India' strategy for electronics industry, boosting manufacturing in states.
- Formulated a national energy policy for the efficient utilisation of the power sector.
- Constructed a developmental strategy for the north-east and hilly areas.

- It recommended closure of sick PSUs, strategic disinvestment of other CPSUs, thereby saving financial resources, which can be diverted for other critical expenditure to the states.
- Formulated a model law on leasing of land and framework of priorities for disinvestment.
- Based on the recommendations of three sub-groups of Chief Minsters, a new Central sector scheme (CSS) sharing system was notified and a transparent formula-based allocation of resources was reached.
- The pursuit of sustainable development goals (SDGs) by the government also needs co-operative federalism at its best. Here, NITI Aayog has played a major goal in the way the states are guided and advised, with a focus on addressing specific challenges and generating lessons for everyone in the form of best practice documentation.

15th Finance Commission

The Finance Commission is a constitutional body formulated under Article 280 of the Indian Constitution. It makes recommendations regarding the devolution of taxes between the Centre and the states from the divisible pool, inclusive of all Central taxes, excluding surcharges and cess. The Centre is transferring a bigger share of the central pool of taxes to the states– a 10 percentage point jump to 42% from a previous 32% as suggested by the 14th Finance Commission. This move, thereby, enhances the share of unconditional transfers to the states. The Modi-led government, in the spirit of treating states as partners in the long-term development agenda, had accepted the key recommendation.

The 15th Finance Commission (XVFC) Report, released in February 2021, was unique and wide ranging in many ways due to the ongoing Covid pandemic and its resulting impact on the country's overall economic growth. In total, the

Commission put forward 117 core recommendations in addition to numerous suggested reforms for the Union ministries and state governments respectively. To maintain predictability and stability of resources, especially during the pandemic, the report recommended maintaining the vertical devolution at 41% as in 2020-21. On horizontal devolution, while the report agreed upon the Census 2011 data as best representing the needs of states, the Commission assigned a 12.5% weight to the demographic performance criterion.

The Commission also recommended grants worth Rs. 4,800 crore from 2022-23 to 2025-26 for incentivising the states to enhance educational outcomes. An additional Rs. 6,143 crore has been proposed for online learning and development of professional courses (medical and engineering) in regional languages. A total of Rs. 45,000 crore is to be kept as performance-based incentive for all the states for carrying out agricultural reforms, and for amending their land-related laws on the lines of NITI Aayog's model law.

Snapshot of Grant Recommendations under 15th Finance Commission[318]	
Grant Components	**2021-26 (in crore)**
Revenue deficit grants	2.94
Local governments grants	4.36
Disaster management grants	1.22
Sector-specific grants	1.29
State-specific	0.49
Total in crore	10.33

For the health sector, the Commission has recommended health spending by states to be increased to more than 8% of their budget by 2022. The total grants-in-aid support to the health sector over the award period works out to Rs. 1.06 lakh crore, or 10.3% of the total grants-in-aid recommended by the Commission. Under Disaster Risk Management, Mitigation Funds have been proposed at the national and state levels, in line with the provisions of the Disaster Management Act. The funds could be used for those local level and community-based interventions that promote environment-friendly settlements and livelihood practices. The 15th Finance Commission recommended the total corpus of Rs. 1.60 lakh crore for states for disaster management for the duration of 2021-26, inclusive of the Union's share of Rs. 1.22 lakh crore. It has recommended six earmarked allocations for a total amount of Rs. 11,950 crore for certain priority areas as well.

Keeping in view the strategic requirements for national defence in the global context, it re-calibrated the relative shares of the Union and states in gross revenue receipts. This has enabled the Union to set aside resources for the special funding mechanism that XVFC has proposed. The Union Government may constitute in the Public Account of India, a dedicated non-lapsable fund, Modernisation Fund for Defence and Internal Security (MFDIS). The total indicative size of the proposed MFDIS over the period 2021-26 is Rs. 2.38 lakh crore.

The 15th Finance Commission Report provided range for fiscal deficit and debt path of both the Union and states with additional borrowing room to states based on performance in power sector reforms. In view of the uncertainty prevailing due to the Covid pandemic, XVFC suggested that the FRBM Act should undergo major restructuring and recommended that the time-table for defining and achieving debt sustainability may be examined by a high-powered inter-governmental group. It has strongly recommended that the Union and state governments amend their FRBM Acts, based on the recommendations of the group, so as to ensure that their legislations are consistent with the fiscal sustainability framework put in place.

Rationalisation of Centrally-sponsored Schemes (CSSs)

Major recommendations of a sub-group of Chief Minsters on rationalisation of Centrally-sponsored Schemes (CSSs) was accepted by the Central Government in 2016. The sub-group was set up after the decision was taken in the first meeting of the Governing Council of NITI Aayog.

One of the major recommendations accepted was to change the focus of CSSs. It was decided that the major focus should be on schemes that comprise the National Development Agenda where the Centre and states will work together in the spirit of Team India. The states will have autonomy in choosing schemes, which they wish to implement as per their need. Funds for these schemes would be allocated to states by the Ministry of Finance. The reduction in the number of schemes and the increase in devolution of resources by the Finance Commission further reduces the dependency of states on the Centre. States with sufficient financial coffers are allowed to borrow directly from the bilateral Official Development Assistance (ODA) partners. The financially capable states will not be dependent on Centre for the funds needed for infrastructure or welfare spending anymore.

In its report, the 15th Finance Commission has proposed that a threshold amount of annual appropriation should be fixed below which the funding for a CSS may be stopped. Below the stipulated threshold, the administrating department should justify the need for the continuation of the scheme. As the life cycle of ongoing schemes has been made co-terminus with the cycle of Finance Commissions, the third-party evaluation of all CSSs should be completed within a stipulated timeframe. The flow of monitoring information should be regular and should include credible information on output and outcome indicators.

From Co-operative Federalism to Cooperative, Competitive Federalism

"We want to promote cooperative federalism in the country. At the same time, we want a competitive element among the states. I call this new form of federalism co-operative and competitive federalism."[319]

— Prime Minister Narendra Modi

"In every state, there are a few districts where development parameters are strong. We can learn from them and work on weaker districts. A spirit of competitive and co-operative federalism is very good for the country."[320]

—Prime Minister Narendra Modi

PM Modi has been an ardent advocate of 'co-operative, competitive federalism'. The competitive spirit among the states to outperform each other on the trajectory of development would enhance shared prosperity and would enable collective upliftment of states. That competitive spirit is indispensable for a sustainable co-operative federalism. 'Sabka Saath, Sabka Vikas' (collective development through collective co-operation) will be possible only if healthy competition thrives between the states. Collective co-operation implies collective competition too.

For example, Vibrant Gujarat has been competing against the Sunrise State of Andhra Pradesh, Resurgent Rajasthan, Invest Madhya Pradesh, or UP Investors Summit, Credible Chhattisgarh, or a Happening Haryana. All these states are consistently working on strategies to attract foreign investors to put money into their local economies. A successful model of one state automatically entices other states to organise similar summits or festivals to gain access to multiple resources and the state-of-the-art technologies.

Keeping with the times, the new slogan of 'Sabka Saath, Sabka Vikas, Sabka Vishwas aur Sabka Prayas' also came through. The latter two, vishwas, i.e. trust and prayas, i.e. effort, signal the next step that is needed when it comes to co-operative federalism.

While the Centre and the states work to ensure that trust in relations is maintained and enhanced, the two also make efforts to take the lead on the direction decided on mutually, creating a win-win formula.

This sense of co-operative federalism has been a foundation stone for rolling out reforms over the years as well. For a federal country of continental dimensions, finding policy instruments at the national level to promote reforms by state governments is indeed challenging. However, the Modi government is firm in its belief that the spirit of Centre-state bhagidari can bring transformations. This approach was seen in various major initiatives like the 'one nation one ration card'; improving ease of doing business at state levels; getting states to uniformly notify floor rates of property tax and of water and sewerage charges in urban areas; or even the introduction of Direct Benefit Transfer (DBT). As PM Modi said while crediting the states for accepting this co-operative approach:[321]

> *"This was made possible due to our approach of 'Sabka Saath, Sabka Vikas aur Sabka Vishwas'. Officials who have been working on these reforms suggest that without this incentive of additional funds, enactment of these policies would have taken years. India has seen a model of 'reforms by stealth and compulsion'. This is a new model of 'reforms by conviction and incentives'."*

Pandemic that Unites a Nation

The Covid-19 pandemic exposed the inadequacy of public health systems worldwide and drew attention to the fact that governance matters. This emergency required meticulous, intricate, well-thought and coordinated, multi-sectoral response across the national, state and local level. Already overstretched due to an insufficient health infrastructure catering to the world's second-largest population, India has had to contend with two fierce waves of the pandemic within a year that forced the nation and its people to test their resolve to overcome all economic and personal odds and emerge as survivors.

Under the leadership of PM Modi, a task force was constituted to conduct research on Covid vaccines as early as April 2020. In November 2020, the Atmanirbhar Bharat Package 3.0 earmarked Rs. 900-crore under the Covid Suraksha Mission for Research & Development of an Indian Covid vaccine. Next, the Union Budget 2021-22 made provision of Rs. 35,000-crore for Covid-19 vaccines. From the beginning of the pandemic, PM Modi displayed confidence in the capabilities of Indian scientists and forwarded every possible support for the development of India-made Covid vaccines. Administrative processes, bureaucratic approvals and financial supports were all fast-tracked to support the development of these vaccines. Regular discussions with the states allowed the Central Government to remove any roadblocks that would otherwise have arisen in the logistics and distribution chain. Even when the economy was opened up again, the constant guidance and handholding of the states was pursued.

The state governments were kept in loop at all stages, and were made a part of the decision-making process or given appropriate guidance whenever it was sought. Even at the peak of the pandemic, PM Modi was involved in at least 25 meetings with important stakeholders, reviewing the oxygen and medicines situation, interacting with CMs, meeting the nation's leading doctors and pharma companies, engaging with leading oxygen manufacturers, involving Armed Forces in Covid assistance, connecting with state and district officials.[322] At his behest, the Group of Ministers (GoM) overseeing Covid management efforts conducted 24 meetings and the Health Ministry 97 review meetings with states, while administrators conducted over 120 meetings for coordinating a timely response and providing technical support at the height of the pandemic. This 'whole of government' approach adopted by the Modi government was particularly useful in the pandemic and fit right into the co-operative federalism model that PM Modi has referred to repeatedly.

The 'Covid-19 Vaccines Operational Guidelines' released in December 2020 is an example of the efficiency, far-sightedness and coordination among the various government bodies, ministries, market players and experts at the local, state and Central levels. Since the launch of India's vaccination drive on 16th January, 2021, till 15th March, 2022, the vaccination drive has covered more than 84% of the eligible population with both doses, while 100% of the eligible population had received atleast one dose. More than 2 crore people had taken the precautionary dose. Between the 15-18 group, 3.4 crore children had become fully vaccinated. The world's largest vaccine drive that happened in India is a prime example of the power that Team India can manifest, if the Centre and states come together.

In order to securely deliver the vaccines to the remotest corners of the country, the entire government machinery including the Indian Railways and the Indian Air Force, was activated. As per need, various ministries went beyond their piece of work to adapt to extraordinary circumstances. For example, when the country faced shortage of oxygen supply, the Indian Railways stepped up to run exclusive 'Oxygen Expresses' across the country. Public sector enterprises also stepped up to manufacture the much-needed medical equipment, PPE kits and even medical grade oxygen. All this was being done with PM Modi at the helm, who, through his leadership qualities, took a strictly apolitical view despite some provocations by certain quarters to politicise the pandemic response and vaccination drive.

Conclusion

The various spectrums of Indian federalism are unique and fit perfectly for a diversified country like ours. The gradual shift from a textbook definition of federalism to a dynamic co-operative and competitive federalism is worth mentioning. This change has been possible due to commitment of the Modi-led government towards adapting and effecting change for a better India, at the same time upholding and adopting tenets of Dr. Babasaheb Ambedkar's vision and his wisdom on the federal polity of the country.

> *"Dual polity under the proposed Constitution will consist of the Union at the Centre and the states at the periphery, each endowed with sovereign powers to be exercised in the field assigned to them respectively by the Constitution."*[323]
>
> **— Dr. B.R. Ambedkar**

□

Reference

Foreword

1. https://www.narendramodi.in/pm-modi-at-the-inauguration-of-maritime-india-summit-2016-in-mumbai-440341

Chapter-1

2. Central Water Commission (2016). Ambedkar's Contribution to Water Resources Development, 2nd ed., Delhi: Central Water Commission, pp.15-16
3. ISBN 0231136021, 9780231136020, Columbia University Press, 2005
4. Moon, V. (Ed.), (2014). Dr. Babasaheb Ambedkar: Writings and Speeches Vol. 9. 1st ed., New Delhi: Dr. Ambedkar Foundation, p.xvi
5. Dr. Babasaheb Ambedkar: Writings and Speeches, Vol.14, Part II, https://www.mea.gov.in/Images/CPV/Volume14_Part_II.pdf
6. Dr. Babasaheb Ambedkar Writings and Speeches, Vol.14, Part II, https://www.mea.gov.in/Images/CPV/Volume14_Part_II.pdf
7. Moon, V. (Ed.), (2014). Dr. Babasaheb Ambedkar: Writings and Speeches, Vol. 8, 1st ed., New Delhi: Dr. AmbedkarFoundation, p.117
8. S.N. Busi, Dr. B.R Ambedkar: Framing of Indian Constitution,Vol. 4, p. 472
9. Khapre, S. (2015). Congress never did B R Ambedkar justice, why recall him now, asks his grandson. [online],The Indian Express. https://indianexpress.com/article/india/india-others/congress-never-did-ambedkar-justice-why-recall-him-now/
10. Mann Ki Baat, (2018). [Radio] A.I.R. 25 March

Chapter-2

11. Moon, V. (Ed.), (2014). Dr. Babasaheb Ambedkar : Writings and Speeches, Vol. 1, 1st ed., New Delhi: Dr. Ambedkar Foundation, p.477
12. Moon, V. (Ed.), (2014). Dr. Babasaheb Ambedkar : Writings and Speeches, Vol. 10, 1st ed., New Delhi: Dr. Ambedkar Foundation, p. 124-127
13. https://www.narendramodi.in/text-of-prime-minister-shri-narendra-

modis-address-at-the-launch-of-make-in-india-global-initiative-2867
14. https://www.narendramodi.in/english-rendering-of-prime-minister-shri-narendra-modi-s-address-to-the-nation-on-12-5-2020-549627
15. https://twitter.com/narendramodi/status/1370224633572511749
16. https://twitter.com/narendramodi/status/1370224809666252807
17. https://pib.gov.in/PressReleasePage.aspx?PRID=1628344
18. https://dot.gov.in/sites/default/files/Public%20Procurement%20Notification3.pdf
19. https://pib.gov.in/newsite/PrintRelease.aspx?relid=229256
20. https://pib.gov.in/PressReleseDetailm.aspx?PRID=1810166
21. https://pib.gov.in/FactsheetDetails.aspx?Id=148581
22. https://www.pib.gov.in/PressReleasePage.aspx?PRID=1710134
23. PTI (2018), 'India exporting bulletproof jackets of international standard to over 100 nations: BIS', The Economic Times, Sept. 2013, available at: https://economictimes.indiatimes.com/news/defence/india-exporting-bulletproof-jackets-of-international-standard-to-over-100-nations-bis/articleshow/71099991.cms?from=mdr
24. https://pib.gov.in/newsite/PrintRelease.aspx?relid=229256
25. https://pib.gov.in/PressReleaseIframePage.aspx?PRID=1795541
26. https://newsonair.com/2022/01/01/make-in-india-for-the-world-india-to-export-brahmos-supersonic-missile-to-philippines/
27. https://www.livemint.com/news/india/india-exported-defence-equipment-worth-over-rs-8-434-crore-in-2020-21-govt-11639396078180.html
28. https://twitter.com/amitabhk87/status/1487854345521483776
29. https://icea.org.in/wp-content/uploads/2022/01/FinalReport_VisionDocument_24012022.pdf
30. https://icea.org.in/wp-content/uploads/2022/01/FinalReport_VisionDocument_24012022.pdf
31. Ministry of Commerce &Industry, DIPP Annual Report 2021-22, 'Industrial Corridors', https://dpiit.gov.in/sites/default/files/IPP_ANNUAL_REPORT_ENGLISH.pdf
32. Ibid.,Moon, Vol.10. p. 237-239.
33. Ministry of Coal, Year End Review (2021), https://pib.gov.in/PressReleseDetail.aspx?PRID=1785444
34. Ministry of Mines, GOI (2018). Year End Review 2018-19: Ministry of Mines. [online] Pib.gov.in. https://pib.gov.in/PressReleasePage.aspx?PRID=1559311
35. Ministry of Mines, Year-wise/Sate wise Auction Summary, https://mines.gov.in/writereaddata/Content/Yearwise-Statewise%20Summary.pdf
36. ibid., Moon, Vol 10, p.125-126.
37. https://www.hindustantimes.com/environment/india-only-g20-nation-to-meet-climate-goals-101629061426571.html
38. https://www.euronews.com/green/2020/11/19/india-the-only-g20-nation-on-track-to-meet-2c-global-warming-targets

39. https://powermin.gov.in/en/content/power-sector-glance-all-india
40. http://rchiips.org/nfhs/NFHS-5_FCTS/India.pdf
41. https://www.eprmagazine.com/industry-analysis/industry-seeks-encouragement-domestic-manufacturing-and-sustainable-wires-and-cables/
42. https://www.ceew.in/publications/state-electricity-access-india#:~:text=96.7%20per%20cent%20of%20Indian,Indian%20households%20still%20remain%20unelectrified.
43. https://pib.gov.in/PressReleasePage.aspx?PRID=1787594#:~:text=Ministry%20of%20Power%20has%20successfully,India%20on%20January%205%2C%202015.
44. Krishnamurthy, J. (2008). The Indian Antecedents of Disguised Unemployment and Surplus Labour. In: N. Jayaram and R.S. Deshpande (Eds.), Footprints of Development and Change, Academic Foundation, p.479.
45. https://www.ibef.org/industry/msme.aspx#:~:text=India%20has%20approximately%206.3%20crore,Udyog%20Aadhaar%20Memorandum%20(UAM).
46. https://www.statista.com/statistics/718319/india-number-of-employees-msmes-by-type/#:~:text=Number%20of%20employees%20at%20MSMEs%20in%20India%20FY%202021%2C%20by%20type&text=Over%20110%20million%20Indians%20were,higher%20than%20in%20rural%20areas.
47. https://pqars.nic.in/annex/256/AU2141.pdf
48. https://sbi.co.in/documents/13958/10990811/060122-Impact_of_ECLG_Scheme.pdf/81078df7-e31a-6f89-6289-f5aecb5b715d?t=1641466592115
49. 2014-15 https://msme.gov.in/schemes/pm-employment-generation-program-and-other-credit-support-schemes
2016-20 https://pib.gov.in/PressReleasePage.aspx?PRID=1620015
2020-21
https://pib.gov.in/PressReleasePage.aspx?PRID=1776784#:~:text=Prime%20Minister's%20Employment%20Generation%20Programme,through%20establishment%20of%20micro%2Denterprises
50. https://pib.gov.in/Pressreleaseshare.aspx?PRID=1786356
51. https://gem.gov.in/statistics
52. https://pib.gov.in/PressReleseDetailm.aspx?PRID=1810166
53. Narke, Hari (2014). 'r. Babasaheb Ambedkar: Writings and Speeches', Vol. 3, 2nd ed., Mumbai, Dr. Ambedkar Foundation, p. 627
54. New India Buzz, February14, 2022
55. https://www.indiatoday.in/business/story/india-crosses-400-bn-milestone-in-exports-1928750-2022-03-23
56. https://economictimes.indiatimes.com/news/economy/finance/indias-total-fdi-inflow-of-usd-60-3-billion-in-april-dec-21-down-10-6-per-cent-govt-data/articleshow/89809337.cms

57. Moon, V. (Ed.), (2014). Dr. Babasaheb Ambedkar : Writings and Speeches, Vol. 1, 1st ed., New Delhi: Dr. Ambedkar Foundation, p.455

Chapter-3

58. https://twitter.com/narendramodi/status/1308776451974467584
59. https://labour.gov.in/ebook/wage/index.html
60. https://labour.gov.in/ebook/SS/index.html
61. https://labour.gov.in/ebook/OSH/index.html
62. https://labour.gov.in/ebook/IR/index.html
63. Ministry of Labour & Employment, GoI (2017). Year End Review-2017. [online] Pib.gov.in. Available at: https://pib.gov.in/PressReleseDetail.aspx?PRID=1512998
64. Ibid.
65. https://pib.gov.in/PressReleasePage.aspx?PRID=1679180
66. https://pib.gov.in/PressReleaseIframePage.aspx?PRID=1699094
67. https://www.esic.in/Dashboard/Default.aspx
68. https://pib.gov.in/PressReleaseIframePage.aspx?PRID=1778601#:~:text=More%20than%201.2%20crore%20benefited%20under%20Pradhan%20Mantri%20Rojgar%20Protsahan%20Yojana&text=Government%20is%20implementing%20Pradhan%20Mantri,workers%20to%20the%20formal%20workforce.
69. https://eshram.gov.in/e-shram-objectives
70. https://app.powerbi.com/view?r=eyJrIjoiNTRjOGEwMmEtYmJlMC00NGZkLWJkNDItNTgwZTA2MzBkZWNlIiwidCI6IjA2ZjUzMmJmLTk3NTItNG VjNi04Y2Y4LTIzYTM3YmM2ZDQ2MSJ9
71. https://www.iralr.in/post/women-in-the-unorganised-sector-does-the-law-protect-them
72. Sreelatha Menon (2013). SCs & STs lose out on NREGA. [online] @bsindia. Available at: https://www.business-standard.com/article/economy-policy/scs-sts-lose-out-on-nrega-113081600358_1.html.
73. https://pib.gov.in/PressReleaseIframePage.aspx?PRID=1806266
74. https://pib.gov.in/PressReleasePage.aspx?PRID=1743300
75. https://rural.nic.in/sites/default/files/GKRA_A_Perspective.pdf
76. https://www.indiabudget.gov.in/doc/eb/sbe87.pdf
77. https://nrega.nic.in/Nregahome/MGNREGA_new/Nrega_home.aspx
78. https://rural.nic.in/sites/default/files/GKRA_A_Perspective.pdf
79. https://dbtbharat.gov.in/
80. https://www.india.gov.in/spotlight/pradhan-mantri-garib-kalyan-package-pmgkp
81. https://www.esic.nic.in/attachments/pressfile/65b11920beb294c0a3cbe687afa387fd.pdf
82. Moon, V. (Ed.), (2014c). Dr. Babasaheb Ambedkar: Writings and Speeches, Vol. 10, 1st ed., New Delhi: Dr. Ambedkar Foundation, pp.182-183
83. Ibid.

84. Meenakshi Meena (2017). Ambedkar: an Educationist of the Marginalized. [online] Forward Press. Available at: https://www.forwardpress.in/2017/10/ambedkars-thoughts-on-education-an-overview/#_edn6 [Accessed 23 Jan. 2020].
85. https://pib.gov.in/newsite/PrintRelease.aspx?relid=178974
86. https://pib.gov.in/PressReleasePage.aspx?PRID=1788919
87. https://www.pmkvyofficial.org/dashboard
88. https://pib.gov.in/PressReleaseIframePage.aspx?PRID=1807667
89. https://www.ncvtmis.gov.in/Pages/ITI/Count.aspx
90. Indian Information, May 15, 1945, pp. 639-40.
91. Legislative Assembly Debates (Central), Vol. 1 (1945), p.584
92. Ministry of Labour & Employment, GoI (2016). National Career Service. [online] Pib.gov.in. Available at: https://pib.gov.in/newsite/PrintRelease.aspx?relid=154498
93. The Times of India, September 22, 1944
94. https://financialservices.gov.in/sites/default/files/Website%20January%202022_compressed.pdf
95. https://pib.gov.in/PressReleaseIframePage.aspx?PRID=1783535
96. https://maandhan.in/scheme/pmsym
97. https://pmjay.gov.in/
98. https://www.pib.gov.in/PressReleasePage.aspx?PRID=1740316
99. https://maandhan.in/stats/state/pmsym
100. https://pib.gov.in/PressReleasePage.aspx?PRID=1693908

Chapter-4

101. Dhananjay Keer: Dr. Ambedkar : Life and Mission. 1954, Mumbai, Popular Prakashan, May, 2005, p.60
102. ibid., p.71
103. Mann Ki Baat, (2018) [Radio] A.I.R. 25 March
104. Ibid
105. Deshpande, Tanvi: Standing Committee Report Summary: Industrial Policy in the Changing Global Scenario. PRS Legislative Research, Dec. 2016
106. https://www.pmkvyofficial.org/dashboard
107. https://pib.gov.in/FactsheetDetails.aspx?Id=148562
108. https://jss.gov.in/
109. https://www.startupindia.gov.in/content/sih/en/startup-scheme.html
110. Ministry of Commerce & Industry,Facilities for New Start-Ups.PIB, Nov 20. 2019, Available at: https://pib.gov.in/PressReleasePage.aspx?PRID=1592372
111. https://www.indiabudget.gov.in/economicsurvey/doc/eschapter/echap09.pdf
112. https://financialservices.gov.in/sites/default/files/Website%20January%202022_compressed.pdf

113. https://www.standupmitra.in/
114. https://financialservices.gov.in/sites/default/files/Website%20 January%202022_compressed.pdf
115. www.scsthub.in
116. MUDRA (2017), Success Stories, Available at: www.mudra.org

Chapter-5

117. Moon, V. (Ed.), (2014). Dr. Babasaheb Ambedkar: Speeches and Writings, Vol.4,1st ed., New Delhi: Dr. Ambedkar Foundation, pp.125-126
118. Modi, N. (2017). Launch of Pradhan Mantri Sahaj Bijli Har Ghar Yojana. [In-person] Available at: https://www.youtube.com/watch?v=e05QhdhZ7bM&feature=emb_title [Accessed 11 Jan. 2020]
119. Ministry of Power, GoI (2019), GARV Dashboard. Available at: http://garv.gov.in/dashboard (Accessed: November 2019)
120. https://saubhagya.gov.in/
121. Yardley, J. and Harris, G. (2012),Power Failures Hit Millions in India https://www.nytimes.com/2012/08/01/world/asia/power-outages-hit-600-million-in-india.html
122. ET Bureau (2018). IEA finds India's rural electrification one of greatest success stories this year. [online] The Economic Times. [Accessed 11 Jan. 2020]: https://economictimes.indiatimes.com/industry/energy/power/iea-finds-indias-rural-electrification-one-of-greatest-success-stories-this-year/articleshow/66583514.cms
123. https://archive.doingbusiness.org/en/data/doing-business-score?topic=getting-electricity
124. https://www.ibef.org/industry/power-sector-india.aspx
125. Modi, N. (2018). Reply on Motion of Thanks in Lok Sabha
126. https://pib.gov.in/PressReleasePage.aspx?PRID=1786527
127. http://omms.nic.in/dbweb
128. https://pmgsy.nic.in/sites/default/files/PMGSY_III_guidelines.pdf
129. Ministry of Shipping, GoI (2017). Transportation Through Waterways and Coastal Shipping. [online] Available at: https://pib.gov.in/newsite/PrintRelease.aspx?relid=160237 [Accessed 11 Jan. 2020].
130. Also, the World Bank, which funds a part of India's inland waterways development, estimates that the cost of transport of 1 tonne of freight over 1 kilometre of road is Rs 2.28, by rail it is Rs 1.41 and by waterways, only Rs 1.19.14, World Bank, http://www.worldbank.org/en/country/india/brief/developing-india-first-modern-inland-waterway
131. Ministry of Shipping, GOI (2017). Developing waterways for sustainable transport in the North East. [online] Available at: https://pib.gov.in/newsite/PrintRelease.aspx?relid=163229 [Accessed 11 Jan. 2020]
132. https://pib.gov.in/PressReleaseIframePage.aspx?PRID=1777764
133. http://mofapp.nic.in:8080/economicsurvey/pdf/120-150_Chapter_08_Economic_Survey_2017-18.pdf

134. https://pib.gov.in/FactsheetDetails.aspx?Id=148570
135. https://pib.gov.in/FactsheetDetails.aspx?Id=148570
136. Modi, N. (2018). Public Meeting in Mysuru, Karnataka.
137. Economic Survey http://mofapp.nic.in:8080/economicsurvey/pdf/120-150_Chapter_08_Economic_Survey_2017-18.pdf
138. https://core.indianrailways.gov.in/
139. https://pib.gov.in/PressReleasePage.aspx?PRID=1709184
140. https://www.ibef.org/industry/indian-railways.aspx
141. https://news.railanalysis.com/year-end-review-2021-major-transformation-achievements-of-indian-railways/
142. Sinha, S. (2018). India to be world's third largest aviation market by 2024-25: IATA - Times of India. [online] Available at: https://timesofindia.indiatimes.com/business/india-business/india-to-be-worlds-third-largest-aviation-market-by-2024-25-iata/articleshow/66351652.cms [Accessed 13 Jan. 2020].
143. https://www.iata.org/en/iata-repository/publications/economic-reports/air-passenger-monthly-analysis---january-2022/
144. https://www.tribuneindia.com/news/nation/1-security-lapse-every-month-at-airports-reveals-govt-data-47345
145. https://pib.gov.in/PressReleaseIframePage.aspx?PRID=1779817
146. https://timesofindia.indiatimes.com/india/efforts-on-to-make-network-of-200-airports-operational-pm-narendra-modi/articleshow/87161283.cms
147. https://www.civilaviation.gov.in/
148. https://www.civilaviation.gov.in/sites/default/files/annual_report-2017_18_en.pdf
149. https://pib.gov.in/newsite/PrintRelease.aspx?relid=229275
150. https://pib.gov.in/PressReleasePage.aspx?PRID=1776091
151. https://www.civilaviation.gov.in/sites/default/files/annual_report-2017_18_en.pdf
152. Modi, N. (2015c). Speech at the Launch of Digital India
153. http://bbnl.nic.in//admnis/admin/showimg.aspx?ID=1513
154. https://pib.gov.in/PressReleasePage.aspx?PRID=1785452
155. https://www.trai.gov.in/sites/default/files/YIR_15092021_0.pdf
156. https://www.trai.gov.in/sites/default/files/QPIR_10012022_0.pdf
157. https://meity.dashboard.nic.in/DashboardF.aspx
158. https://pib.gov.in/PressReleasePage.aspx?PRID=1785452
159. https://pib.gov.in/PressReleaseIframePage.aspx?PRID=1778566
160. https://pib.gov.in/PressReleasePage.aspx?PRID=1748297#:~:text=The%20aggregate%20asset%20pipeline %20under,more%20than%2020%20asset%20classes.

Chapter-6

161. Modi, N. (2016). Address at the Launch of Smart City Projects in Pune

162. Planning Commission (2013). Twelfth Five Year Plan (2012-2017). New Delhi: SAGE Publications India Pvt Ltd, p.318
163. https://www.pib.gov.in/PressReleasePage.aspx?PRID=1741942
164. The Associated Press (2013). India census says 1 in 6 lives in unsanitary slums. [online] CBC. Available at: https://www.cbc.ca/news/world/india-census-says-1-in-6-lives-in-unsanitary-slums-1.1403897
165. https://smartcities.gov.in/
166. http://amrut.gov.in/content/
167. https://unctad.org/system/files/official-document/wir2021_overview_en.pdf
168. https://pmay-urban.gov.in/about
169. https://www.pib.gov.in/PressReleasePage.aspx?PRID=1740316
170. Modi, N. (2015). Address at the Launch of the Smart Cities Mission, AMRUT & Housing for All Mission
171. http://swachhbharaturban.gov.in/Home.aspx
172. http://ab-hwc.nhp.gov.in/
173. http://dashboard.mohua.gov.in/
174. https://pib.gov.in/Pressreleaseshare.aspx?PRID=1693893
175. https://www.pib.gov.in/PressReleasePage.aspx?PRID=1794165
176. https://pib.gov.in/PressReleaseIframePage.aspx?PRID=1794164
177. http://ras.org.in/b_r_ambedkar_on_caste_and_land_relations_in_india#bib1

Chapter-7

178. https://www.mea.gov.in/Images/CPV/Volume17_Part_III.pdf
179. https://www.mea.gov.in/Images/CPV/Volume17_Part_I.pdf
180. http://www.cscsarchive.org/dataarchive/otherfiles/TA001003/file
181. https://www.mea.gov.in/Images/CPV/Volume17_Part_III.pdf
182. https://pib.gov.in/PressReleseDetail.aspx?PRID=1582107
183. https://ejalshakti.gov.in/jjmreport/JJMIndia.aspx
184. https://ejalshakti.gov.in/jjmreport/School/JJMSchool_India.aspx
185. https://static.pib.gov.in/WriteReadData/specificdocs/documents/2021/sep/Jal%20Jeevan%20Eng.pdf
186. https://jalshakti-ddws.gov.in/samvad/JalJeevanSamvad-February-2022-en.pdf
187. https://jaljeevanmission.gov.in/sites/default/files/publication_and_reports/two-years-of-jal-jeevan-mission_0.pdf
188. https://static.pib.gov.in/WriteReadData/specificdocs/documents/2021/sep/Jal%20Jeevan%20Eng.pdf
189. https://static.pib.gov.in/WriteReadData/specificdocs/documents/2021/sep/Jal%20Jeevan%20Eng.pdf
190. https://cdn.cseindia.org/userfiles/Politics%20of%20Environment%20-%20Anil%20Agarwal.pdf
191. https://static.pib.gov.in/WriteReadData/specificdocs/documents/2021/

sep/Jal%20Jeevan%20Eng.pdf
192. https://jaljeevanmission.gov.in/sites/default/files/manual_document/FFC_22-10-21_English.pdf
193. https://pib.gov.in/PressReleaseIframePage.aspx?PRID=1805746
194. https://cdma.cgg.gov.in/cdma/Circulars/344913JalJeevanMission AMRUT2.0withdraftproposal.pdf
195. https://pib.gov.in/PressReleasePage.aspx?PRID=1694420
196. https://pib.gov.in/PressReleseDetail.aspx?PRID=1786616
197. https://nmcg.nic.in/
198. Ministry of Water Resources, River Development and Ganga Rejuvenation (2017). Year End Review 2017. https://pib.gov.in/PressReleasePage.aspx?PRID=1514500
199. Ministry of Water Resources, GOI (2018). Year end Review, 2018. https://pib.gov.in/newsite/PrintRelease.aspx?relid=186602
200. https://nmcg.nic.in/
201. https://pib.gov.in/PressReleasePage.aspx?PRID=1805945
202. https://www.indiabudget.gov.in/doc/Budget_Speech.pdf
203. https://pib.gov.in/PressReleseDetail.aspx?PRID=1786616
204. https://pib.gov.in/PressReleasePage.aspx?PRID=1794274

Chapter-8

205. Inaugural address of Maritime India Summit, 2016
206. http://www.cwc.gov.in/sites/default/files/ambedkars-book_1.pdf
207. First Odisha Conference, 1945 on the Hirakud river valley project
208. Ambedkar, Dr. B.R. (1945) 'Presidential Speech at Cuttack Conference', presented at the Conference on Multi-Purpose Plan for Development of Orissa Rivers
209. Ibid.
210. Modi, N. (2017). Inauguration of Ro-Ro ferry Service in Gogha, Gujarat
211. https://pib.gov.in/PressReleaseIframePage.aspx?PRID=1777764
212. https://www.thestatesman.com/india/cargo-movement-inland-waterways-increases-2-76-times-1503044600.html
213. https://www.livemint.com/news/india/25-national-waterways-found-fit-for-cargo-or-passenger-movements-11638888104386.html
214. http://jmvp.nic.in/about-us
215. https://www.sentinelassam.com/guwahati-city/work-started-on-dredging-brahmaputra-union-minister-sarbananda-sonowal-572302
216. India Aiming To Reduce Logistics Cost To Less Than 10% Of GDP By 2022. https://www.business-standard.com/article/news-cm/india-aiming-to-reduce-logistics-cost-to-less-than-10-of-gdp-by-2022-118082400367_1.html [Accessed 7 Nov. 2019]
217. PTI (2019). Sardar Sarovar dam water level touches its highest mark. [online] Available at: https://economictimes.indiatimes.com/news/politics-and-nation/sardar-sarovar-dam-water-level-touches-its-highest-

mark/articleshow/71140009.cms?from=mdr
218. https://www.indiatoday.in/india/story/pm-narendra-modi-inaugurate-saryu-nahar-national-project-up-balrampur-farmers-water-agriculture-1886651-2021-12-11
219. https://www.thestatesman.com/india/modi-govt-will-complete-projects-pending-decades-anurag-thakur-1503031077.html
220. Ministry of Water Resources, GoI (2017). Dam Rehabilitation and Improvement Project. https://pib.gov.in/newsite/PrintRelease.aspx?relid=169539
221. https://pmksy.gov.in/mis/frmDashboard.aspx
222. https://navbharattimes.indiatimes.com/elections/assembly-elections/uttar-pradesh/news/saryu-canal-project-was-stuck-from-last-44-years-what-will-it-benefit-to-bjp-in-up/articleshow/88222662.cms
223. https://pib.gov.in/PressReleasePage.aspx?PRID=1780456

Chapter-9

224. Narke, H. ed., (2014a). Dr. Babasaheb Ambedkar : Writings and Speeches, Vol. 2, 2nd ed., New India: Dr. Ambedkar Foundation, p.40
225. Modi, N. (2016). Dr. Ambedkar Memorial Lecture
226. Welcome speech by Dr. Babasaheb Ambedkar at Milind Mahavidyalaya Aurangabad, 1951, as mentioned in Thoughts of Dr. Baba Saheb Ambedkar (Ed.). Yashwant Daulatrao Sontakke, 2004, Samyak Prakashan
227. https://pib.gov.in/FactsheetDetails.aspx?Id=148590
228. Narke, H. ed., (2014). Dr. Babasaheb Ambedkar: Writings and Speeches, Vol. 2, 2nd ed., New Delhi: Dr. Ambedkar Foundation, pp.40–42.
229. https://pib.gov.in/PressReleaseIframePage.aspx?PRID=1786630
230. https://pib.gov.in/PressReleaseIframePage.aspx?PRID=1583418
231. https://fitindia.gov.in/schooldashboard
232. Keer, D. (2005). Dr. Ambedkar: Life and Mission. Mumbai: Popular Prakashan, p.84
233. https://pib.gov.in/PressReleasePage.aspx?PRID=1740382#:~:text=Key%20Highlights%3A,suitable%20land%20by%20the%20States.
234. https://pib.gov.in/PressReleseDetail.aspx?PRID=1659029
235. Ministry of Human Resource Development (2016). Initiatives and Achievements of Ministry of Human Resource Development. [online] Available at: http://pib.nic.in/newsite/PrintRelease.aspx?relid=155999 [Accessed 15 Jan. 2020]
236. https://pib.gov.in/PressReleseDetail.aspx?PRID=1789398
237. https://pib.gov.in/PressReleaseIframePage.aspx?PRID=1766061
238. Modi, N. (2014). Independence Day Address.
239. Modi, N. (2015). Independence Day Address.
240. https://dashboard.udiseplus.gov.in/#/home
241. https://nsp.gov.in/dashboard/
242. Ambedkar, Dr. B.R. (1944). Address to the Technical Training Scheme

Advisory Committee
243. Ministry of Skill Development and Entrepreneurship (2015). Ministry of Skill Development and Entrepreneurship: Key Achievements and Success Stories in 2015. [online] Available at: http://pib.nic.in/newsite/PrintRelease.aspx?relid=133233
244. Modi, N. (2017). Opening Remarks During Smart India Hackathon.
245. https://pib.gov.in/PressReleaseIframePage.aspx?PRID=1695636
246. Moon, V. (Ed.), (2014). Dr. Babasaheb Ambedkar: Writings and Speeches, Vol. 10, 1st ed., Mumbai: Dr. Ambedkar Foundation, p.431
247. https://www.apprenticeshipindia.gov.in/
248. https://www.education.gov.in/sites/upload_files/mhrd/files/steps_sel.pdf
249. Lok Sabha Unstarred Question No. 4708 Answered on: July 22, 2019.
250. https://static.pib.gov.in/WriteReadData/specificdocs/documents/2022/feb/doc20222519701.pdf

Chapter-10

251. Raghavendra, R.H. (2016). 'Dr. B.R. Ambedkar's Ideas on Social Justice in Indian Society', Contemporary Voice of Dalit, 8(1), p.24-29
252. ibid
253. Chakrabarty, B. (2018). Constitutional Democracy In India, New York: Routledge
254. Ambedkar, B.R. (1989). Constituent Assembly Debates Vol. XI, New Delhi: Lok Sabha Secretariat, p.978
255. Modi, N. (2016). Speech at Digidhan Mela
256. Modi, N. (2017). Speech at BJP Headquarters Following Win in State Elections.
257. Modi, N. (2015). Independence Day Address
258. Ministry of Tribal Affairs, GOI (2019). Facilities in Scheduled Tribes Areas. [online] Pib.gov.in. Available at: https://pib.gov.in/newsite/PrintRelease.aspx?relid=192060
259. https://pib.gov.in/PressReleasePage.aspx?PRID=1740382#:~:text=Key%20Highlights%3A,suitable%20land%20by%20the%20States.
260. https://pib.gov.in/PressReleseDetail.aspx?PRID=1786612
261. Modi, N. (2014). PM's Message to the Nation on Good Governance. Available at: https://www.narendramodi.in/pms-message-to-the-nation-on-good-governance-7080
262. https://transformingindia.mygov.in/performance-dashboard/
263. https://www.pib.gov.in/PressReleseDetailm.aspx?PRID=1786560
264. http://www.drbrambedkarcollege.ac.in/sites/default/files/Dr.%20B.%20R.%20Ambedkar%20A%20Farsighted%20and%20Forgotten%20Economist.pdf
265. https://www.narendramodi.in/text-of-prime-minister-shri-narendra-modi-s-address-in-hindi-to-the-nation-from-the-ramparts-of-the-red-

fort-on-the-69th-independence-day-211475
266. https://transformingindia.mygov.in/performance-dashboard/
267. http://rchiips.org/nfhs/NFHS-5_FCTS/India.pdf
268. https://www.npci.org.in/what-we-do/bhim/product-statistics
269. https://dbtbharat.gov.in/
270. https://static.pib.gov.in/WriteReadData/specificdocs/documents/2022/jan/doc2022l207101.pdf
271. https://pib.gov.in/PressReleseDetail.aspx?PRID=1781676
272. https://wcd.dashboard.nic.in/view_detail/eyJpdiI6IjZlb3RabGlVSlF4RTNuV0kwSU9mZGc9PSIsInZhbHVlIjoiellSXC8yd2JiRmtkV0dqZENxNnA1bGc9PSIsIm1hYyI6IjE1MGUzYjc0NjkyY2E2ODUzMTZlYTg4MTkxZTFjZDE1ODc5OGM3MWI5YWQ4NzQxYjFjNGRkNDkzNTMwOTM1ZGQifQ==/2
273. https://pib.gov.in/PressReleasePage.aspx?PRID=1785589#:~:text=Age%20of%20Marriage%20of%20Women%3A%20The%20Bill%20on%20Prohibition%20of,18%20years%20to%2021%20years.
274. Modi, N. (2017). Address at the 50th Year Celebrations of the IMC Ladies Wing
275. https://transformingindia.mygov.in/performance-dashboard/
276. https://pib.gov.in/PressReleaseIframePage.aspx?PRID=1783923
277. President's Secretariat (2019): https://pib.gov.in/PressReleaseIframePage.aspx?PRID=1562085
278. https://archive.pib.gov.in/ndagov/Comprehensive-Materials/compr34.pdf

Chapter-11

279. Mann Ki Baat, (2018). [Radio] A.I.R. 25 Feb.
280. IANS (2018). Credit to PM for rise in girl child ratio: Maneka Gandhi. [online] Available at: https://www.business-standard.com/article/news-ians/credit-to-pm-for-rise-in-girl-child-ratio-maneka-gandhi-118030800890_1.html
281. https://static.pib.gov.in/WriteReadData/specificdocs/documents/2022/jan/doc2022l207101.pdf
282. Ministry of Women and Child Development, GoI (2018). Beti Bachao Beti Padhao : Achievements and Progress. [online] Available at: https://pib.gov.in/newsite/PrintRelease.aspx?relid=177109
283. https://www.indiabudget.gov.in/economicsurvey/doc/eschapter/echap10.pdf
284. https://pib.gov.in/PressReleasePage.aspx?PRID=1782601
285. Ahir, D.C. (1990). The legacy of Dr. Ambedkar (Bharat Ratna). Delhi: B.R. Pub. Corp.
286. Narke, H. (Ed.), et.al. (2014). Dr. Babasaheb Ambedkar: Writings and Speeches, Vol. 17, Part 3, 1st ed., New Delhi: Dr. Ambedkar Foundation, p.283

287. ibid., p. 411
288. Moon, V. ed., (2014). Dr. Babasaheb Ambedkar: Writings and Speeches, Vol. 8, 1st ed., New Delhi: Dr. Ambedkar Foundation, p.227
289. https://www.pmuy.gov.in/index.aspx
290. https://sbm.gov.in/sbmreport/home.aspx
291. https://pib.gov.in/PressReleasePage.aspx?PRID=1787361
292. https://pib.gov.in/PressReleaseIframePage.aspx?PRID=1796099
293. https://pib.gov.in/Pressreleaseshare.aspx?PRID=1797685
294. https://pib.gov.in/PressReleasePage.aspx?PRID=1805731
295. https://pib.gov.in/PressReleasePage.aspx?PRID=1805731
296. Moon, V. ed., (2014). Dr. Babasaheb Ambedkar: Writings and Speeches, Vol. 10, 3rd ed., New Delhi: Dr. Ambedkar Foundation, pp 139-143
297. https://pmjdy.gov.in/account
298. https://pib.gov.in/PressReleasePage.aspx?PRID=1783537
299. https://www.standupmitra.in/
300. https://pib.gov.in/Pressreleaseshare.aspx?PRID=1703083
301. https://pib.gov.in/PressReleasePage.aspx?PRID=1788900
302. Dhananjay Keer (2005). Dr. Ambedkar : Life and Mission, Mumbai: Popular Prakashan, p.111
303. The Times of India, June 17, 1936, vide Das, B. ed., (n.d.). Thus Spoke Ambedkar Vol. 3. p.195
304. https://pib.gov.in/PressReleseDetail.aspx?PRID=1786640

Chapter-12

305. Ambedkar, Dr. B.R. (1949). Constituent Assembly of India Debates (Proceedings) - Vol. XI
306. Ambedkar, Dr. B.R. (1948). Constituent Assembly of India Debates (Proceedings) - Vol. VII
307. http://164.100.47.194/loksabha/writereaddata/cadebatefiles/C04111948.html
308. ibid
309. ibid
310. Ambedkar, Dr .B.R. (1949b). Speech in The Constituent Assembly on Adoption of the Constitution
311. https://www.narendramodi.in/text-of-pm-s-speech-at-gajwel-telangana-511398
312. https://www.narendramodi.in/text-of-pm-s-remarks-after-dedication-to-the-nation-of-2-5-mt-steel-plant-at-iisco-burnpur-10498
313. https://www.narendramodi.in/pm-delivers-opening-remarks-at-3rd-meeting-of-governing-council-of-niti-aayog--535165
314. https://www.cbic.gov.in/resources//htdocs-cbec/press-release/46th%20GST%20Council%20Press%20Release%20final.pdf
315. https://gstcouncil.gov.in/gst-revenue
316. https://pib.gov.in/newsite/PrintRelease.aspx?relid=108819

317. https://www.narendramodi.in/pm-chairs-first-meeting-of-governing-council-of-niti-aayog-7240
318. https://pib.gov.in/PressReleasePage.aspx?PRID=1693868
319. https://www.narendramodi.in/text-speech-of-pm-modi-at-vibrant-gujarat-global-summit-2926
320. https://www.narendramodi.in/text-of-pm-s-address-at-the-national-legislators-conference--539264
321. https://www.linkedin.com/pulse/reforms-conviction-incentives-narendra-modi
322. https://www.narendramodi.in/vikasyatra/articledetail/india-fights-corona/complete-commitment-to-the-battle-against-covid-19-555572
323. http://164.100.47.194/Loksabha/Debates/Result_Nw_15.aspx?dbsl=144&ser=&smode

□□□